LOVE THEM IN

LOVE THEM IN

The Life and Theology of D. L. Moody

By

STANLEY N. GUNDRY

Foreword by

FRANK E. GAEBELEIN

BAKER BOOK HOUSE
Grand Rapids, Michigan 49506

Printed in the United States of America

CONTENTS

FOREWORD

BY ANY RESPONSIBLE ESTIMATE, Dwight L. Moody remains a major figure in American church history. The literature about him is still growing, and Dr. Gundry has added to it a landmark study of the great evangelist's theology. This revision of his doctoral dissertation from the Lutheran School of Theology at Chicago goes beyond the usual competent academic research. It presents valuable and authentic insight into Moody's thought and practice. For me the book was important reading, and I believe it will be so for others.

There are several reasons for this. For one thing, Dr. Gundry understands his subject. While being aware of Moody's shortcomings and dealing honestly with them, he knows from within the kind of theology that undergirded his ministry. Dr. Gundry also writes out of an exemplary knowledge of his sources. Where others have written about Moody out of partial knowledge of the voluminous records of his preaching and the extensive contemporary information about him, Dr. Gundry has gone further and has written an inductive study based on the whole body of available Moodyana.

Thus at point after point this book sets the record straight—not in an oracular way but modestly, courteously, and through the weight of the facts. Especially impressive is the section dealing with the contention of Mead, McLoughlin, Weisberger, and (to a lesser degree) Findlay that Moody's evangelistic technique determined his theology and that, following Finney's theories, he made revivalism a big business enterprise in which the end justified the means. Here, as in other instances, the rigorous analysis of the evidence as a whole leads to a telling defense of the evangelist's integrity.

The book is balanced, and the author avoids lapsing into adulation of Moody. It shows him as he really was—with his great educational

7

limitations, his ungrammatical speech and letters, and with the complete lack of theological sophistication with which he began his ministry. In a moving way it tells of his unremitting efforts to learn from the distinguished ministers and scholars who were drawn to him. Above all, it faces us with the extent to which a man of inferior education and humble background, yet one wholly dedicated to Christ and relying fully on the Scriptures, could develop and express with compelling power a theology that so successfully avoided vagaries and heresies.

Step by step, Dr. Gundry leads us in an analysis of Moody's thought in relation to basic themes like the fall of man, redemption, regeneration, faith, repentance, the will, election, assurance, Christian life and service, and eschatology. He is not content with simplistic answers about such things as Moody's supposed Arminianism but shows the tension between Arminianism and Calvinism in the evangelist's preaching. At this point, the discussion of the influence of Spurgeon and the Plymouth Brethren on Moody is enlightening.

I believe that this is a book no student of evangelism in America should leave unread. Its tone is admirable and its research thorough. It is not every writer who can make ideas interesting and even at times exciting. This is what Dr. Gundry has done in his study of Dwight L. Moody's theology.

FRANK E. GAEBELEIN

PREFACE

AN ENTIRE BOOK devoted to the theology of Dwight L. Moody? He was an evangelist, not a systematic theologian. The sum of his formal academic training has been estimated not to exceed the fifth-grade level.[1] A close look at his sermon notes and personal letters suggests that even that estimate may have been overly optimistic. He never had any formal theological education. He never wrote books or articles for himself, and even his published sermons were recorded stenographically and usually edited by others. His sermons consist primarily of anecdotes and exhortations. They are not exegetical and doctrinal, and they usually lack a carefully elaborated form or outline. Those outlines evident in the published sermons are often editorial creations. For him to have set forth consciously a carefully worked out systematic theology would have been out of character and possibly beyond the range of his capabilities. This man who simply signed his name D. L. Moody and declined ordination, insisting that he be called only Mr. Moody, probably would have been the first to admit this.

Why then presume to investigate Moody's theology? Did he even have one? For the moment this question and the matter of Moody's own attitude toward theology will be deferred with the observation that any Christian, and especially a preacher of the Gospel, has an implicit theology, no matter how inadequately it may be worked out and expressed. Moody is no exception. There is a theology to be found in his published sermons and informal remarks that have been preserved. But is it significant?

If for no other reason, this question must be answered in the affirmative because of the influence wielded and the place occupied by Moody in the last quarter of the nineteenth century. From his rise to fame in late 1873 to his death in 1899 he preached far and wide across North America and the British Isles to audiences usually numbering in the

---

1. James F. Findlay, Jr., *Dwight L. Moody: American Evangelist, 1837-1899* (Chicago: U. Chicago, 1969), pp. 40-41, cited as *Dwight L. Moody*.

9

thousands. The services were reported in the local papers and religious periodicals, often with the sermons reproduced in their entirety. These same sermons were then collected by those wanting to make a fast dollar (or pound), or by Moody's own trusted associates, and published in book form to extend his message. Because of the pirating of material, publication without copyrights, revisions, and reissuing of collections under new titles, definitive description of the published sermons presents the bibliographer with an impossible task. Nevertheless, some idea of its volume can be formed from the fact that Wilbur M. Smith lists some 113 titles containing sermons, addresses, and anecdotes by D. L. Moody.[2]

This number is significantly increased if one includes those biographies which included sermonic material. At Moody's funeral service Theodore Cuyler estimated that at times Moody spoke to 40,000 or 50,000 people a week, an estimate not at all unreasonable in view of the fact some single services had 10,000 to 20,000 in the audience.[3] This evidence would seem to indicate that A. T. Pierson's calculation that Moody brought the claims of Christ by voice and pen to the attention of 100 million people, if anything, errs on the conservative side.[4]

Charles R. Erdman, an admiring biographer, claimed Moody at the close of his life was the "most famous and influential evangelist in the world."[5] Ernest Sandeen speaks of Moody as "the most influential 'clergyman' in America" in the last two decades of the nineteenth century, and Martin E. Marty says that at a critical stage of American religious history he "could plausibly have been called Mr. Revivalist and perhaps even Mr. Protestant."[6] Both eulogistic biographers and more dispassionate observers agree that Moody is a figure to be reckoned with in late nineteenth-century American Christianity.

It is not surprising, then, that Moody has had so many biographies. Eulogistic accounts of his life and work appeared very soon after his

2. Wilbur M. Smith, *An Annotated Bibliography of D. L. Moody* (Chicago: Moody, 1948), pp. 97-108, cited as *Annotated Bibliography*.
3. J. Wilbur Chapman, *The Life and Work of Dwight L. Moody* (Philadelphia: International, 1900), p. 466.
4. Will H. Houghton and Chas. T. Cook, *Tell Me About Moody* (London: Marshall, Morgan & Scott, 1936), p. 117; for similar statistical estimates see J. C. Pollock, *Moody: A Biographical Portrait of the Pacesetter in Modern Mass Evangelism* (New York: Macmillan, 1963), pp. 166, 242, 283-84, cited as *Moody: A Biographical Portrait*.
5. Charles R. Erdman, *D. L. Moody: His Message for To-day* (New York: Revell, 1928), p. 11.
6. Ernest R. Sandeen, *The Roots of Fundamentalism: British and American Millenarianism, 1800-1930* (Chicago: U. Chicago, 1970), p. 172, cited as *Roots of Fundamentalism;* Martin E. Marty in the foreword to Findlay, *Dwight L. Moody*, p. 1.

rise to fame in 1873, and they continued to come off the press until his death, even though he personally would have preferred that the account of his life and work be deferred till after his death and then be produced by one who knew him well, his older son, William R. Moody. Moody's death was the catalyst producing another spate of biographies, and this time a son-in-law and two sons were among the authors. Though he lists some works which are not biographies in the strictest sense, Smith gives the titles of 113 works relating to the life and work of Moody appearing between 1874 and 1948; and I have found at least three which Smith overlooked from that period.[7]

Treatments of Moody's life have continued to appear in the years since Smith's bibliography. Not only are there the histories of revivals by Bernard A. Weisberger and William G. McLoughlin, containing significant chapters on Moody and his work, but three full-length biographies also have appeared.[8] Though Richard K. Curtis and J. C. Pollock are among the eulogists, they did attempt to produce serious studies on their subject.[9] Most recently, James F. Findlay, Jr., has written what will undoubtedly remain Moody's definitive biography for years to come. Based on extensive research, Findlay successfully avoids the extremes of bias and considers Moody within his historical context, two points at which most other books have fallen short.[10]

Recently Moody also has been the subject of a number of theses and dissertations, most of which remain unpublished.[11] Moody's social views, speech techniques, and work as an educator are the focus of most of these studies. These treatises, along with the recent biographies, are not merely curiosities testifying to the fascination that Moody exerts over those who have come in contact with him even indirectly; they are part of the recent interest in late nineteenth-century British and American Christianity in general, and in particular they evidence the renewed interest in late nineteenth-century Evangelicalism and the origins of Fundamentalism.[12]

7. Smith, *Annotated Bibliography*, pp. 1-25; those of significance for this book are cited later.
8. Bernard A. Weisberger, *They Gathered at the River: The Story of the Great Revivalists and Their Impact upon Religion in America* (Boston: Little, Brown, 1958), cited as *They Gathered at the River*; William G. McLoughlin, Jr., *Modern Revivalism: Charles Grandison Finney to Billy Graham* (New York: Ronald, 1959), cited as *Modern Revivalism*.
9. Richard K. Curtis, *They Called Him Mr. Moody* (New York: Doubleday, 1962); Pollock, *Moody: A Biographical Portrait*.
10. Findlay, *Dwight L. Moody*.
11. See lists of Dissertations and Theses in Sources Consulted at the back of this book.
12. Much of this literature is briefly surveyed in Findlay, *Dwight L. Moody*, pp. 9-21.

But there is a strange gap in this vast literature surrounding Moody. As far as I have been able to discover, no one has ever written a full-length critical analysis of the whole range of Moody's theology.[13] This is not to say that the question of Moody's theology has been totally ignored. As a matter of fact, nearly every writer of theses, dissertations, and books on Moody devotes a few pages to the basic beliefs he preached. In addition, there are popular-level articles and sermonic material by Moody's friends and associates which briefly explain those doctrines he held. However, none of this literature is based on a thorough examination of his sermons and recorded statements. Often it is characterized by borrowing from others who have spoken or written on Moody's beliefs, or by impressions that Moody left on those who heard and associated with him.

Very early there were also those who wrote against the theology implicit in Moody's preaching. There is not an overabundance of this kind of literature, but I have examined such material by Universalists, Unitarians, Anglicans, Particular Baptists, "Campbellites," and by writers who were satirical skeptics claiming to give a rational refutation of the revivalistic madness.[14] Though this material sheds light on the message that Moody preached, it is basically polemical in nature and cannot be considered scholarly in its analyses of Moody.

In spite of the inadequacies of previous treatments of Moody's theology, a brief survey of some of the highpoints will help put this study in proper perspective. One of the very earliest and still the longest presentation of that theology was compiled by W. H. Daniels, a Methodist minister in Chicago who apparently knew Moody well. He presented Moody's beliefs sympathetically, although he expressed reservations about what he regarded as Calvinistic elements in Moody's preaching. Daniels' method was to give a nine-page introduction to

13. This conclusion was verified by Wilbur M. Smith in a telephone conversation on Feb. 3, 1972, and by James F. Findlay, Jr., in a letter dated Feb. 25, 1972.
14. When appropriate to the concerns of this book, some of this material is examined. At this point the following typical examples are cited: Universalist: W. H. Ryder, *An Open Letter from W. H. Ryder, D.D., of Chicago, Ill., to D. L. Moody, Esq., The Evangelist* (Boston: Universalist, 1877). Unitarian: John Cuckson, *Religious Excitement, A Sermon on the Moody & Sankey Revival* (Birmingham: A. J. Buncher, 1875). Anglican: A. Williams, *Weak Points in Mr. Moody's Teaching* (London: William MacIntosh, 1875). Particular Baptist: J. K. Popham, *Moody and Sankey's Errors Versus the Scriptures of Truth* (Liverpool: J. K. Popham, 1875). "Campbellite": John Tomline Walsh, *Moody versus Christ and His Apostles: A Vindication of the Truth of the Gospel* (St. Louis: John Burns, 1880). Satirical skeptic: "By a Descendant of the French Protestant Refugees," *The Moody & Sankey Humbug: Recent Ridiculous Religious (?) Revivals Rationally Reprobated* (London: *The West End News*, 1875).

Moody's theology and then to arrange excerpts from Moody's sermons under a simple outline of basic theology drawn up by Daniels himself, without editorial comment. He does not identify his sources, but at times whole sermons appear to be reproduced and the material extends for over 200 pages.[15] Also in 1877, a volume was published under Moody's name entitled *Arrows and Anecdotes*, containing a section of "Illustrations of Scriptural Theology," but this material is anecdotal.[16]

After Moody's death, it was customary for biographers to include a brief description of his theology as they remembered it. Typical here are the recollections of his two sons, William and Paul, and of Charles F. Goss and J. Wilbur Chapman.[17] In a Founder's Week sermon delivered on February 3, 1907, A. C. Dixon, pastor of the Moody Church in Chicago and later editor of the first five volumes of *The Fundamentals*, summarized the message of D. L. Moody based on several years of intimate acquaintance.[18] Again directed toward a lay audience, but this time written by men who had not known Moody intimately, articles by James M. Gray and W. H. Griffith Thomas appeared in 1920 and 1923 in *The Moody Bible Institute Monthly*, expounding the virtues of what he had believed.[19] A short time later, biographer Gamaliel Bradford gave a not-so-friendly resumé of Moody's theology, but within ten years Moody's friends again were relating "Things Moody Most Surely Believed."[20]

No one to this point had written a carefully researched summary and analysis of Moody's theology, but in the mid-1940s the appearance of theses and dissertations on Moody indicated a developing interest in the evangelist. In 1945 James M. Nelson submitted a Th.M. thesis which

15. W. H. Daniels, ed., *Moody: His Words, Work, and Workers* (New York: Nelson & Phillips, 1877), pp. 253-478.

16. D. L. Moody, *Arrows and Anecdotes* (New York: Henry Gurley, 1877), pp. 104-60.

17. William R. Moody, *The Life of D. L. Moody* (New York: Revell, 1900), pp. 494-501, cited as *Moody* (1900); Paul D. Moody, *My Father: An Intimate Portrait of Dwight Moody* (Boston: Little, Brown, 1938), pp. 176-99, cited as *My Father*; Charles F. Goss, *Echoes From the Pulpit and Platform* (Hartford, Conn.: A. D. Worthington, 1900), pp. 93-95, cited as *Echoes*; J. Wilbur Chapman, *The Life and Work of Dwight L. Moody* (Philadelphia: International, 1900), pp. 396-413.

18. A typed manuscript of the sermon is in the Moodyana Collection, Moody Bible Institute, cited as Moodyana.

19. James M. Gray, "D. L. Moody's Theology: A Finger Post for Christian Workers," *The Moody Bible Institute Monthly*, Feb., 1920, pp. 455-58; also reprinted as No. 1 in *The D. L. Moody Pamphlets Christian Faith Series* (Chicago: BICA, n.d.); W. H. Griffith Thomas, "What D. L. Moody Believed and Taught, and How He Taught It." *The Moody Bible Institute Monthly*, Nov., 1923, pp. 101-6.

20. Gamaliel Bradford, *D. L. Moody: A Worker in Souls* (New York: George H. Doran, 1927), pp. 57-66; Will H. Houghton and Chas. T. Cook, *Tell Me About Moody*, pp. 102-16.

claimed to be "a critical study of the theologies of Dwight L. Moody and his successors in urban evangelism. It does contain a basically accurate summary of Moody's message, although it sheds no new light on the subject.[21] By 1955 August J. Fry had written what he called a B.D. "dissertation," which discussed Moody's theology before 1873, the year of his rise to international fame as an evangelist. This study is brief and of only limited value, but at least it did go back to the few source materials available prior to 1873.[22] In 1963 John Wesley White submitted a doctoral thesis to Mansfield College, Oxford, entitled "The Influence of North American Evangelism in Great Britain between 1830 and 1914 on the Origin and Development of the Ecumenical Movement." A great deal of attention was devoted to Moody in this work, but mostly in terms of his relationship to the ecumenical movement. Nevertheless, there was some analysis of Moody's theology, although much too brief to be of real value.[23]

The first attempt to deal with Moody's theology which is worthy of being taken seriously is a chapter in Findlay's definitive biography of Moody, published in 1969, being based on his 1961 Ph.D. dissertation submitted to Northwestern University. Though not as thorough a treatment as it could have been, this thirty-five-page chapter wrestles more seriously with Moody's theology than previous attempts and is characterized by its appeal to the source materials. Findlay's forte, however, is history, not theology, and serious questions must be raised concerning his understanding of some points of Moody's theology. This chapter is the weakest in the book.[24]

There has been an even more recent attempt to examine Moody's theology seriously, the 1973 M.A. thesis of Stan Nussbaum.[25] The early pages of the thesis sketch the broad outlines of Moody's theology, but that is all it is, a sketch.[26] Later pages in the thesis go into detail

21. James Melvin Nelson, "The Theological Significance of City Evangelism" (Master's thesis, Princeton Theological Seminary, 1945). Cf. Dissertations and Theses in Sources Consulted at back of this book.
22. August J. Fry, "D. L. Moody: The Formative Years, 1856-1873" (B.D. thesis, U. Chicago, 1955).
23. John Wesley White, "The Influence of North American Evangelism in Great Britain between 1830 and 1914 on the Origin and Development of the Ecumenical Movement" (Ph.D. diss., Mansfield College, Oxford, 1963), 4:10-15.
24. Findlay, *Dwight L. Moody*, pp. 227-61. On p. vii Findlay comes close to admitting his own sense of inadequacy in treating Moody's theology.
25. Stan Nussbaum, "D. L. Moody and the Church: A Study of the Ecclesiological Implications of Extra-Ecclesiastical Evangelism" (Master's thesis, Trinity Evangelical Divinity School, 1973), cited as "D. L. Moody and the Church."
26. Ibid., pp. 10-34.

with reference to the church in Moody's ministry and theology.[27] The scope of this study is quite narrow; further, as I will show later in this book, Nussbaum does not examine all the evidence, does not use his sources as critically as he should have, and tends to find or not to find what he wants.

In short, a full-length critical analysis of the whole range of Moody's theology has yet to be written. This book is an attempt to fill that gap. The need for such an analysis, together with my interest in late nineteenth-century American Christianity motivated me to research this subject. Association with the Moody Bible Institute as a member of the faculty provided a unique opportunity to examine carefully the wealth of material in the Moodyana Collection of the institute's library. The Moodyana Collection has always been important, but as a result of recent acquisitions anyone engaging in serious Moody research will find it necessary to spend a great deal of time there. Indeed, so far as sermonic material and other materials relating to Moody's theology, either directly or indirectly, it is hardly necessary to go elsewhere. There is more than enough material to satisfy the most insatiable researcher.

The primary purpose of this book, then, is to set forth Moody's understanding of theology, thereby correcting any misconceptions that may exist, and casting light on the context of the evangelical Protestantism in which Moody lived and moved in the last quarter of the nineteenth century. The most valuable source will be the sermons and public statements that were printed from 1873 through 1899. Some of his sermon notes still exist and have been carefully examined; they are, however, so sketchy and ill-organized as to be of little value, except to confirm that published reports of his sermons are basically accurate. Moody's personal correspondence is also extant, but upon examination failed to reveal much of significance theologically. Evidence of Moody's theology prior to 1873 is scant, but there is some, such as that reported in *The Advance* (Chicago) concerning his noon prayer-meeting talks in the local YMCA. Light is cast on some points of Moody's theology by what he did as much as by what he said. The source materials are vast, and it appears that no one has carefully sifted through them up to this point with the purpose in mind of analyzing Moody's theology.[28]

27. Ibid., pp. 63-102.
28. Note the annotations of the entries in Sources Consulted and its Introductory Essay at the back of this book.

Drawing upon these materials, this book will expound the theological themes that characterize Moody's preaching, especially the controlling and unifying theme. The possibility that his theology changed or developed in the years 1873 through 1899 will be considered, especially as during this time he became aware of and interacted with trends within and without Protestant Evangelicalism and society at large.

I gratefully acknowledge my indebtedness to Wilbur M. Smith. Although our contacts have been infrequent, in the early stages of this project he gave the encouragement needed to carry it through. Probably no living person has spent more time studying Moody in library stacks and archives.

The library staff at Moody Bible Institute deserves a special word of thanks. They have gone the extra mile many times over in acquiring new materials relating to Moody from other libraries by Xerox, microfilm, and interlibrary loan. Other libraries are to be commended for their cooperation with the efforts of the institute library to build its collection of Moody materials using modern means of copying. Many institutions could be cited, but several deserve special mention: the Northfield Schools, the Library of Congress, the New York City Public Library, the library of Yale University, the library of the Chicago Theological Seminary, and the British Museum. To Mr. Richard Schock, Mr. Wally Osborne, and Miss Henrietta Watts of the library staff of Moody Bible Institute, I extend my special thanks.

I also gratefully acknowledge all that my advisor at the Lutheran School of Theology at Chicago, Dr. Robert Fischer, has contributed to this project and to me personally in seminars and in person-to-person contact. This book began as a doctoral dissertation. Dr. Fischer's guidance and encouragement in the doctoral program and while working on the dissertation have been above and beyond the call of duty and have been rendered with sincere interest. His exactitude was demanding but most helpful. Whatever sense of critical historical judgment I may have acquired can be attributed in large measure to him. However, responsibility for any errors or shortcomings rests squarely on my own shoulders.

Finally, I thank my wife, Pat, for enduring the research and writing and for helping to put the finishing touches on the book.

1

MEET MR. MOODY

D. L. MOODY's theology was neither formed nor preached in a vacuum, and it cannot be done justice without tracing the broad outlines of his life and the ideas and conflicts of his times socially, economically, and intellectually. This book is neither a biography nor a study of the times per se; such works already exist in great abundance.[1] But the nature of the case demands that such considerations be given their due place. Though more detailed treatment of appropriate subject matter is reserved for later chapters, the purpose of this introductory chapter is to establish a context for the book as a whole.

D. L. MOODY: HIS LIFE AND CAREER

THE EARLY YEARS: NORTHFIELD AND BOSTON, 1837-56

Northfield. Moody's early years contain no clues indicative of the place he was to occupy in the religious life of Great Britain and the United States in the last quarter of the nineteenth century. However, the influences of his home and the small community of Northfield nestled in the rural environment of the Connecticut Valley undoubtedly remained throughout his life. Born on February 5, 1837, in Northfield, Massachusetts, Dwight Lyman was the sixth child and the fifth son in the family.[2] His father, Edwin, apparently never had provided amply

1. The most recent and helpful of these are: James F. Findlay, Jr., *Dwight L. Moody* (1969), and Paul A. Carter, *The Spiritual Crisis of the Gilded Age* (DeKalb, Ill.: Northern Illinois U., 1971).
2. I have not documented every factual statement concerning Moody's life. Such tedious footnoting when the facts are readily accessible in any one of a number of volumes would serve no useful purpose. However, I readily acknowledge my indebtedness to James Findlay's *Dwight L. Moody* for most information not otherwise documented. Readers desiring more detailed information and documentation should consult that volume first. Footnotes are used when the information is not widely available or when the information is of special interest for this study.

for the large family, and his sudden death when Dwight was only four years old plunged the family into dire financial stress. It was Betsy Moody's determination and hard work, the cooperation of the remaining family unit, as well as the helpful interest of the local Unitarian minister, Oliver Everett, which held the family together through those difficult years when the children were growing up.

It was probably Everett's genuine concern for the widow and her family that caused her to become a member of the local Unitarian church on January 1, 1843. At that same time Dwight, then five years old, and the other children were baptized as Unitarians. The family's circumstances suggest that their alignment with Unitarianism was more a matter of convenience and respect for their minister than concern for theological controversy. In fact, the Unitarian church which had begun in 1827 was originally a split from the "orthodox" church effected by a group of discontents who were at odds with the "orthodox" minister. Thus it seems that the church itself did not originate from purely theological considerations. Most people assumed the two groups would reunite when Thomas Mason, the pastor in question, left. However, when the Unitarian fellowship received a substantial endowment in 1836, its continued existence was assured.[3]

Unitarianism itself was in a transitional period at the time, there being a more radical, liberal wing and a more traditional and conservative wing which Timothy L. Smith calls "Evangelical Unitarianism."[4] The Northfield Unitarian congregation seems to have been aligned with the more traditional, conservative group, but in any case theological distinctions were not the talk of the town in Northfield, and they were even less so in the Moody family.

The Moody children were sent to Sunday school and church, and the family library consisted of a family Bible, a catechism, and a book of devotions. Betsy gathered the children daily for readings and prayers, but what evidence is available indicates there was little if any attempt to acquaint them with Christian doctrine.[5] Even if there had been such

---

3. Findlay, *Dwight L. Moody*, pp. 35-39.
4. Timothy L. Smith, *Revivalism and Social Reform in Mid-Nineteenth-Century America* (New York: Abingdon, 1957), pp. 31-32, 95-102, cited as *Revivalism and Social Reform*; cf. William R. Moody, *D. L. Moody* (New York: Macmillan, 1930), pp. 17-19, cited as *Moody* (1930). In later life Moody was asked if he was satisfied with baptism at the hands of a Unitarian minister. He replied, "I found I was baptized in the name of the Father, Son and Holy Ghost. I couldn't see that anyone could add to this," W. R. Moody, *Moody* (1930), p. 14.
5. W. R. Moody, *Moody* (1900), pp. 25-26.

attempts, Moody's absolute ignorance of theological matters when he began attending Boston's Mount Vernon Congregational Church and his own admission of such indicate that his childhood contact with Unitarianism had no enduring effect on his theology as a mature man. Even Findlay's hesitant suggestion that this milieu is a hazy though necessary backdrop to Moody's later decisions which cannot be entirely dismissed is too strong. The fact is, at this time Moody was religiously and theologically unaware, and also probably basically unconcerned. Certainly to say that his contact with Unitarianism as a youth had any significant impact upon his mature thinking and outlook would be an overstatement. As will be seen shortly, from the very earliest time Moody chose for himself to follow the Christian way, he consistently moved in the milieu of evangelical Protestantism and embraced this doctrinal viewpoint. Very shortly after his own conversion, Moody was writing home expressing concern for the souls of his loved ones.[6] A letter apparently written in the early 1860s by Moody's bride-to-be, Emma Revell, to his mother suggests something of Moody's changed relationship toward the family's Unitarianism and the resultant tension. Emma, a lifelong Baptist, wrote:

> I thought also that you might have thought that because Mr. Moody was of a different denomination to what I had been trained in youth that his love and respect for his mother had abated, but I know such is not the case. Besides some of Mr. Moody's warmest friends are Unitarian.[7]

Moody's educational debt to Northfield was similarly quite limited. He did attend the grammar school, but that was intermittent, and his contemporaries remembered him more for his practical jokes than his learning. The estimate that the sum of his formal academic training may have been five years would probably strike those who examine his notes and letters as overly optimistic.[8] They are barely legible, abound in grammatical errors and misspellings, and are deficient in punctuation and capitalization. One lengthy letter dated "Jany 13/62" and addressed "Dear Brother" is totally without punctuation![9]

Findlay emphasizes that Northfield was typical of small-town Amer-

6. Findlay, *Dwight L. Moody*, pp. 52, 67.
7. Quoted in W. R. Moody, *Moody* (1930), p. 81.
8. Findlay, *Dwight L. Moody*, pp. 40-41.
9. Moodyana; see pp. 37-38.

ica at mid-century, making a distinction between small town and rural.
Here elements of city and farm life existed side by side and cast their
influence on the town's inhabitants. Northfield was peaceful and slow,
and yet it was a meeting point between the modes of urban life and rural
life. Whether it was the youthful desire to go to Boston and launch out
on his own or his evangelistic concern for the urban masses, Moody
heard and heeded the call of the city. But at the same time, his roots
and heart were in the slow-paced life of Northfield and its value system,
and so it was to Northfield, not his adopted Chicago, that he returned
when he needed a respite from his two-year preaching tour of Great
Britain in 1875. He purchased property there and established a home
base to which he normally returned at least in the summers. It was
there he chose to rear his children. It was there he ultimately founded
the Northfield Schools and there he started the summer conferences,
including the student conference from which the famous Student Volunteer Movement sprang. When he became ill in the midst of a huge
evangelistic effort in Kansas City in 1899, it was to Northfield he returned for what he thought was to be a recuperation, but which was his
death. Moody lived his life with this dual attraction and attempted to
live and work in both worlds.[10] It may be that this tension, this dual
outlook, was Northfield's most significant contribution to Moody's mature viewpoint.

    Boston. In early 1854 Moody answered the call of the city for the
first time. He went to Boston seeking his fortune and a more exciting
way of life than was to be found in Northfield, thus becoming a part of
the movement to the urban centers so characteristic of the nineteenth
century. But like so many, he found city life had its problems. Employment did not come quickly, and his letters and later statements in
sermons tell of the loneliness he experienced in those early days away
from home. The YMCA had come into existence to serve the needs of
young men in Moody's situation, and Boston had its association.
Though vague religious influences from childhood may have made
Moody receptive to joining, the meager remains of his correspondence
at the time indicate that religious concern was not a significant factor in
his joining the Boston YMCA in mid-1854.[11] The social and intellectual advantages were what attracted him. But if spiritual concern was

    10. Findlay, *Dwight L. Moody*, pp. 41-43.
    11. Ibid., pp. 45-46.

not yet a factor, this contact served to put him into the context of Protestant Evangelicalism. It was also his first relationship with the association with which he was to work so frequently the rest of his life. Indeed, within a very few years, Moody himself was to become a leading personality and influence in the YMCA both in Chicago and throughout America.

Another contact with mainstream American Evangelicalism was established very quickly after his arrival in Boston. When Moody failed to find employment in Boston, he went to his uncle, Samuel Holton, who owned a retail shoe and boot store, and asked for work. His uncle gave him a job, but made Moody promise to attend one church regularly. This agreement was fulfilled when Moody began attending the Mount Vernon Congregational Church.

No evidence indicates any religious commitment yet on Moody's part, but there is a clue to his biblical illiteracy at the time he began going to the church. When Moody attended his first Sunday school class, Edward Kimball, the teacher, announced that everyone should turn to the Gospel of John, from which the day's lesson was taken. Moody, having been handed a Bible by Kimball, began thumbing through Genesis, looking for the appropriate text, as his classmates began to snicker.[12] Moody was rescued from the situation by the alert teacher, who traded Bibles, handing Moody one already opened to the text.

Regular attendance at the services did begin to make their mark on Moody though, and on April 21, 1855, this same Sunday school teacher called on Moody while he was working in his uncle's shoe store. Moody responded positively to Kimball's simple appeal to accept God's love by committing his life to Christ. Although Moody always regarded this as the time of his conversion, it was not a highly emotional experience, and events soon to follow show that Moody had hardly any understanding of the basic doctrines of evangelical Protestantism. Perhaps this partially explains his brand of evangelism in which there was no attempt to produce a highly emotional response and in which fine points of theology normally were not stressed so long as the Gospel presentation was in the mainstream of evangelical understanding.

Within four weeks he presented himself to the church's deacons for examination for membership. Church records indicate that the deacons

12. Pollock, *Moody: A Biographical Portrait*, p. 11.

were impressed with his sincerity, but Moody came far short of the doctrinal understanding then required of prospective members. His Sunday school teacher, Kimball, was present at the examination, and twenty-one years later he wrote an article in which he explained and defended the deacons' action in rejecting this first request for membership.

> I remember the chief question and its answer—the longest he gave: "Mr. Moody, what has Christ done for us all—for you—which entitles Him to our love?" "I don't know;" he said, "I think Christ has done a good deal for us; but I don't think of anything in particular as I know of."

Kimball then went on to say:

> I can truly say (and in saying it I magnify the infinite grace of God as bestowed on Mr. Moody) that I have seen few persons whose minds were spiritually darker than was his when he came into my Sunday-school class, and I think the committee of the Mt. Vernon Church seldom met an applicant for membership who seemed more unlikely ever to become a Christian of clear and decided views of Gospel truth, still less to fill any sphere of public or extended usefulness.[13]

In a sermon preached in Boston in late 1876 or early 1877, Moody himself admitted that when he first became a Christian he "knew nothing of the Bible." He went on, "I was not acquainted with this precious Word. I do not think there were a dozen passages in the whole Word of God that I had committed to memory, and that I could quote."[14] Hoping to correct these deficiencies, the deacons committed him to the instruction of two individuals. About a year later he appeared before the committee again. The church records reveal that the examination results were not significantly better, though he was admitted to membership on the basis of his "evident sincerity" and "earnest determination to be a Christian." He became a member May 3, 1856.[15]

Moody's ignorance of doctrine and Scripture at that time confirms the earlier conclusion that his mature religious and theological views

13. Edward Kimball, "Mr. Moody's Admission to the Church," *New York Witness Extra,* Apr. 1876 (11th week).

14. Dwight Lyman Moody, *New Sermons, Addresses and Prayers* (St. Louis: N. D. Thompson, 1877), p. 634, cited as *New Sermons.* After first footnote citation, volumes of sermons published under Moody's name will be referred to by title only.

15. Findlay, *Dwight L. Moody,* pp. 50-51; W. R. Moody, *Moody* (1930), p. 34, cf. p. 110; David O. Mears, *Life of Edward Norris Kirk, D.D.* (Boston: Lockwood, Brooks, 1877), pp. 225-27.

owed little, if anything, either to his home training or the Northfield Unitarian Church. In fact, the above information suggests that the contributions by Moody's evangelical associations in Boston to his theological understanding were minimal, beyond leading to his conversion and drawing him into the mainstream of evangelical life. Even though Moody's pastor, E. N. Kirk, had been a well-known and successful revivalist before settling in Boston, given Moody's ignorance before the membership committee, it is highly unlikely Moody would have derived much of substance theologically from the preaching of Kirk and then have incorporated it into his own theology.[16] Moody sat under Kirk's preaching only four more months after finally getting his name on the church roll, for the desire to escape the tensions that had developed between him and his uncle and the appeal of opportunities in Chicago drew him West. Examination of Kirk's *Lectures on Revivals* confirms the conclusion that Moody owed little by way of understanding of doctrine to Kirk, for this volume contains nothing of striking similarity to Moody's later beliefs which cannot as well be explained by his later contacts.[17] But the young man had been quickened spiritually in the milieu of Boston Evangelicalism, and it was only natural that he would continue to move in this sphere after his arrival in Chicago on September 11, 1856.

IN BUSINESS: CHICAGO, 1856-1860

Moody was always a man of energy, drive, and ambition, whether as a salesman of shoes or of salvation. That he would move to Chicago and work his way into the business world to make his fortune is not surprising. His aggressive salesmanship, already evident in Boston, served him well in Chicago's thriving shoe business. He became a clerk for E. E. Wishall, a retailer of shoes and boots. Moody did well in this position and in his later employment with C. N. Henderson. Abundant evidence exists which indicates Moody's improved financial position, increased affluence, and preoccupation with making money.[18]

But more significant is the fact that this spirit did not totally possess him to the exclusion of his newborn religious interests. Not only do his letters continue to show his concern for his loved ones, but they indicate

16. McLoughlin, *Modern Revivalism*, p. 171.
17. Edward Norris Kirk, *Lectures on Revivals*, ed. David O. Mears (Boston: Congregational Pub. Soc., 1875).
18. Findlay, *Dwight L. Moody*, pp. 58-62.

that as soon as he arrived in Chicago he began to become involved in the city's Protestant Evangelicalism. A letter to his mother on January 6, 1857 refers to the "great revival of Religion in this city," a revival he was to look back upon longingly in 1899 in these words: "I would like, before I go hence, to see the whole church of God quickened as it was in '57.[19] In May of 1857 he transferred his membership to the Plymouth Congregational Church in Chicago, and at least by 1859 he was deeply involved in the Chicago YMCA work. As in Boston, these associations drew him into the mainstream of American Evangelicalism.

Since it is in this context that Moody began to work and in which his own views of Christianity and theology began to be formed, it is appropriate to take a closer look at what has been called, up to this point, American Evangelical Protestantism.[20] Actually, it is wrong to suggest that a strict definition of American Evangelicalism can be formulated. No one sharply defined theological system can be said to be held by American Evangelicals, though generally speaking, one could say that Evangelicals hold the doctrines of traditional Protestant orthodoxy. But this begs the question by pushing it further back in time and fails to state which doctrines all Evangelicals would hold. But the difficulty of strict definition need not deter description of historical roots, theological tendencies, religious attitudes, and ecclesiastical principles.

The Evangelicalism that characterized most American Protestantism by the middle of the nineteenth century had its roots in colonial Puritanism and even beyond this in seventeenth-century Protestant orthodoxy and the pietistic reaction. Protestant orthodoxy in the late sixteenth century and the seventeenth century tended to harden into a Protestant scholasticism and a formalism in the churches. At the same time it fragmented into rival theological systems having ecclesiastical counterparts. Two significant reactions to this state of affairs were rationalism and pietism. They were two sides of the same coin, both being weary of an orthodoxy which seemed to them to be more productive of division and debate than unity and peace. Both tended to shrug off the theological questions that had seemed so important to their counterparts in Protestant orthodoxy.

19. Letter cited by Findlay, *Dwight L. Moody*, p. 63; *Northfield Echoes, 1899*, 6:382.

20. The following discussion of American Evangelicalism is dependent on Sidney E. Mead's analysis contained in *The Lively Experiment: The Shaping of Christianity in America* (New York: Harper & Row, 1963), especially chaps. 3 and 7, pp. 38-54, 103-33, cited as *The Lively Experiment*.

But the nature of these two reactions was quite different and ultimately incompatible. Rationalists tended to put ultimate confidence in autonomous human reason as the judge of all truth. Among them divine revelation became less significant as opposed to the claims of reason, and the essence of true religion was reduced to a set of intellectual propositions (all very rational, of course) about God, immortality, and a life of virtue and morality. In short, the theology of orthodoxy with its claim to be based on divine revelation in Scripture was rejected in favor of what seemed to be a more rationally acceptable and more practical view of God and virtue.

While rationalism was more of a reaction of the head against dead orthodoxy, pietism was a reaction of the heart, although this does not necessarily suggest that pietists were unlearned. H. R. Mackintosh's description of pietism as "a recoil of living faith from a dead and rigid orthodoxy" is not too far off the mark.[21] The pietists were seeking a spiritual nourishment they did not find in the formal creeds and the systematic theologies of the churches. They fought the worldliness and apathy which they felt had worked its way into the churches. But their purpose was not to remodel doctrine; it was to quicken the spiritual life of the Church on both the corporate and individual levels. Nevertheless, the tendency was to downgrade the importance of creeds and theologies and to minimize the intellectual content of faith. This, in turn, tended to break the pietists' sense of continuity with the Christian past. In other words, though the religious and intellectual outlooks of pietists and rationalists were fundamentally different, the end results were often the same or similar when viewed from the perspective of the place theology occupied.

That members of pietistic groups immigrated to the American colonies in the late seventeenth century and throughout the eighteenth century and became quite strong in Rhode Island and the middle colonies is well known. Nor were the American colonies immune to the then current forms of rationalism; some of the best-known leaders in the revolutionary period belonged to this mind-set. The eighteenth-century revivals increased the size of the pietistic sects both by conversions and schisms from the entrenched right-wing churches, and these sectarian groups spread widely through the colonies. Conflict between groups with a pietistic orientation and the established or dominant churches in

21. H. R. Mackintosh, *Types of Modern Theology* (London: Collins, 1964), p. 19.

the colonies was almost inevitable, with the Establishment fighting to retain its privileged position at the expense of the pietists. It was in this situation that an unequal yoke between pietists and rationalists was formed in the eighteenth century in the American colonies. Sidney Mead's summary is to the point:

> The struggles for religious freedom during the last quarter of the eighteenth century provided the kind of practical issue upon which rationalists and sectarian-pietists could and did unite, in spite of underlying theological differences. The positive thrust for the separation of church and state and the making of all religious groups equal before the civil law came from the sectarian-pietists both within and without the right-wing churches, and from the rationalistic social and political leaders.[22]

The final disestablishment of churches and the declaration of national religious freedom which came in the early days of the new nation owed most to the coalition into which pietists and rationalists had been pushed by the pressure of circumstances. But their success broke the bond holding them together, and a major realignment was very quickly to take place. Pietists and traditionalists were soon to be arrayed against the rationalists.

Practical and political agreements made it possible for rationalists and pietists to work together for full religious liberty. However, there were significant differences between them. Sociologically, the rationalists, in spite of their affirmations for liberty, tended to be elitists by birth, breeding, wealth, and education. Pietism was more a religion of the common man. But the theological difference was more significant. Rationalists argued for the autonomy and sufficiency of human reason to interpret the universal revelation of God in creation. Traditional concepts of supernaturalism were incompatible with "reasonable" concepts of the world order. The actual break between the rationalists and the pietists came when nonrationalists looked at the course of the French Revolution and came to the conclusion that infidel rationalism led to the anarchy and atrocities of the later phases of the French Revolution. The views of Jefferson and other leaders of the Jeffersonian party were labeled "French."[23]

22. Mead, *The Lively Experiment*, p. 43. For a detailed treatment of "infidelity" and its temporary alliance with the dissenters, see Martin E. Marty, *The Infidel: Freethought and American Religion*, Meridian Books (Cleveland: World, 1961), pp. 43-70.
23. Mead, *The Lively Experiment*, pp. 45-46.

It is not necessary to go into the details of the rationalistic attack on the institutional church or the subtle interplay of personalities and events. Nor is it important at this point to determine whether the conclusions of nonrationalists about the end results of rationalistic religious, social, and political theory were correct or justified. The important point is that the radical attack on revelation was interpreted by nearly all religious leaders as subversive, not just to the traditionally authoritarian churches, but to Christianity itself, indeed to society.

A contest then developed between rationalists and orthodox for the allegiance of the masses of the people. Ethan Allen and Thomas Paine popularized the rationalists' position with tracts like *Reason the Only Oracle of Man* and *Age of Reason*. The defenders of orthodoxy likewise took the battle to the people, and their tool in the ideological warfare was the revival. In this battle for the mind at the turn of the century a new alignment of religious and intellectual forces was taking shape. Sectarian pietists and orthodox traditionalists, so recently disestablished, joined forces against the rationalists. This constituted a major turning point in the history of Christianity in America, and the new shape of things was to influence profoundly the development of Protestantism throughout the nineteenth century and into the twentieth. This new union was to give birth to denominationalism and what has been called American Protestant Evangelicalism within these churches. Since the new alignment of pietists and traditionalists generally won the battle for the mind of the people, this was to be the dominant characteristic of American Protestantism through the nineteenth century.

Though it is not here suggested that this was an incompatible union, the nature of the union from which American Evangelicalism sprang explains the previously mentioned difficulty in sharply defining what it is. Pietists as such had never necessarily discarded the doctrinal baggage of the dead orthodoxy they had reacted against. They had just said that it was not enough. So doctrinally they experienced little difficulty in the realignment. Traditionalists found themselves uncomfortable with revivalism and gradually came to see an already weakened Calvinistic theology further eroded in the first half of the nineteenth century in the theologies of Timothy Dwight, Charles Finney, and others. Arminianism with a residue of Calvinism was to become more and more characteristic of American Evangelicalism. Not only did the union of traditionalism and pietism produce a new breed, but the fact that nearly

every Christian European group had been transplanted to what was
now the United States contributed to the multifaceted character of
American Evangelicalism.

Again, Mead's analysis of the distinctive character of typical American Christianity as it had emerged by 1850 is helpful, for it was in this
mainstream American Evangelicalism that Dwight L. Moody had
gotten his feet wet in Boston, and it was into this stream that he was
steadily and inexorably drawn when he moved to Chicago. This would
be the sphere in which he would develop his religious views. Mead lists
six basic characteristics that mark the denominations and, by virtue of
that, American Protestant Evangelicalism.[24]

First is the tendency of each denominational group to justify its distinctives of doctrine and practice as conforming more closely to those of
the Church of the New Testament than the doctrine and practice of
rival denominations. This tended to ignore the developments of the
intervening centuries, with the result that it amounted to an antihistorical
bias. This was a tendency that had a long history in Protestantism with
its emphasis on the authority of Scripture and the right of private judgment. Right-wing Protestants had tried to preserve a sense of historical
continuity, but the left-wing groups, taking no creed but the Bible,
radically left the appeal to Church and historical tradition and claimed
to appeal directly to the beliefs and practices of New Testament Christianity.

In the American experience, this appeal to Scripture found its most
frequent expression. One thing that the many Christian groups shared
in common was the Bible and respect for it as the highest authority.
Shorn of coercive powers that some groups had once enjoyed, and
sharing a common sense of opportunity to begin anew in the new land,
the denominations that grew up in the post-revolutionary era under-
standably lacked a sense of history and appealed back over the centuries
to first-century Christianity as the justification for their peculiar beliefs
and practices. What became true of denominations in particular was
true of American Evangelicalism in general.

The second element noted by Mead is the principle of voluntaryism.
With disestablishment of the churches and equality before civil law,
one's association with a church became free and uncoerced—voluntary.
This in turn meant that in the effort to obtain the free consent of indi-

24. Ibid., pp. 108-33.

viduals to a particular church, practical considerations came to the fore with promotion of the group and its purposes. Discussion of theology which might be divisive and consequently retard realization of the group's purposes or alienate prospective recruits tended to fade into the background.

Emphasis on the missionary enterprise was a third characteristic of the denominations and a natural concomitant of voluntaryism. Converts had to be won by persuasion, not coercion. This sense of mission not only characterized the denominations but also the evangelical interdenominationalism into which Moody himself was being drawn.

The fourth element in Mead's scheme is revivalism as the accepted technique of recruitment. This, of course, tied in with voluntaryism and the tendency to put doctrinal discussion into the background. Old-line traditionalists sensed that revivalists put the expediencies of evangelism above creed, and eventually Moody himself was to be criticized by the old guard on this point. The evangelistic stress on "whosoever will" placed the emphasis on man's initiative in salvation. This in turn tempted revivalists to justify whatever means would produce conversions, and it was largely on this ground that the "new measures" of Finney were justified.

This emphasis on man's role in his own salvation and on aggressive evangelism steadily became more characteristic of American Evangelicalism in the nineteenth century. It commonly has been identified as Arminianism and has been set in opposition to the Calvinism of the Puritan forefathers and later Presbyterian immigrants. Used in this manner, Arminianism usually denotes a view of salvation that is synergistic, that is, God and man working together in salvation. In such a view the effects of sin on the human will were thought either to be not totally disabling or sufficiently counteracted by God's grace so that man could cooperate with God. But grace was also resistible. Election was conditioned on God's foreknowledge of who would believe. The benefits of Christ's death were sufficient for all and genuinely offered to all. Anyone could accept or reject the offer of salvation. And those who accepted might fall from grace later of their own choice. Those who held such views normally argued that if man did not have the power of free choice, God could not justly hold him morally responsible. In brief, these ideas are the core of what has come to be known commonly as Arminianism.

In opposition to Arminianism, Calvinism stresses a divine monergism that seems to leave the sinner totally passive in his own salvation and at the mercy of the elective choice of a sovereign God. The acronym, TULIP, describes the five-point Calvinism that excluded the Arminian Remonstrants from the Reformed churches after the Synod of Dort (1619). The TULIP doctrines serve as a convenient means of contrasting Calvinism with Arminianism: *T*otal depravity, *U*nconditional election, *L*imited atonement, *I*rresistible grace, *P*erseverance of the saints. When theologians in the Calvinistic tradition toned down some of the harshness of these points, they would promptly be accused of Arminianism by those who thought of themselves as purists, as happened in the history of New England theology.

This is what has been meant when historians have described Arminian tendencies in American Evangelicalism vis-à-vis Calvinism. The same usage will be maintained here. To depart from it would make interaction with other historians of the period difficult; furthermore, this does generally conform to the nineteenth-century usage of the terms. Recent studies, however, have emphasized the limitations of this way of looking at Arminianism and Calvinism. It has become increasingly clear that Calvin must be distinguished from the Calvinists and Arminius from the Arminians. For instance, Carl Bangs' recent study of Arminius cogently argues that he was a Reformed theologian and that his views must not be identified with the synergistic views of some later Arminians. Others would ask if it is possible to be truly Calvinist or Arminian in soteriology without also being Calvinist or Arminian in the other branches of theology, such as ecclesiology. Still others, out of regard for the conditioning that the times exert on all theological efforts, would deny that anyone can speak to his own time and wholly adopt an earlier theology. There is another problem. These labels tend to ignore different strands within the theological traditions denoted by the labels, as well as similar emphases outside those traditions.[25]

25. Ibid., pp. 33, 124. For recent discussions of Calvinism and Arminianism, see Carl Bangs, *Arminius: A Study in the Dutch Reformation* (Nashville: Abingdon, 1973), pp. 186-221, 332-55; John T. McNeill, *The History and Character of Calvinism* (New York: Oxford U., 1954), pp. 201-23, 426-38; Carl Bangs, "Arminius as a Reformed Theologian," in *The Heritage of John Calvin*, ed. John H. Bratt (Grand Rapids: Eerdmans, 1973), pp. 209-22; C. C. Goen's editorial introduction to *Jonathan Edwards: The Great Awakening*, pp. 4-18, 25-32; Sidney Earl Mead, *Nathaniel William Taylor, 1786-1858: A Connecticut Liberal* (Chicago: U. Chicago, 1942), pp. 87-89, 95-127, 189-99; Basil Hall, "The Calvin Legend" and "Calvin against the Calvinists" and J. I. Packer, "Calvin the Theologian," in *John Calvin*, ed. G. E. Duffield (Grand Rapids: Eerdmans, 1966), pp. 1-37, 149-75.

In spite of these difficulties, the terms *Arminian* and *Calvinist* will be used in this study as functionally useful to denote two significant strands in Evangelicalism. But description of trends or people as Arminian or Calvinistic must be tempered by recognition of the limitations of the terms. They are helpful if not pressed too far, but it must be remembered that they also may be simplistic and inaccurate. With this warning in mind, we repeat that American Evangelicalism had Arminian tendencies.

A fifth element characteristic of the American churches was the flight from reason. Except for Unitarians, especially left-wing Unitarians, American Protestantism turned against the rationalism of the Enlightenment when the pietists joined forces with traditional orthodoxy and pitted revelation against reason. The distinctive pietistic emphasis on heart rather than head generally won the day in American Evangelicalism, so that not only was rationalism skirted, but subjective religious experience became basic, whereas traditional orthodoxy had tended to make theological content basic. This in turn contributed to the "amorphous" character of American Evangelicalism.

Mead's final characteristic of American Christianity as it grew out of the new alignment is the competition that existed among the denominations. Again this is related to the principle of voluntaryism in that the denominations were competing for converts. Though this was competition among Christian groups that held more in common than not, the animosity could become intense. It will be discovered in due course that this was an aspect of American denominationalism that Moody not only experienced, but reacted against. To him it was a curse.

Mead's analysis of the roots and character of the American Evangelicalism into which Moody was being progressively drawn has been employed because of its utility in portraying a complex historical development. Of course, it runs the risk of oversimplification, and this summary has undoubtedly aggravated that problem. For instance, one might want more development of the motif of perfection in American religious life from the very earliest days. Or where is mention found of industrialization and urbanization? What about the more recent concern to see American life, culture, and religion as part of a broader Atlantic community? There is ample evidence of the interchange of people and ideas between American Christians and Christians in the British Isles. How did this shape American Evangelicalism?

The experience of Moody himself soon will be seen to be a good case in point, for he not only made three trips across the ocean to learn from the British brethren he had already heard and read of, but he was readily accepted, in spite of his Yankee peculiarities, in his famous 1873-1875 tour of Scotland, Ireland, and England. Why? Apparently American Evangelicalism did not develop in total isolation, nor was it absolutely unique. While Mead's description is helpful in understanding what is unique in American Christianity of the mid-nineteenth century, one must guard against the unwarranted conclusion that forces that shaped the evangelical orbit into which Moody was moving were exclusively American; nor should one conclude that American Evangelicalism was absolutely unique.[26]

As already noted, the points of contact that Moody had had with Evangelicalism in Boston were taken up again in Chicago shortly after his move in the late summer of 1856. In fact, the evidence testifies to a deepening involvement in evangelical causes and to his acceptance of evangelical concerns and viewpoints. In addition to his transfer of membership to Plymouth Congregational Church, probable involvement in the revival of 1857, and membership in the YMCA, Moody was becoming increasingly concerned for the salvation of individuals.

James Findlay, who has carefully sifted through the remaining letters written shortly after Moody's arrival in Chicago, has established that Moody's central concern for his family in New England was that they stood in need of conversion, an indication of his estimate of the family's Unitarianism.[27] Activist by temperament, it is not surprising that Moody showed this quality so typical of Evangelicalism.

Since matters of eternal destiny hung in the balance, Evangelicals emphasized the necessity of aggressive work to obtain converts. This theme of work which Moody was to emphasize so frequently in his attempts to move Christians to action in the early phases of a series of meetings or in his instructions to new converts at the close of a series, very quickly manifested itself in his own activities in Chicago. Typical of Moody is the title of a widely circulated volume of his sermons with

26. This warning has been elaborated by Winthrop S. Hudson, "How American is Religion in America?" and Martin E. Marty, "Reinterpreting American Religious History in Context," in *Reinterpretation in American Church History*, ed. Jerald C. Brauer. (Chicago: U. Chicago, 1968), pp. 153-67, 195-218.

27. Findlay, *Dwight L. Moody*, p. 67.

the title, *To the Work! To the Work!* Moody's comments in the preface have special significance:

> During the years that I have been privileged to labor for God, in this country and in England, I have strongly and increasingly felt that the task of arousing Christians to a deeper sense of their responsibility is even a more important one than that of the simple evangelist. As I have frequently had occasion to remark: It is far better to get a hundred men to work, than to do the work oneself. Only when the rank and file of the Christian churches are enlisted in active service for Christ, will His Kingdom advance as it ought.[28]

Shortly after arriving in Chicago, Moody rented a pew in the Plymouth church and filled it with people brought in from street corners and boarding houses. It was to be some time yet before he began teaching and preaching, but he could bring them in to hear. Years later he said his efforts to speak in these meetings were met with irritation and boredom by the older church people. Eventually he was renting four pews which he managed to keep full. This apparently was not a sufficient outlet for his energies, for he next offered his services to a mission Sunday school on North Wells Street, only to be told no class was available. He would have to provide his own class, which is precisely what he proceeded to do, recruiting children from the streets and bringing them to the school.[29]

Sometime in 1858 or early 1859, without support from any church or society, Moody began his own mission Sunday school on Chicago's North Side in a deserted saloon near the North Side Market. During this same period he worked with a group of young men from the First Methodist Church, visiting hotels and saloons, distributing tracts, and inviting people to church. He had chosen one of the most difficult sections of Chicago for his Sunday school. "The Sands" abounded with crime and prostitution, and young urchins swarmed the streets; the area was infested with saloons and gambling houses. The wooden shanties that were the housing in the area were primarily inhabited by German and Scandinavian immigrants.

Moody apparently served mainly as the organizer and recruiter of both the teaching staff and students. His aggressive methods were so

28. D. L. Moody, *To the Work! To the Work!* (Chicago: Revell, 1884), p. 3.
29. W. H. Daniels, *D. L. Moody and His Work* (Hartford, Conn.: American, 1875), pp. 31-32.

successful that the school outgrew the facilities in the saloon and moved to a large hall above the North Market. Facilities were somewhat better there, and regular classes were formed and additional teachers obtained, with permanent organization probably taking place in late 1859.[30]

From his arrival in Chicago in 1856 throughout the rest of the 1850s, Moody steadily became more and more involved in missionary outreach among the city's masses, especially among the deprived children of the North Side. Initially he worked through his church, filling pews; but experiencing frustration here, he moved into mission work to children, eventually starting his own school. Relatively uneducated in doctrine and untrained, he himself did little actual teaching, relying on his staff of teachers while he devoted most of his energies to administration and outreach. In a sermon probably preached in Boston in January, 1877, Moody took a few moments to talk "to you Christians and stir you up to work." His recollections of these early years in Chicago serve well to summarize his concerns, activities, state of learning, and the direction in which he was moving.

> If the church people do not like to see you trying to work, you can go into some of these lanes, you can go out upon the streets and gather there little boys and bring them into the Sabbath-school. The first two or three years that I attempted to talk in the Meeting I saw that the older people did not like it. I had sense enough to know that I was a bore to them. Well, I went out upon the street and I got eighteen children to follow me the first Sunday and I led them into the Sunday-school. I found that I had something to do. I was encouraged and I kept at that work. And if I am worth anything to the Christian Church to-day, it is as much due to that work as to anything else. I could not explain these Scriptural passages to them, for I did not then comprehend them, but I could tell them stories; I could tell them that Christ loved them and that He died for them. I did the best I could. I used the little talent I had, and God kept giving me more talents, and so, let me say, find some work.[31]

But during these years Moody not only became more involved in work for Christ among the city's masses, he was also becoming more and more successful in business. He had come to Chicago to make money, and he was doing just that. In 1859, as a salesman on commission he had made $5,000 above his salary. He had moved from the

30. Ibid., pp. 45 ff.; Findlay, *Dwight L. Moody*, p. 77.
31. *New Sermons*, pp. 577-78.

business of his friend Wishall to the business house of C. N. Henderson. In this position he had to travel extensively in the Midwest. Even though the superintendent of the Chicago, Burlington, and Quincy Railroad provided him with a pass to get back to Chicago for the Sunday school, it obviously worked something of a hardship on Moody. When Henderson died, Moody moved to the firm of Messrs. Buel, Hill, and Granger.

During this time Moody was apparently coming to feel that he could no longer carry on both interests and do them justice, and so in June of 1860 he abandoned the shoe and boot business to devote his future to religious work. A few days after he quit, he was to tell Mr. Hill who had asked him what he was now doing, "I am at work for Jesus Christ."[32]

Not much is known of the details surrounding Moody's decision to take this new course. The fact that Moody's commitment to a cause he believed in was never halfhearted must have been a significant factor. His religious work which had started as an after-hours project had come to occupy more and more of his time and attention. Moody himself often told the story of the influence on him of a young victim of tuberculosis. Moody testified that for a long time after his conversion he really didn't accomplish anything. He'd get up and pray, but he did not yet have the courage to "go up to a man and take hold of his coat and get him down on his knees. . . . It was in 1860 the change came."

A young teacher of a girls' class in Moody's Sunday school came to see Moody at the store, saying, "I have been bleeding at the lungs, and they have given me up to die." His request was that Moody would help him work for the conversion of each of the girls in his class. Moody was to later say that this was "how I got the first impulse to work solely for the conversion of men." "I myself was led by this incident—this wonderful blessing of God on individual effort—to throw up my business and give my whole strength to God's work."[33]

Sixteen years later Moody was found warning his auditors in the Boston Tabernacle not to "give up their business and their worldly occupation" to "go into the work of the Lord entirely." "It is too high a calling, it seems to me, for men to be influencing one another to go into

32. Daniels, *D. L. Moody and His Work*, p. 81; cf. Findlay, *Dwight L. Moody*, pp. 88-91.
33. *New Sermons*, pp. 295-96.

it," he said. Wait until God calls and sends, he advised.[34] Moody apparently felt that God had so called him, and acting on the basis of his own personal faith that Christ would guide and provide, he left his successful start in the shoe business. With characteristic decisiveness, he devoted all his time and energies to the work of his Sunday school and eventually to other endeavors growing out of his widening contacts with evangelicals and evangelical causes. This new departure set the course of the rest of his life. It was devoted to Christian work; he was without regular income and he refused to profit personally either from offerings taken in meetings or from the income from his song and sermon books. He was totally dependent on the confidence and goodwill of individual benefactors.

THE SCHOOL OF EXPERIENCE: CHICAGO AND BEYOND, 1860-1873

When Moody decided to give his "whole strength to God's work," he was totally without formal training for the work he had chosen and only had a bare minimum of practical experience to draw on. Yet within fourteen years reports of his meetings would fill the front pages of newspapers in Great Britain and the United States. Whatever views he had of the Christian faith and whatever skills he had as an evangelist were basically formed in these intervening years. They were the formative years, years spent in the school of experience.

The Moody who is to be seen in this period, especially in the earlier years, is a colorful, unorthodox, at times even crude individual who was working with every fiber of his being to bring souls into the Kingdom and to alleviate the hardships of the less fortunate. One finds Moody buttonholing total strangers and confronting them with the question, "Are you saved?" He is to be seen pouring out the whiskey of a drunken father. He is to be found riding his pony through the slums with ragged children riding and running alongside. He can be seen chasing a prospective Sunday school scholar wildly through the streets and alleys. Anecdotes abound relating those antics that gave him the name "crazy Moody" in some circles. But Moody was to mellow, and the rough edges were to be knocked off. In this period Moody's efforts to reach the masses of Chicago intensified. He was able to identify with their plight both spiritually and materially. At the same time he was

34. D. L. Moody, *To All People* (New York: E. B. Treat, 1877), p. 279; cf. p. 490.

able to enlist the support of the well-to-do in Chicago, both for his Sunday school and the YMCA.

Work for the YMCA began informally, consisting of encouraging people to attend and take part in the noon prayer meeting. Soon he was given the formal position of librarian of the association, thus becoming the first full-time employee of the Chicago YMCA, though without pay. That little matter was handled individually by such well-to-do businessmen connected with the Y as John V. Farwell. Moody's organizational abilities and personal drive were what held the Chicago YMCA together in the early sixties, and he was to prove to be its chief fund-raiser.

The start of the Civil War in 1861 brought opportunities for both the YMCA and Moody in the form of work among the troops of the North and captured soldiers from the Southern army. From the YMCA's involvement as the link between the evangelical churches and the soldiers grew the United States Christian Commission in which Moody played a very active role. Moody spent time near the front lines and back at the Chicago home base. These war experiences were later to serve as a rich source of illustrations for his sermons. Camp Douglas to the south of Chicago was the main scene of Moody's efforts for the commission and the association during the war; he conducted frequent meetings and distributed songbooks and tracts to the men. At this same time the YMCA in Chicago expanded its relief work to the needy of Chicago, and Moody was deeply involved in that, merging his previous efforts with those of the association. The best description of Moody's life and activities at this time is to be found in a letter to his brother Samuel dated "Jany 13/62." An unretouched excerpt follows:

> I am very sorry I have not answered your 3 last letters but I have had so much to do I could not find time you seem to be very ancious to know what I am doing this winter well I will tell you I am agent for the City Relief Society that is to take care of the poore of the city I have some 500 hundred or 800 people that are dependent on us for their daily food & new ones coming all of the time I keep a Saddall horse to ride around with to hunt up the poore people with & then I have a man to waite on the folks as they come to my office I make my head quarters at the rooms of the Young Mens Christian association & then I have just raised money enough to erect a chapell for the Soldiers

at the Camp 3 miles from the city I hold a meeting down there every day & 2 in the city so you see I have 3 meetings to attend to every day bes side calling on the sick & that is not all I have to go into the country every week to buy wood & provisions for the poore also coal wheet meal and corn then I have to go to hold meetings I was sent for last month to go to [?] Elgin to a prayer meeting 36 miles just to one prayer meeting I had a very good time I have not told you all I am doing I am also raising money to buy Himbooks for the soldiers I am one of the army Commitey [?] & we hold meetigs once a week & then we have to distribute the books to the different companeys you do not know how much I have to do I speak about 3 times a day from 10 minuets to one hour I do not get 5 minuets a day to study so I have to talk just as it happens & now I have told you what I am a doing. . . .[35]

One wonders how Moody in this helter-skelter round of activities had time for anything else, especially when occasional trips to the war front are thrown in for good measure. But he somehow did find the time, and the Sunday school in the hall of North Market continued to grow and evolve. By mid-1862, there were 450 children attending, with Moody also conducting a prayer meeting for the parents. In the winter months there was an evening class meeting three nights a week "for instruction in the common English branches." By 1863 the school had outgrown its North Market facilities and a lot was purchased at the corner of Illinois and Wells streets with substantial gifts from Farwell. By February, 1864, a large brick building was completed with an auditorium seating 1,500, a chapel, and numerous classrooms. At the end of 1865 the weekly Sunday school attendance averaged 750, being the second largest Sunday school in Chicago.

When the school moved into its own building, it quickly evolved into a church, which came into being officially as the Illinois Street Church on December 30, 1864.[36] The church was nondenominational, though the Congregationalists in the city provided assistance in its formative stages. This was reflected in its doctrinal statement and bylaws.[37] How much of this statement was consciously formulated by Moody, and how much was due to the outside Congregational influences, is impossible to say, but these articles of faith are the first extant concrete clue

35. Moodyana.
36. Findlay, *Dwight L. Moody*, pp. 106-9; cf. W. R. Moody, *Moody* (1930), pp. 98-99.
37. August J. Fry, "D. L. Moody: The Formative Years, 1856-1873" (B. D. thesis, U. Chicago, 1955), pp. 12-17.

of Moody's own beliefs. Though the church did not affiliate with the Congregationalists, it probably would have been readily accepted by them. The articles of faith were clearly evangelical but strictly non-denominational. This is indicative of the direction in which Moody himself was moving, at least in terms of his public efforts and allegiances.

Moody's horizons had been expanded somewhat beyond Chicago by virtue of his work with the Christian Commission during the Civil War, but new responsibilities taken on after the war were to broaden further his opportunities, contacts, and experience. In 1866 he was chosen president of the Chicago YMCA, a position he was to hold for four years. In this post he promoted personal evangelism and frequently took the leadership of the noon prayer meetings conducted daily in the association's headquarters. The format of these meetings was very flexible, but often Moody, along with others, would take the opportunity to offer comments.

The reports of these meetings in *The Advance* (Chicago) contain the earliest clear clues of the religious beliefs that Moody was in the process of forming.[38] One even begins to encounter in these talks the illustrations that Moody was to frequently repeat in his later preaching. Not to be ignored is the building program taken up during Moody's presidency of the YMCA. But of greater significance for this study is the fact that his position as president of the Chicago association, one of the most important and active in the country, meant that he had to travel extensively all over the country. He made contacts that were not only going to help him in the future, but which were also molding him at that time. In 1870 he gave a major address at the national meeting in Indianapolis.[39]

Other interdenominational involvements were also broadening his contacts, contributing to the forging of his own views and affording him more frequent opportunities to speak. Specifically, Moody became more and more involved in the interdenominational conventions for the promotion and improvement of Sunday schools. Two movements of similar aims emerged, the "Christian conventions" and Sabbath school conventions. Conventions would normally be held annually at the

---

38. These reports are to be found in the issues of *The Advance* (Chicago), 1867-70. Chicago Theological Seminary has a file of them, and Xerox copies of certain key issues are in Moodyana.

39. Findlay, *Dwight L. Moody*, pp. 117-18.

state and county levels for the purpose of inspiring the participants to
new heights of achievement and comparing curricula and methods. It
was natural that Moody would become involved in both these movements for they emphasized lay leadership and were interdenominational
in nature. Furthermore, Moody's reputation as a young, aggressive
leader in the Chicago YMCA and as the founder and guiding light of
a highly successful mission Sunday school in Chicago marked him as
a leader in the movement. By 1868 he was a much sought-after speaker. Again, this expanding circle of contacts and acquaintances was not
only to serve him well in his future evangelism, but was also a significant influence upon his developing understanding of the Bible and
doctrine.

When Moody stopped searching for dollars to search for souls, he
also found ever-expanding opportunities to speak. In more or less this
order, his audiences had expanded from one-to-one witnessing, to informal comments in praise and prayer meetings, to stories told to
children in Sunday school, to teaching adults, to street preaching, to
preaching to soldiers, to leading and addressing YMCA prayer meetings, to preaching in his church, to preaching to large interdenominational Sunday school conventions. Though extant records of what
Moody was preaching toward the end of this period and before the
first meetings in England in 1873 are very limited, they are sufficient
to show that Moody had developed an articulated evangelical understanding of the Christian faith and that he was using illustrations and
other materials in his sermons that were used after he came to international fame.

Largely ignored up to this point has been the question, "Where and
how did the young man who was practically illiterate biblically and
doctrinally in 1860 acquire his religious understanding?" From what
sources had Moody acquired the knowledge and understanding to be
able to preach at all?

Moody's own admission was that in the early days, 1862 to be
specific, he was speaking three times a day for periods from ten minutes
to one hour, yet with all his other activities to attend to, "I do not get
5 minutes a day to study so I have to talk just as it happens."[40] W. H.
Daniels, who had known Moody in Chicago, said of Moody's preaching in those early years:

40. From a 1862 letter to his brother, Samuel, Moodyana, and quoted on p. 38.

His sermons and addresses, though often founded upon a text of Scripture, were largely made up of personal incidents, arguments drawn from surrounding scenes and circumstances; fervid personal appeals to Christians, inciting to greater activity; and earnest calls to sinners, urging them to repent and believe the Gospel.[41]

Given his state of understanding, Moody at this point hardly had any other alternative in his preaching. However, Moody's reference to not having five minutes a day to study is of the nature of a complaint and suggests that Moody was not satisfied to go on in ignorance. Moody never was one who could spend long hours in tedious study, though he did later develop a certain regimen of study. But he developed a method of educating himself theologically that was to stay with him to the end of his days.

The first element of the method was that he carried with him a notebook in which he jotted down information that struck him as helpful and then filed it away in large linen envelopes marked with textual or topical headings, and there the notes remained until needed for a sermon on that topic or text. Taking notes on sermons or Bible studies which he attended, he did not hesitate to take such material and make it his own. Even in the 1880s and 1890s he could be seen at his summer Northfield conferences taking notes on the messages of such noted yet diverse men as A. T. Pierson, William Rainey Harper, Henry G. Weston, or Henry Drummond.

The second element of his method for educating himself consisted of forming impromptu bull sessions whenever he found himself among persons, especially ministers, from whom he thought he could learn. Moody would often advise his converts to keep in the company of more experienced Christians from whom they could learn. And then Moody would say, "I like to keep in the company of those who know more than I do; and I never lose a chance of getting all the good I can out of them." And then he might add, "I get the best of the bargain that way."[42]

Whether with one or ten such companions, he might say, "Give me something out of your heart. Tell me something about Christ." Or he might ask, "What has been your best thought to-day?" At other times

41. Daniels, D. L. Moody and His Work, p. 174.
42. D. L. Moody, Pleasure and Profit in Bible Study (Chicago: BICA, 1895), p. 9; D. L. Moody, Glad Tidings: Comprising Sermons and Prayer-Meeting Talks Delivered at the N.Y. Hippodrome (New York: E. B. Treat, 1876), p. 452, cited as Glad Tidings.

the question would be "What does this verse mean?" as Moody would go around the circle of participants on one verse after another.[43] One such occasion in Peoria, Illinois, was later recalled by D. W. McWilliams. Several ministers and two laymen were dining with Moody. "The entire conversation that day was exposition of Scripture in reply to Mr. Moody's rapid questions." "The impression made upon us all that day . . . was . . . his intense desire for Bible knowledge."[44]

J. V. Farwell, businessman and financial supporter of Moody since the early 1860s, told of a similar meeting in London with "ten or a dozen eminent ministers" where he was asking them "questions to enlarge his own knowledge of the Word of God." At such a meeting he remembered Moody saying, "I have never been through a college or a theological seminary, and I have invited you here to get all the valuable teaching I can out of you to use in my work."[45]

Though he would have admitted himself that this was a poor substitute for formal training, this method of learning was suited to Moody's aptitudes; and Moody must be credited with making the most of the opportunities for such interchange of ideas as his circle of acquaintances enlarged through the 1860s, and indeed, throughout his life. In this way Moody attempted to compensate for what he recognized as his own deficiencies, and through this means primarily he acquired his understanding of evangelical doctrine.

This is not to suggest that Moody never read books, but book study certainly was not his forte; and it is not known when he began to make significant use of such helps. However, in an 1876 address to young converts in the New York Hippodrome, he advised:

> I have one rule about books. I do not read any book, unless it will help me to understand *the* book. . . . It is a great pleasure to get a book that helps unfold the blessed Bible. It is manna to my soul.[46]

At the top of such a list of books, Moody would have placed *Cruden's Concordance* and a topical textbook, two books which he often said every Christian should have in addition to a Bible. Moody himself apparently began Bible study with the use of a concordance

43. Daniels, *D. L. Moody and His Work*, p. 175.
44. Handwritten recollections of D. W. McWilliams, Moodyana; cf. Pollock, *Moody: A Biographical Portrait*, p. 44.
45. John V. Farwell, *Early Recollections of Dwight L. Moody* (Chicago: Winona Pub., 1907), p. 192.
46. *Glad Tidings*, p. 452.

about 1861.[47] In the study of the home that he later purchased in Northfield he had a sizable library, but many of these volumes were donated by friends. In view of the demands made on Moody's time by his many activities, the conjecture of W. H. Daniels in the mid-1870s that Moody did not really know more than half a dozen of these books is probably pretty close to the truth.[48]

His son W. R. Moody testified that in 1876 Moody began to try to compensate for his lack of training by enlarging his reading. The extended meetings in Great Britain had depleted his supply of fresh sermon material. Moody came to the place that he did not hesitate to repeat sermons he felt to be effective scores of times, but after his return from Great Britain it became his practice to retreat to Northfield for the summer months where he spent some time each morning in study.[49] Glimpses are to be had of Moody studying in Baltimore in 1878-79; in fact, Moody went to that city primarily for rest and study, though he soon became involved in preaching.[50]

There are other clues indicating that from the late 1870s Moody was reading more widely than he had in his earlier years. Joseph Parker reported an occasion when Moody took Parker into his study, pointed to Parker's commentaries and said, "I never travel without these books; they have been more to me than any other books of these days." Parker examined the volumes and found that Moody had not only read them, but had marked "little sentences which I thought he would never have seen."[51] However, one should not conclude too much from this evidence of somewhat wider reading on Moody's part in later years. In fact, his younger son, Paul, did not remember Moody reading much in his later years, and concluded that since his father knew the gist of some of these books and had marked them, he must have done so in earlier years. However, the older son, William, suggested the opposite.[52]

Perhaps the best conclusion is that though Moody came to read more than he had in the 1860s, he read and studied so little that even those who were closest to him were never sure when he did it or how much he did it. And in terms of the interests of this study, most of his reading was done after his basic understanding of doctrine had been formed,

47. *Pleasure and Profit in Bible Study*, p. 54.
48. Daniels, *Moody: His Words, Work, and Workers*, p. 39.
49. W. R. Moody, *Moody* (1930), pp. 303, 507.
50. Pollock, *Moody: A Biographical Portrait*, p. 206; Findlay, *Dwight L. Moody*, pp. 303-4.
51. Joseph Parker, "Reminiscences of Mr. Moody," *The Institute Tie*, Feb. 1902, p. 195.
52. Paul Moody, *My Father*, p. 114; cf. W. R. Moody, *Moody* (1900), p. 526.

and even the later reading was probably done in the search for preach-able material. That it significantly affected his theology is highly un-likely. Moody's library has been scattered to the four winds so that it is nearly impossible to locate his books for markings and other indica-tions of what may have influenced him in reading and study.

He seldom referred to books or other sources in his sermons, and of those he did mention it still remains a question of how carefully they had been read.[53] In fact, books of sermons published with Moody's approval are not only more polished in style, but also contain more literary allusions than newspaper versions. This suggests the possibility that Moody's editorial associates may have occasionally "spiced up" the original sermons with references to Hodge and others. Given his method of pumping information from those with whom he came in contact, this must be regarded as the most obvious and strongest ex-ternal doctrinal influence brought to bear upon him, especially in the years 1860-1873, the years under consideration here.

If Moody's personal acquaintances in the circle of Evangelicalism are the most significant outside doctrinal influence molding him in these years, who were they? It is possible to identify some of these people. In this country, Moody seems to have felt most at home among the Congregationalists and Methodists. He also had associations with the Plymouth Brethren. Among the more interesting and readily identi-fiable are those that Moody established in England. Prior to the begin-ning of his meetings in 1873, he had made three trips to the British Isles, the main purpose of these being to learn from his British counter-parts. He met with remarkable success in making these acquaintances and in becoming known to British Evangelicals. His list of contacts almost reads like Who's Who in British Evangelicalism. From his first trip in 1867 he established close ties with both the personnel and work of the YMCA in Great Britain, including George Williams. His pri-mary purpose had been to hear and meet C. H. Spurgeon, the great Baptist preacher, and George Müller, a Plymouth Brother who had become well known for his orphanage work.

But his contacts among the Brethren there were more extensive than that, and Moody came to appreciate them, though he did not adopt all of their views. Moody also made the acquaintance of Henry Varley, a

53. The writings of C. H. Mackintosh on the Pentateuch and the published sermons of C. H. Spurgeon figure most prominently among those mentioned by Moody.

leading Nonconformist layman; T. B. Smithies, editor of a leading
evangelical periodical; R. C. Morgan, editor and publisher of evangelical periodicals and books; and Henry Moorhouse, another member
of the Plymouth Brethren and popularly known as "the boy preacher."

This first visit in 1867 lasted four months. Moody was to return
briefly in 1870 and again in 1872. On his third trip he spent most of
his time in or near London, participating in the noon prayer meetings
of the YMCA, preaching in Nonconformist chapels, and renewing
acquaintances. In late July, 1872, he delivered a major address at the
annual Mildmay Conference, which exposed him to hundreds of Evangelicals from all over England. These associations in England were
informative to Moody theologically. Initially this had been his prime
motive in making the trips, but they also served as a base from which
Moody could move in the evangelistic campaigns which began in
1873.[54]

Of the above-mentioned individuals, it was Henry Moorhouse who
was to have the most profound influence on the outlook and preaching
of Moody, and Moody was to refer often to it in later messages. Their
meeting in 1867 in Ireland was only brief and incidental, but the next
year Moorhouse came to the United States and prevailed upon Moody
to let him fill the pulpit of his Chicago church. Though Moody hardly
knew the young preacher and initially was very unimpressed, Moody's
attitude toward him quickly changed and there developed between the
two men a very close friendship in which Moody confessed to being
profoundly influenced by Moorhouse.

Specifically, Moody came to place a new emphasis on the Bible in
the preparation of his sermons as a result of the prodding of Moorhouse. "Stop preaching your own words and preach God's Word" was
the advice he gave Moody.[55] Though Moody's personal study of the
Bible and his own faith response to it had already been a significant influence on his beliefs (a fact which it is all too easy for those looking
for doctrinal influences to ignore), Moody's professed dependence on
and study of the Bible took on new dimensions as a result of the influence of Henry Moorhouse in 1868 and the years following till Moorhouse's death.

54. Findlay, *Dwight L. Moody*, pp. 124-31; W. R. Moody, *Moody* (1900), pp. 129-43, 152-
54; W. R. Moody, *Moody* (1930), pp. 112-22.
55. Geo. C. Needham, *Recollections of Henry Moorhouse, Evangelist* (Chicago: Revell,
1881), p. 118.

Just as profound in its influence on Moody was Moorhouse's emphasis on love as the essence of the Gospel message. It was his preaching from John 3:16 and consequent discussion with Moody that radically transformed Moody's evangelistic approach. Prior to this encounter with Moorhouse, Moody had appealed to sinners to repent out of fear of God's judgment. Now he came to believe that God hates sin but loves the sinner; sinners should be drawn to God by love, not driven by fear of hellfire and damnation; God wants sons, not slaves.[56] Moody's evangelistic preaching was to take on a different tenor than that of so much previous revivalistic preaching in the American tradition.

Aside from the influences already mentioned, two factors stand out when one steps back and looks at the men and movements among which Moody had been moving since he gave up the shoe business in 1860. Though the Evangelicalism in which Moody moved had long been leaning in an Arminian direction, Moody himself came under the spell of such species of Calvinism as were to be found among the Plymouth Brethren in general and Henry Moorhouse in particular. By the same token one cannot discount the influence that the Calvinism of Charles Haddon Spurgeon may have had on Moody. This is not to suggest that Moody was a consistent Calvinist; but in view of his high regard for Moorhouse and Spurgeon, it would be surprising if Moody were an unreconstructed Arminian. Indeed, his early Methodist admirer and biographer, W. H. Daniels, spoke of his "strong points of Calvinism" and "Calvinistic theology."[57] From the Plymouth Brethren, Moody also learned "dispensational truth." Moody was never enough of a systematic thinker to spell out a dispensational interpretation of the Bible. But a few of the motifs of dispensationalism rubbed off on him and he was the first American evangelist of note to follow the premillennial scheme of eschatology. These two, elements of Calvinism and dispensational premillennialism, in conjunction with Moorhouse's emphasis on love and the Bible stand out as the most obvious theological debts that Moody incurred in the formative years, 1860-1873.

Toward the end of this period Moody passed through a spiritual crisis which had doctrinal implications, though Moody never claimed to have received new truth as a result of the experience.[58] Moody felt

56. This theme is developed in later chapters.
57. Daniels, *D. L. Moody and His Work*, pp. 107, 249.
58. W. R. Moody, *Moody* (1930), p. 130.

that a spiritual coldness had crept over him in which there was too much of ambition and not enough of Christ. Self-examination told him that there was much in his heart that should not be there. He felt that the anointing of God did not rest on him. In short, he testified, he was miserable.

But after four months a crisis experience came which he variously spoke of as anointing, filling of the Spirit, baptism by the Spirit, unction, and empowerment for service.[59] Moody was later to preach that such an experience was necessary to truly effective Christian service. This raises the question of Moody's position with reference to what is often called the doctrine of the second blessing and what later became known as Pentecostalism and its concomitant, speaking in tongues. Involved here also is the question of perfectionism and "higher life," a discussion that occupied Evangelicals on both sides of the Atlantic. Thorough investigation of this problem will be necessary. But whatever its theological implications for Moody, the experience came to him in the winter of 1871 and his interests turned even more in the direction of preaching Christ and working for souls.

He had already started to rid himself of some of the responsibilities that had taxed even his prodigious energies, by giving up the presidency of the Chicago YMCA in 1870. But other burdens had fallen on Moody, namely, the loss of his family's personal belongings in the Chicago fire in October 1871, as well as the destruction of the YMCA's Farwell Hall and the destruction of the building that had been erected for his church. These events probably contributed to the sense of spiritual depression he felt in 1871. Moody now moved to rid himself of these entanglements and burdens and made his previously mentioned third trip to England in 1872.

In June of 1873 he made his final break with the burdens of Chicago, leaving the city for England, accompanied by his singing associate, Ira D. Sankey. Whether he was conscious of it or not, Moody was moving into the field of urban evangelism, having trained himself both in methodology and doctrine in the school of experience. Arriving in England on June 17, 1873, Moody not only had a method and a message, but a network of previously established contacts throughout the

59. *Glad Tidings*, pp. 471-72.

British Isles, as well as in America, that served as a framework for his mission.[60]

MASS EVANGELISM: ABROAD AND AT HOME, 1873-1878

Though Moody was to branch out into new fields of endeavor later, and though his methods of evangelism were not to remain static from this point on, I have been unable to discover any significant shifts in Moody's doctrinal beliefs as expressed in his preaching or evidenced in his actions. This conclusion grows out of research that placed primary importance on those printed versions of sermons than can be more or less precisely dated. This is not to suggest that Moody's sermons do not reflect the developing controversies of his times. They do give evidence of the ferment, socially and theologically. He became involved either directly or indirectly in such movements as the Student Volunteer Movement, Keswick, and the prophetic conferences. He established a unique circle of friendships that included such diverse personalities as Henry Drummond and R. A. Torrey, George Adam Smith and A. T. Pierson, William Rainey Harper and G. Campbell Morgan.

Yet through all of this it is difficult to discover an appreciable change in Moody's theology after he got into the full swing of the British mission. Sermons preached in the British meetings of 1873-1875 were still being preached in 1899, the last year of his life. This fundamental absence of change in the midst of change will become abundantly evident in succeeding chapters. Consequently, this biographical sketch which has been preoccupied with the search for possible influences upon the developing beliefs of D. L. Moody will now become more of a skeletal chronicle to serve as a framework for considering the theology revealed in his sermons and other extant statements of belief.

Moody and Sankey arrived in England in the summer of 1873 only to find that the two supporters who had promised to back them had died. But Moody also had in his pocket an almost forgotten invitation from the director of the YMCA in York to conduct evangelistic meetings there. Without prior preparations, Moody contacted the director by telegraph, announcing that he had arrived and was ready to begin meetings. The director, a Mr. Bennett, replied that things were so cold in town that it would take at least a month to prepare for the meetings. He told Moody to name a date. Moody did name a date—he tele-

60. Findlay, *Dwight L. Moody*, pp. 131-35.

graphed Bennett early in the day that he was coming immediately; Moody arrived that evening at ten o'clock. The meetings began in York as soon as Sankey could be summoned from Manchester.

To repeat the details of the development of this mission from its humble and inauspicious beginnings in York to its triumphal and spectacular progress through Scotland, Ireland, and England would not serve the purposes of this study and would repeat what is so readily available in other sources. Suffice it to say that what began in York, grew in Sunderland, budded in Newcastle, and came to full bloom in Scotland. Five months were spent that winter in Scotland, two in the churches and secular auditoriums of Edinburgh, and three months in Glasgow. Huge crowds attended the meetings to hear the Gospel preached by an uneducated Yankee and sung by a bewhiskered Sankey who accompanied himself on a pump organ.

Estimates of the lasting results of these meetings differ, as they do of Moody's other efforts, but there can be no doubting the fact that for at least five months there was some sort of revival spirit in Scotland. Here Moody acquired his reputation as an evangelist, and here also the friendship with Henry Drummond was established that endured through a lifetime. In fact, Moody enlisted the young Drummond in the work with young men. Though the two were very different by culture and education and were eventually to grow apart theologically, Moody probably had few friends with whom he had a closer attachment.

Drummond had interrupted his studies at New College, Edinburgh, to work with Moody as a student evangelist. Drummond was not the only person at New College with whom Moody had a close relationship. William Garden Blaikie, professor of apologetics and pastoral theology at New College, served as the host of Moody and his family during the winter of 1873-1874 in Edinburgh. The Blaikies had made Moody's acquaintance several years earlier in Chicago; in fact, Moody had called upon him to preach in his church one Sunday.[61] As a result of this earlier association, Blaikie felt free to invite the Moodys to live with them during their time in Edinburgh, and Blaikie and Moody became

61. There seems to be disagreement as to the date of this first contact between the two men. In his autobiography Blaikie gives two different dates, 1869 and 1870. Cf. William Garden Blaikie, *An Autobiography: "Recollections of a Busy Life,"* ed. Norman L. Walker (London: Hodder & Stoughton, 1901), pp. 331, 343. White gives the date 1868. Cf. John Wesley White, "The Influence of North American Evangelism in Great Britain between 1830 and 1914 on the Origin and Development of the Ecumenical Movement," 2:35.

the closest of friends. In the spring of 1880 Blaikie visited Moody in Northfield where Moody arranged for Blaikie to give a week of Bible readings. What discussions of theology may have transpired between these two men in the two months that they were so close together in Edinburgh, one can only guess at. It is inconceivable that Moody would not have availed himself of this opportunity to pump such a learned man; but in his autobiography Blaikie says nothing of any such discussions, though he has a chapter on Moody.

Moody also became closely attached to the Scottish clergyman, Andrew Bonar. Moody expressed indebtedness to him in his sermons more than to any other person, and Bonar told how he helped Moody.[62] Moody probably interacted with many of his supporters and hosts throughout the months in Scotland, indeed throughout the entire British tour, though the lineaments of these discussions and their influence on Moody are now impossible to recover.

Through the late spring and summer months Moody and Sankey worked their way through the smaller towns of Scotland. After spending most of September, October, and November in Ireland, they moved on to England. From late November to early March they conducted evangelistic meetings in Manchester, Sheffield, Birmingham, and Liverpool. Systematic preparations were made in each city with a great deal of care devoted to the securing of appropriate halls, publicity, and enlistment of support of the clergy. The popular excitement continued and even winter cold and meetings conducted at unseasonable hours did not abate the huge crowds. No less a church leader than R. W. Dale, the well-known English Congregationalist, was won over to the cause and became an admirer of Moody. The British tour reached its climax in the four months of meetings held in London from early March to early July of 1875. The city was divided into four sections, and large halls were either rented or constructed in each section to accommodate the meetings. The sermons delivered in these meetings are of special interest for this study, for many of them form the substance of three volumes which were the earliest *extensive* verbatim reports of Moody's sermons available to me.

Evaluation of the long-range results of these meetings in the British Isles and the factors producing whatever measure of success Moody and

62. Cf. comments in this connection in W. R. Moody, *Moody* (1900), pp. 257, 299; Marjory Bonar, ed., *Andrew A. Bonar: Diary and Life* (London: Banner of Truth Trust, 1960 reprint), pp. 333-34, 528-35.

Sankey had are not a part of the purpose of this investigation. However, it cannot be denied that few in the British Isles in July of 1875 were unaware that for two years they had been subjected to American evangelism, and the two returned to America as popular religious heroes, their fame having preceded them.

Even before Moody left England, he had been approached about conducting revivals in New York, Chicago, and Philadelphia. By the time he arrived back in New York, the secular and religious press by its accounts of the British meetings had created a great deal of public interest. But on his return, Moody retreated to the quietude of Northfield. This in itself was significant, for Moody did not return to Northfield just to visit relatives; he was eventually to put his own roots back into his native soil. Northfield was the place he established as the home base and to which he returned for rest and contemplation.

But Moody was not one to take extended periods of rest, and he began to consider where he should begin his American campaigns. Representatives of the cities vying for his services and friends helping him plan for future campaigns began making the trek to Northfield, and by the middle of October the basic plans had been drawn up. The requirements that had to be met before Moody agreed to conduct a series of meetings were that there be united support of the evangelical churches, that adequate buildings be available to accommodate the huge crowds, and that the churches avoid programs and activities that would be in direct competition with the evangelistic effort.

The plan called for Moody to begin in Brooklyn, which he did on October 24, 1875. From there he moved to Philadelphia, New York City, Chicago, and Boston. These were the major meetings held in the rest of 1875, 1876, and the first part of 1877, though other smaller meetings were held at Princeton, Nashville, St. Louis, and Kansas City. In 1878 he moved on through Providence, Springfield, Hartford, and New Haven. These meetings attracted the same vast audiences as in the British Isles. Meetings in the larger cities lasted two or three months and were held in large halls, accommodating several thousands, usually in the downtown section of the city. Concomitant with the major evening meeting were meetings during the day with smaller groups not of the general public.

Though Moody did not feel bound by his own precedents and was open to innovation, he basically used the methods employed in the

British Isles. The accounts of these meetings are copious. The major city newspapers carried reports of the meetings daily, often including what were reputed to be verbatim reports of Moody's sermons. These newspaper versions would then be incorporated into books such as *Holding the Fort, Glad Tidings, The Gospel Awakening, Great Joy,* and *The Great Redemption.*[63] These and similar volumes obviously constitute the major sources for the early preaching of Moody.[64]

NEW APPROACHES: 1878-1899

If one judges in terms of public visibility and notoriety, the years 1873-1878 were the high-water mark of Moody's career as an evangelist. However, the advertisement of Moody's name was enough to pack out auditoriums to the end of his days, and he continued to be one of the most significant personalities in American Evangelicalism to the end of the century.

The date 1878 has been selected as the *terminus a quo* of this period of Moody's life, for late in 1878 he evidenced the flexibility that permitted him to take new approaches to the work of preaching the Gospel. In October he went to Baltimore to rest and study, but within a few days he was meeting with local ministers and laymen who wanted counsel from him as to how they themselves could carry on effective work. From these small meetings larger meetings developed to the point that Moody was holding one meeting a day in one of the evangelical churches of the city. This plan originally was apparently an attempt to preserve a semblance of time for rest and study, but from it evolved a new approach to urban evangelism. This method had the advantage of using existing structures without the necessity of renting or erecting large halls. It also had the advantage of extending the mission into the warp

63. For full bibliographic information and annotations on these volumes, see the entries in the Source List.

64. Remember that this summary of Moody's early evangelistic work in Great Britain and the United States has only been a cursory survey. Chaps. 4-6, pp. 136-226, of Findlay, *Dwight L. Moody,* give this period the kind of treatment it deserves. Reading the accounts in the religious periodicals and secular newspapers also helps give one a feel for what was happening. In addition to many clippings not in a continuous series, researchers will be interested to know that Moodyana has a run of *The Christian: A Weekly Record of Christian Life, Christian Testimony, and Christian Work,* January 1, 1874—Dec. 31, 1875, containing regular reports of the meetings through Scotland, Ireland, and England; also available in that collection are copies of the *New York Witness Extra,* Feb. 14, 1876—Apr. 1876, and *New York Witness Extra* (Chicago series), Nov.—Dec., 1876. Moodyana also contains photostats of the *New Haven Daily Palladium,* Mar. 20—May 13, 1878, with reports of the meetings in that city.

and woof of the city, as in the case of Baltimore which was thoroughly canvassed by May, 1879.

This is not to say that he never used the large central meeting place again; he did periodically, including his last series in Kansas City which was interrupted by his illness. But this new approach did become a method that Moody continued to use as he felt appropriate. Findlay suggests that this reflects a deepening of Moody's understanding of his own faith, that is, that mass meetings did not accomplish all they were reputed to. If effective work was to be done, it should be done in the churches; and members in churches needed to be awakened to go out in personal witness. Though this is only conjecture, Findlay does cite evidence to justify the suggestion and it does have some cogency. The more recent research of Donald Wells tends to support this suggestion.[65]

The establishment of the Northfield School for Girls in 1879, followed by the Mount Hermon School for Boys in 1881, marked another new departure for Moody, this time into the field of education more than evangelism. The fundamental purpose of the Northfield Schools, as they came to be called, was to provide a prep school education that would promote the development of well-rounded Christian character. Moody himself had no illusions of being an educator, but he saw a need and obtained funds, property, buildings, and personnel for the schools. He did not handle the details of day-to-day administration, but his presence on the campuses was certainly felt and he was the guiding light of both institutions. It was Moody's intention that the Bible and study of Christian doctrine be the core of the curriculum in both the schools, and his hope was that they would serve as training schools for evangelists and feed competently trained people into the churches. Again this suggests Moody was reassessing the effectiveness of mass meetings and was coming to realize that the churches themselves needed to be revived to become the centers of work and outreach in the last two turbulent decades of the century.[66]

The existence of these campuses and physical facilities at Northfield also allowed Moody to move in another direction, the inauguration of the summer Bible conferences for adults and college-age young people.

65. Findlay, *Dwight L. Moody*, pp. 304-5. Donald Austin Wells, "D. L. Moody and His Schools: An Historical Analysis of an Educational Ministry" (Ph.D. diss., Boston U., 1972), pp. 93-99.

66. Findlay, *Dwight L. Moody*, pp. 312-13; for more detailed information on the Northfield Schools, cf. pp. 306-21 and W. R. Moody, *Moody* (1930), pp. 301-29. Wells' dissertation cited in note 65 devotes more than 150 pages to these two schools.

This again came at the time when other considerations indicate that
Moody was rethinking his approaches to evangelism. In November of
1879 he conceived the idea of a summer Bible conference at Northfield
for laymen that would augment their understanding of the Bible and
Christian faith and serve the purpose of spiritual renewal. These people
would then go back into the churches and exert their influence. In
September, 1880, the first such conference was held, lasting for ten
days, with Moody and his trusted friends as the speakers. The next
such conference was in August, 1881.

Shortly after this Moody left for three years of meetings in Great
Britain, and during Moody's absence the conferences were suspended.
But in 1885 the summer conferences resumed, and they were expanded
the following year to include a month-long conference for college students. From the first college conference in 1886, a total of 100 students
dedicated themselves to foreign missionary service when they completed
college. This was the beginning of a movement among college students
that included 2,000 students by the following June, and out of it grew
the Student Volunteer Movement, seeking "the evangelization of the
world in this generation."

For the most part the speakers at these conferences were men for
whose theology Moody had a great deal of sympathy, men like A. T.
Pierson, A. J. Gordon, D. W. Whittle, George Needham, and W. G.
Moorehead. Many of the speakers had a strong Keswick-type emphasis,
and dispensationalism and premillennialism tended to be emphasized.
But examination of lists of speakers at these conferences, especially the
student conferences held in succeeding years, reveals some surprises
such as William Rainey Harper, George Adam Smith, and Henry Drummond, whose theology had undergone quite a metamorphosis since his
days of conducting young men's meetings for Moody in the first British
Isles campaigns.[67] Many of Moody's conservative supporters and associates did not appreciate these invitations and no little controversy
arose from them; reverberations from them were still being heard in the
1920s at the height of the Modernist-Fundamentalist controversy. Who

67. For a narrative of the activities of the student conferences and reports of the major
addresses, 1886-1889, see T. J. Shanks, *D. L. Moody at Home: His Home and Home Work*
(Chicago: Revell, 1886); Shanks, ed., *A College of Colleges: Led by D. L. Moody* (Chicago:
Revell, 1887); Shanks, ed., *College Students at Northfield; or, A College of Colleges, No. 2*
(New York: Revell, 1888); Fred L. Norton, ed., *A College of Colleges, Led by D. L. Moody*
(New York: Revell, 1889). The last three titles will be cited as *A College of Colleges*, with
the date in parentheses.

were the true heirs of D. L. Moody, the Fundamentalists or the Modernists? Where would Moody have stood had he been twenty-five years later? Or would the controversy have broken out as it did? These questions are explored when Moody's response to the liberal trends in theology is discussed in chapter 10.

The Northfield Schools were not Moody's only ventures into education. Many of Moody's friends in Chicago had long hoped that he would establish in that city a work of more permanent nature than a brief evangelistic campaign. Some of these were businessmen; among them was Cyrus McCormick, with the money to get any such project off the ground. Miss Emma Dryer was another person determined and hopeful that Moody would establish some work in Chicago besides his church, which had been rebuilt and renamed the Chicago Avenue Church. She had already established a little training school. In 1886 Moody began to move in this direction. On January 22, 1886, he announced to a group of Chicago businessmen that he intended to establish in Chicago a school for the "training of Christian workers," primarily for the purpose of city missions.[68] This school was to train men and women to stand in the gap between the clergy and the laity, a concept that had been in Moody's mind at least since May of 1874.[69] The next summer Moody explained this concept of theological education to a group of students at Northfield thus:

> Some of you may think I oppose theological seminaries. I want to say I believe we want thoroughly trained men. I don't think we have enough trained men. At the same time, we want some men to stand between the laity and the ministers—I don't know what you would call them—gap men. We want men to stand in the gap. There is such a thing as educating a man away from the rank and file. There is a class of men, I believe, that have got to be raised up to do what we used to call in the war bushwhacking. We want irregulars—men that will go out and do work that the educated ministers can't do: get in among the people, and identify themselves with the people.[70]

Because of personality clashes among Moody's friends in Chicago and the failure of Moody himself to follow through aggressively in implementing his proposals, the first years of what was later to become

68. *Chicago Tribune,* Jan. 23, 1886.
69. *The Christian,* May 7, 1874, pp. 382-83.
70. Shanks, ed., *A College of Colleges* (1887), pp. 212-13.

known as Moody Bible Institute were both stormy and fragile. The first major step was the charter given to the Chicago Evangelization Society on February 12, 1887. This organization was to bring to reality the envisioned training school. But it was not until October, 1889, that the Chicago Bible Institute officially opened its doors. From that time on its existence was fairly well assured.[71]

The concept behind the Bible institute is another indication of Moody's readiness to try new approaches to evangelism. He appears to have been somewhat disappointed that the Northfield Schools were not turning out more lay evangelists, and the rural setting of Northfield did not lend itself to the students becoming involved in urban evangelism during their training. Furthermore, Chicago contained friends of Moody who not only had the desire to see him establish a work there, but some of them had the money. Chicago also constituted a mission field, and remembering that 1886 was a year of serious labor strife in Chicago, one can understand something of the urgency of the situation that moved Moody to choose that year to implement an idea that he had long held. Unemployment had been rising and labor unrest had been common in the two preceding years. Early in 1886 labor-management problems had erupted at the McCormick harvester factory in Chicago and eventually led to the Haymarket Riot in May. The Bible institute was Moody's effort to reach the seething masses with the Gospel, by which means he felt problems between labor and management and of unemployment would be solved.[72]

In the 1890s Moody's efforts at evangelism took two more new directions. The first of these was a city-wide effort conducted during the 1893 World's Fair in Chicago. His purpose was not only to reach the city, but to bring the Gospel to those who were visiting the fair in the city. Elaborate plans were made and carried out, with churches and halls all over the city being used as the sites of various meetings. Students from the Bible institute were enlisted in the work, and speakers from around the United States, Great Britain, and Europe were brought in to speak to the different linguistic groups and in the various localities.

71. Findlay, *Dwight L. Moody*, pp. 323-28. For more detailed information on the origin of the institute, see Gene A. Getz, *MBI: The Story of Moody Bible Institute* (Chicago: Moody, 1969), pp. 29-46.
72. Cf. Henry F. May, *Protestant Churches and Industrial America* (New York: Harper Bros., 1949), pp. 91-111.

On some Sundays no fewer than 125 meetings were conducted under the auspices of this effort.

In 1894 Moody ventured forth into yet another new effort, publication of colportage books. In 1881 Moody had been instrumental in the inauguration of the periodical, *Record of Christian Work;* eventually it became an organ for the institutions that Moody had founded. From the time of his first tour of Great Britain in 1873-1875, volumes of Moody's sermons had been published, after being collected and edited by others. He had been reluctant to publish them himself, primarily for fear that the public would see it as a money-making scheme on his part. But in 1881, he sanctioned the volume *Twelve Select Sermons,* published by the firm of Fleming H. Revell, his brother-in-law. Convinced that a vast readership could be reached by such books, he issued at irregular intervals other volumes of sermons published in the United States by Revell. In 1894 he became convinced that another innovation in the publication of these and other sermons was needed in order to reach the masses of people. They should be published as paperbacks and sold at the cheapest possible price. He had been told that religious books did not sell in bookstores, so they did not carry them. The answer seemed to be to provide cheap editions. A colportage department was created in connection with the Chicago institute, with students often serving as colporteurs. Many of Moody's own sermon books, which had been published previously by Revell, became standards in the line, though other well-known authors and books were also used. The next year the outreach of the colportage work was extended to the prisons by providing the prison libraries with books from the colportage line. In the last years of his life, Moody developed special interest in the plight of prisoners and the prison work.[73]

During these years from 1878 to 1899, Moody continued his revival preaching, sometimes following the pattern used in Baltimore for two or three nights or two or three weeks in a city. At times they were extended city-wide efforts conducted in some large central hall such as the Auditorium in Chicago in 1897. In these years he made three trips to Great Britain and he traversed North America with his message.[74] During this period, he took innovative approaches to evangelism, and

73. W. R. Moody, *Moody* (1930), pp. 416-25.
74. For a chronological summary of Moody's life with notations of place see Smith, *Annotated Bibliography*, pp. xx-xxv; while Smith's information is substantially correct, I have noted some minor errors.

occasionally interacted with and reacted to the late nineteenth-century social, intellectual, and theological ferment.

D. L. MOODY: HIS LIFE IN CONTEXT

When Moody's fatal illness interrupted his evangelistic campaign in Kansas City in 1899, the last sermon he had preached was "Excuses." Substantially the same sermon had been repeatedly used through the years. The earliest record of its use that I have found is on Tuesday evening, March 23, 1875, in the Agricultural Hall in London. It had almost certainly been used many times before that.[75] Research reveals the same story with reference to many of Moody's sermons. This phenomenon is a paradigm of Moody's unchanging message in an age of change.[76]

The last quarter of the nineteenth century was an age of change from which two challenges to organized Christianity in America emerged. One challenge was to its system of thought and the other was to its social program.[77]

The social program of American Evangelicalism found itself challenged by the difficulties and unrest growing out of immigration, urbanization, and industrialization. Though they did not always capture the headlines or the attention that other evidences of unrest did, the farmers were hard hit by the move to the cities and the industrialization of the country. There were intermittent movements of revolt, such as the Grange movement beginning in 1867, Greenbackism in the 1870s, the Farmers' Alliance following 1880, and the merging of these movements in the 1890s in the People's Party and in the Bryan Democrats in the free silver campaign.

The uprisings of labor and the economic difficulties out of which they grew were more spectacular. There was the panic and crash of 1873, epitomized by the failure of the financial empire of Jay Cooke. With the financial collapse, unemployment and breadlines grew; and with that came unrest. As unemployment grew, wages declined. As the incidence of the failure of businesses increased, homes were abandoned

75. D. L. Moody, *The London Discourses of Mr. D. L. Moody* (London: James Clarke, 1875), pp. 87-107, cited as *London Discourses*.
76. For another example, see p. 122.
77. For the development of this twofold theme, the following section is particularly dependent on Arthur M. Schlesinger, "A Critical Period in American Protestantism, 1875-1900," *Massachusetts Historical Society Proceedings* 64 (June 1932): 523-48, and chapter 9 of Mead, *The Lively Experiment*, pp. 156-87.

and vagrancy spread.[78] The most spectacular explosions growing out of this situation were the railroad strikes of 1877 which involved battles between workers and police, militia, and federal troops. The year 1877 became a symbol of shock and has been described as one of the darkest in the annals of American history.[79] With a revival of prosperity there was a decrease of strife in the early 1880s, but in the middle of the decade depression returned with its attendant evils. The decline reached its crisis in 1886, which is best known for the clashes between police and strikers at the McCormick harvester plant in Chicago. These reached their height in the Haymarket Square Riot in which eight policemen were killed and twenty-seven persons injured. The years 1890 to 1894 taken together constituted a third crisis in the last quarter of the century. Though some calm had returned to the nation after the Haymarket affair, the nation's social ills were far from cured. The year 1892 saw the strike at the Carnegie Steel Plant in Homestead, Pennsylvania, involving 300 Pinkerton "detectives" doing battle with strikers and 8,000 state militiamen who finally put down the strike. In 1893 financial panic again hit the nation followed by prolonged industrial depression with layoffs and wage cuts. Usually originating as efforts to prevent the further fall of wages, the strikes of 1894 were the most widespread yet. The symbol of those strikes was the strike of the Pullman Palace Car Company in Pullman, Illinois, a community that had been a model of employer paternalism. The strike which erupted when wages were reduced by 25 percent was defeated by court injunction and the dispatch of 2,000 federal troops to "guard the mails."

This quarter century of socioeconomic turmoil saw the challenge of prevailing socioeconomic theories, and the thinking and programs of American Protestantism were not immune to review and challenge. Was it enough to try to rescue through the YMCA young men who had moved to the evil city? Was it enough to preach that thrift and hard work would see any man through any time of difficulty? Would individual spiritual renewal cure the ills of society? Were these ills even subject to cure? This was a question raised by premillennialists in particular. Was poverty the result of sin and vice individually conceived, or did it grow out of an evil system?

78. Allan Nevins, *The Emergence of Modern America, 1865-1878*, vol. 8 of *A History of American Life*, ed. Arthur M. Schlesinger and Dixon Ryan Fox (New York: Macmillan, 1927), pp. 290-315.

79. Ibid., p. 304; Henry F. May, *Protestant Churches and Industrial America*, p. 95.

During this period the challenge to the social thinking and program of American Protestantism was matched by the challenge to its system of thought.[80] Specifically, evolutionary theory produced such an impact and presented a challenge to the traditional concepts of Protestant orthodoxy. The concept of biological evolution appeared to erase the line between man and other animals and to question the concept of a creating Deity. The evolutionary view of history and of the development of religion questioned the scheme of history presented in the Bible as well as the concept that God had given this religion by special revelation. The idea of progress applied to anthropology questioned traditional views of sin and grace. Higher criticism of the Bible, which came into its own during this time, was fundamentally the result of the application of the evolutionary model to Christianity's sacred literature.

Three broad strands could be discerned in the thought of American Protestantism during this period, though they had a long history not only in American theology, but indeed in the history of Christian theology in general. There was traditional orthodoxy, the stream in which American Evangelicalism stood. Though the doctrinal outlines were somewhat fuzzy more often than not, it was frankly supernaturalistic and held to the absolute authority of Scripture.

The second strand was romantic liberalism, or progressive religion, which had grown out of early nineteenth-century transcendental Unitarianism. In Horace Bushnell, Calvinism had been transcendentalized, and through him this new liberalism took root in the denominations. In placing an emphasis on the direct, intuitive perception of the Gospel, the romantic liberals tended to abstract religion from the realm of scientific verification, and by that means from criticism. By the doctrine of God's immanence, God was seen as revealing Himself in all history. Through belief in developmental progress, evolution was accommodated as the way in which God had been working in history.

The third strand was scientific modernism, using "the methods of modern science to find, state and use the permanent and central values of inherited orthodoxy in meeting the needs of a modern world."[81] These streams did not always run in clearly defined channels and they were

80. Though no attempt is made here to summarize his presentation, Carter's *Spiritual Crisis of the Gilded Age* is an especially helpful analysis of the challenges to the thinking of American Protestantism.
81. Statement by Shailer Mathews quoted by Mead, *The Lively Experiment*, pp. 173-74.

to cross and recross in different patterns in different individuals and groups.

It was within this context of change and challenge to traditional programs and thought that D. L. Moody carried out his career of evangelism for some twenty-five years or more, being nurtured himself in the stream of orthodox American Evangelicalism. It is to the theology revealed by his messages preached during this era that we now turn our attention. We have attempted to discover the heart of his own faith, and the manner in which his messages reflect the conflicts and challenges of that age.

2

THE ROLE OF THEOLOGY IN
MOODY'S MESSAGE

A DISCUSSION of Moody's theology at some point must consider the role it played in his message and ministry. Evangelists in general have not had a reputation for being theologically acute, and if one is speaking of systematics, Moody certainly fits the stereotype. Neither by training nor interest would Moody have been inclined to formulate a systematic statement of his understanding of theology. If one examines his messages from the standpoint of an organized presentation of doctrine or careful exegesis, nearly all of them are woefully lacking.

But theology does not have to be systematized to be theology, and by the same token, doctrines and creeds do not have to be formally stated for one to have definite beliefs. Fundamentally, no Christian has a choice of having or not having a theology. If he is a Christian, he subscribes to certain doctrines and not to others, and he is a theologian. His theology consists of the statements he makes about the truth he holds. Thus, a certain understanding of theology inevitably shines through in Moody's preaching in spite of his lack of precision. This study attempts to bring to light what that understanding was, and part of that effort involves two questions discussed in this chapter: (1) What was Moody's expressed attitude toward theology? and (2) Did Moody's evangelistic technique determine his theology?

WHAT WAS MOODY'S EXPRESSED ATTITUDE TOWARD THEOLOGY?

While Protestant orthodoxy has always been intent upon defining the intellectual content of Christian theology, pietists have placed primary emphasis upon the subjective religious experience. Though these are not necessarily mutually exclusive concerns, the fact remains that pietism has tended to minimize the importance of theology. The wedding of pietistic and revivalistic concerns with the traditional churches and theology in the denominations which emerged from the revolutionary era produced American Evangelicalism with its tendency to be doctrinally amorphous, though not without doctrinal content.

The doctrinal boundaries tended to be fuzzy, yet they were there.[1] The tendency was to avoid creeds, doctrines, and dogmas, and to concentrate on the practical aspects of saving souls and the nurture of the individual's subjective religious experience.[2] These inherent tendencies were further augmented by a spirit of tolerance among American Evangelicals that grew out of the awakening of 1857-1858. Among those affected by the awakening, the attitude spread that the significance of doctrinal differences should be toned down; the simplicity of the Gospel should be emphasized, compassion should be stressed over creed, and divisions should be minimized[3]

Moody had been converted under evangelical influences. Even more significantly, in the years prior to 1873, he came to his understanding of Christianity within the circle of American Evangelicalism. This in itself is enough to raise the question of Moody's attitude toward theology. Add to this the fact that Moody's earliest years before leaving home were spent in Unitarianism with its denigration of dogmatic theology, and the question of Moody's attitude toward theology takes on added interest.[4] Indeed, although other Unitarian critiques of Moody's message were decidedly negative, a Unitarian named W. C. Gannet was appreciative of Moody on this point. His remarks, summarized in the *Unitarian Review* of 1877, admit that the whole of Calvinism may be implied in Moody's talk, but practically it is not expressed. "Logically, it may be there, but practically it is not." Gannet implied that Moody's preaching was one with the Unitarians; only his symbols were different. According to Gannet, "The secret of the Evangelist's power . . . is in the fact there is so *little* theology and so *much* morality in his preaching."[5]

1. See pp. 24-31.
2. Cf. William G. McLoughlin, ed., *The American Evangelicals, 1800-1900: An Anthology* (New York: Harper & Row, 1968), p. 10; Mead, *Lively Experiment*, pp. 127 ff.
3. Smith, *Revivalism and Social Reform*, pp. 83-87.
4. Cf. Smith's discussion of Unitarian attitudes toward dogmatic theology in *Revivalism and Social Reform*, pp. 31-32, 46, 95-102.
5. M. P. L., "Things at Home (Freedom with Fellowship)," *Unitarian Review* 7 (May 1877): 560.

That D. L. Moody, a lay evangelist without formal training and spiritually nurtured in pietistic Evangelicalism, did not give evidence in his sermons of a systematically worked-out theology should not be at all surprising. And, following the usual revivalist practice, he was preaching a Gospel message that was calculated not to stir up the underlying theological differences that existed among cooperating evangelical participants in his meetings. His early defenders praised him on that very point. Daniels asserted that "one looks in vain for anything original."[6] E. J. Goodspeed wrote:

> He keeps close to the essentials, and is free from such crotchets as often narrow the sphere and destroy the influence of evangelists. It is not irritation but balm, that he tries to bring to our religious divisions. . . . Though he has introduced some novel methods, he has stuck to the simple old truths, and his convictions are in entire accord with Scottish orthodoxy.[7]

A. G. Sedgwick writing in *The Nation* defended the absence of dogmatic theology and biblical exegesis in Moody's messages by saying, "A revival is not the place to look for these things. A revival preacher is no pundit, but an exhorter to new life, and he is, by the conditions under which he works, constrained to make his exhortations simple and general."[8]

However, once it is granted that for good or for ill Moody was short on systematic theological expression, the question still remains, What was his own attitude toward theology? Did he oppose doctrines and doctrinal preaching, creeds and confessions of faith per se? At least one contemporary apparently had Moody in mind when he criticized those evangelists who have no ecclesiastical connection and hence no accountability to such a connection for teaching and practices; he went on to criticize evangelistic preaching that has an antipathy for doctrine.[9] Stan Nussbaum in his 1973 thesis is even more severe in his assertions of Moody's opposition to systematic theological statements. He claims that one of Moody's basic premises is that "theology, at least as a syste-

---

6. Daniels, *Moody: His Words, Work, and Workers*, pp. 260-61.
7. E. J. Goodspeed, *A Full History of the Wonderful Career of Moody and Sankey, In Great Britain and America* (Cleveland: C. C. Wick, 1876), pp. 107-8, cited as *Wonderful Career of Moody.*
8. A. G. Sedgwick, "Moody and Sankey," *The Nation* 22 (Mar. 9, 1876): 157.
9. J. A. Singmaster, "Modern Evangelism," *Quartrely Review of the Lutheran Church and Lutheran Quarterly* 7 (July 1877): 407-8.

matic discipline, is superfluous to Christian faith." He elaborates his charge thus:

> The importance of reason in systematizing these nuggets of revelation was minimal, according to Moody, and this for three reasons: 1) theology is basically superfluous to salvation and therefore wastes precious time, 2) theology will not stand against the devil because it is based on human reason, and 3) theology tends to divide Christian forces because it obscures the mission of the Church.

Moody supposedly held that formulations of doctrine are not in the sphere of the Spirit but in the sphere of reason and therefore without authority and useless. "The work of systematic theology is a luxurious pasttime [sic] not to be enjoyed while the whole world is going to hell. Perhaps in heaven we will be theologians, but on earth we are called to be evangelists."[10] Though not sharing Nussbaum's negative value judgment, C. Howard Hopkins would have agreed with this interpretation of Moody's attitude toward theology. "To . . . Dwight L. Moody, theology actually meant little."[11] In a similar vein, Lyman Abbott wrote that Moody was "indifferent to theological theories."[12]

When one considers the circumstantial evidence, it is not difficult to discover why some students of Moody have concluded that at worst he opposed theology and that at best he was indifferent to it. His own pietistic evangelical milieu would suggest this as a viable interpretation of his failure to articulate doctrine systematically. His evangelistic message sought for the lowest common denominator and was calculated to be acceptable to all potential supporters who might be included under the evangelical umbrella. Moody frequently spoke to this subject, especially when someone would press him with a question on a controversial topic such as baptism. He usually refused to answer such questions, and the following refusal to be drawn into debate is typical:

> Some people would smash up a work like this in 24 hours. I have not come to preach this or that doctrine; I preach the "whosoever."

10. Nussbaum, "D. L. Moody and the Church," p. 1 of "Abstract" and summary of pp. 15-18. Nussbaum's citations of Moody to establish his point are hardly even relevant to the point when taken in context, and he takes no account of the evidence to follow here. Actually, Nussbaum could have made a much stronger case for his interpretation by citing the superficially anticreedal statements to be referred to below.

11. C. Howard Hopkins, *History of the Y.M.C.A. in North America* (New York: Association, 1951), p. 7.

12. Lyman Abbott, "Snap-Shots of my Contemporaries: Dwight Lyman Moody—Evangelist," *The Outlook* 64 (June 22, 1921): 326.

> Some are always asking, "why I don't specially preach election or sanc-
> tification, or baptism" or this or that. I would say to them, "Why don't
> you go and preach them yourselves?"[13]

There can be no doubt that Moody regarded it as his mission to preach
the Gospel, and his refusal to preach "this or that doctrine" that he
regarded as debatable and on the periphery of the "whosoever" does
lend itself to the interpretation that he was either indifferent to or opposed to doctrine.

Actually, one can build an even stronger case for this position on the
verbal evidence, though it will be seen that it is a superficial interpretation of that evidence. One need only recall, for instance, the occasion
in London in 1875 when an interrogator asked him for his creed. "It is
already in print" was Moody's reply as notebooks came out and inquiry
was made as to where it could be found. Moody continued, "In the
fifty-third chapter of Isaiah."[14] Moody himself told the story of a woman
who came to him after his sermon entitled, "The Elder Brother," and
said, "I want to be frank with you, I want you to know I do not believe
in your theology." "My theology!" Moody exclaimed. "I didn't know
I had any. I wish you would tell me what my theology is."[15] To such
anecdotal statements can be added the scores, perhaps hundreds, of
statements scattered through the published versions of Moody's sermons
which on the surface seem to reflect negatively upon the value of creeds
and doctrine. One such volume may be perused as an example.[16] "It is
not creeds and doctrines we want so much as compassion and sympathy." "He [Jesus Christ] is not a creed, a mere empty doctrine, but it
is He Himself we have." If a person puts his "trust in any church, any
creed, or any minister," he will be disappointed. "The great difficulty
is that people try to get some other physician—they go to this creed or
that creed, to this doctor of divinity and that one, instead of coming
directly to the Master." "The greatest mistake of the present day is the

---

13. *Signs of Our Times* (Mar. 10, 1875), p. 149; cf. Shanks, ed., *College Students at Northfield* (1888), pp. 217-18.
14. W. R. Moody, *Moody* (1930), p. 212.
15. From a sermon preached in Providence, R.I., on Jan. 1, 1894, according to the "Elder
Son" sermon envelope, Moodyana. Quoted from an undated, unidentified clipping from a
Providence newspaper in that envelope.
16. D. L. Moody, *New Sermons, Addresses and Prayers* (St. Louis: N. D. Thompson,
1877). This volume contains 73 sermons and 29 addresses, and is probably the most representative selection of Moody's sermons in one volume. They were preached from mid-1876
to early 1877.

following of this creed and that one, and this and that Church, and a great many listen to the voice of the Church instead of the voice of God." The Bible must be studied from an unbiased viewpoint. People "believe in certain creeds and doctrines, and they run through the book to get Scripture in accordance with them." Instead, "Study it in the light of Calvary." People were warned against "building our hopes of salvation upon some form or creed." "It won't do for them to merely take up with some minister or church or creed." He warned against "head beliefs only." He pitied those about whom he said, "You are living a life of formalism—you are living on doctrines." The person who does not feel like praising God "has been born to some creed or profession, some man or church, and not to the loving Son of God." "We want to lift up this creed, this party, this doctrine. Oh, may God sweep it away, and help us to lift up the Gospel of Christ."[17] These statements are a typical cross section of those made time and again through the span of Moody's ministry.[18]

However, in the attempt to discern the significance of such statements, it must be seriously questioned that they indicate that Moody was either indifferent to or opposed to creeds, theology, or preaching of doctrine. On the very face of these quotations it is evident that Moody was opposed to a dead letter of doctrine that did not also involve a living faith. He was opposed to reading Scripture in the light of doctrine rather than reading it in the light of Calvary. He was opposed to the divisions that resulted from creedal disputes. He was opposed to doctrinal correctness that was devoid of Christian compassion. He was opposed to formalism that lived on doctrines. In short, Moody was insistent that adherence to a creed was no substitute for a personal faith in Christ; and the common bond among those who had such a faith in Christ transcended the party spirit that tended to rise out of creedalism.

It is granted that this is a pietistic concern, a concern that one would expect from a revival preacher; however, there is nothing in these statements to necessitate the conclusion that Moody's pietism was indifferent to creeds, doctrine, or theology. Even his statement that he did not

17. Ibid., pp. 41, 58, 138, 214, 268-69, 347, 357, 382, 415, 618.
18. Cf. "The Revival," *Chicago Tribune*, Oct. 7, 1876; "Moody's Ministrations," *Daily Inter-Ocean* (Chicago), Nov. 9, 1876; "Messrs. Moody and Sankey," *Irish Times* (Dublin), Jan. 11, 1883; "Moody Talks on Faith," *Journal* (New Bedford, Mass.), undated clipping, but probably from 1895; "Dwight L. Moody Again Speaks to Large Congregation," *Post* (Chicago), Oct. 30, 1899; unidentified newspaper clipping, "Wages of Sin," reporting one of the 1897 Moody meetings in the Auditorium, Chicago. All of these are clippings in Moodyana.

know he had a theology when seen in the light of other statements is best understood as a tongue-in-cheek statement. Indeed, even those rare statements that any creed would do that led to Christ or that would prompt a man to put his arm around another man and lead him to God do not imply indifference to doctrine; they simply imply that correct doctrine is correlative with faith in Christ and compassion for people. Often, within the context of such statements, Moody would warn against those who suggest that it does not make any difference what kind of a belief a man has, so long as he is sincere. "My friends, it makes all the difference in the world whether a man believes a truth or a lie."[19]

This suggests that Moody's statements about creeds and doctrine must be examined within both their immediate and broader contexts. Such examination clearly shows that Moody had an appreciation of the role of theology. The very fact that at the time the Illinois Street Church had been constituted it was provided with articles of faith to which would-be members had to subscribe shows that this was not a matter of indifference to Moody. Later in his career Moody would even speak of "my theology"; and repeatedly through this study I have cited Moody's use of theological terms, including such nonbiblical theological terminology as *substitution, satisfaction, trinity, premillennialism, dispensation,* etc.[20] Since Moody did not formally study theology, he must have acquired his theological vocabulary from what reading he did (such as Spurgeon's sermons), from sermons he heard, and from discussions with preachers and Bible teachers. Since Moody was not indifferent to theology, he adopted the theological vocabulary of the living tradition to express his own beliefs.

In his sermon on faith preached in London in 1875 and again at the New York Hippodrome in 1876, Moody spoke of faith as consisting of knowledge, assent, and laying hold; and then he went on to say, as he so often did, that sincerity was not enough—it did make a difference what one believed.[21] In a similar vein, in his sermon notes on "Confessing Christ" there is a sentence in Moody's own hand that refers to a false idea of faith: "It makes no difference what a man believes if he only sticks to it."[22] The sermon on faith was preached again within the year

19. Charles F. Goss, *Echoes*, pp. 317-19.
20. Smith, *Annotated Bibliography*, pp. 150-51, or Daniels, *D. L. Moody and His Work*, pp. 109-10. See p. 102.
21. *London Discourses*, pp. 149-51, and D. L. Moody, *Wondrous Love* (London: J. E. Hawkins, 1875), pp. 261-64; *Glad Tidings*, pp. 270-73.
22. Moodyana

as reported in *New Sermons, Addresses and Prayers,* and on this occasion Moody was even more specific, warning against false ideas of God, the sincere followers of Baal, error, and the folly that "any creed is good . . . if they only believe it." He even is critical of people who "go wandering about without any definite belief—who don't know what they believe."[23] During his last summer at his Northfield General Conference, Moody was saying substantially the same thing:

> People have an idea now that it makes very little difference what a man believes if he is only sincere, if he is only honest in his creed. I have had that question put to me many a time: "Mr. Moody, you don't think it makes any difference what a man believes if he is only sincere?" I believe that is one of the greatest lies that ever came out of the pit of hell. Why they virtually say you can believe a lie just as well as you can believe the truth, if you are only earnest, you know, and stick to it.[24]

In view of these considerations, it is significant that Moody did not regard his own evangelistic ministry as the only valid ministry, or for that matter necessarily the most important type of ministry. As early as 1875, when asked how young converts were to be built up and fed, he simply replied, "That is the work of the pastors."[25] If anything, Moody became more convinced of the importance of the pastor's teaching ministry with the passage of the years. In 1888 he told the college students assembled at Northfield, "I believe that what we want in this country to-day is more teaching and less preaching—or perhaps as much preaching, but certainly more teaching." Too many sermons are all exhortation, and too many are directed to the unconverted when none are present. If a man "is building up those that are in the kingdom of God, he is doing a work that is just as important, if not more so."

Later that summer Moody was to advise the students that in their personal Bible study they would greatly benefit by taking the fundamental doctrines and devoting a month of study to each of them. He specifically mentioned faith, assurance, atonement, justification, and sanctification. He concluded, "You will get a foundation of truth that

---

23. *New Sermons,* pp. 137-40; cf. p. 351.
24. "Address delivered by Mr. D. L. Moody, General Conference, Saturday Evening, August 12, 1899," p. 4 of typed manuscript, Moodyana. Cf. D. L. Moody, *Moody's Latest Sermons* (Chicago: BICA, 1900), p. 27.
25. *Signs of Our Times,* Mar. 10, 1875, p. 149.

will serve you the rest of your life."[26] Eleven years later at the General
Conference in Northfield, Moody was again saying that preachers who
do not feed the flock make a bad mistake and are a big failure.[27] Such
statements reveal in themselves how far off the mark those are who
suggest that theology meant little to Moody or that he felt that perhaps
heaven would contain theologians, but on earth all are called to be
evangelists.[28]

In Moody's thinking, creeds or doctrine were not inconsistent with
a living faith in and relationship with Christ; just because this saving
relationship with Christ was the ultimate goal, it was important to have
right doctrine, or, in Moody's judgment, biblical doctrine. His sermon
on "Faith" in New Bedford, Massachusetts, in 1895 eloquently expressed this complementary relationship as he saw it. The sermon
opened with the twofold warning that faith is not merely intellectual
assent, and yet faith is also not a "leap into the dark." "God doesn't ask
a man or a woman to believe without giving them evidence or something to believe." And then he quoted, "He that hath the son hath life,"
and commented:

> Now notice, it isn't a mere creed or doctrine. Doctrines are all right in
> their places, but when you put them in the place of faith or salvation
> they become a sin. If a man should ask me up to his house to dinner
> tomorrow, the street would be a very good thing to take me to his
> house, but if I didn't get into the house, I wouldn't get any dinner. Now
> a creed is the road or street. It is very good as far as it goes, but if it
> doesn't take us to Christ it is worthless. "He that hath the son hath
> life." Faith in a person, and that person is Jesus Christ. It isn't a
> creed about him, but it is himself.[29]

That Moody would at least attempt to preserve the dynamic relationship between creed or correct doctrine and living faith in and relationship with Christ should not be too surprising. Besides evidencing
his own understanding of the Christian faith, it would seem that he was
being true to his own origins in American Evangelicalism, which was
a combination of pietistic concerns and doctrinal orthodoxy.

26. Shanks, ed., *College Students at Northfield* (1888), pp. 182, 223.
27. "Questions answered by Mr. Moody, at General Conference, Tuesday Afternoon,
August 16, 1898," typed manuscript, Moodyana.
28. See pp. 64-66.
29. "Moody Talks on Faith," *Journal* (New Bedford, Mass.), undated clipping, but probably 1895, Moodyana.

DID MOODY'S EVANGELISTIC TECHNIQUE DETERMINE
HIS THEOLOGY?

D. L. Moody, like so many American revivalists, has been charged with allowing technique to triumph over theology. Precisely what this means is somewhat difficult to determine, especially in the case of Moody. But it is clear that those making the charge make it in a pejorative sense. The basic implication of the more radical statements is that in his determination to win souls at all costs, Moody severely truncated the Gospel message and employed methods which fundamentally shaped or altered it. Such charges have usually come from those unsympathetic to Moody because they saw him as a threat to their own brand of rigid orthodoxy, or from those simply unsympathetic to any form of orthodoxy. These charges need to be investigated, and the best place to start is with the critique of James F. Findlay in his recent biography.

To Findlay's credit, it needs to be pointed out that his book attempts to be sympathetic without being uncritically eulogistic, and objective without using that objectivity as a screen for either hostility or aloofness. Furthermore, he normally proceeds very cautiously, documenting carefully as he goes. Consequently, what Findlay says on this matter deserves more careful consideration than the statements of others mentioned later.

In a concluding statement to his chapter on Moody's theology, Findlay says that Moody has deserved the criticism directed toward him by theologians and many secular historians that for him technique had triumphed over truth rigorously examined. By looking back over the chapter, one can discover what this apparently means to Findlay. Technique is said to have been Moody's great strength as a revivalist and preacher, whereas theology was a noticeable weakness. His success is said to have come by creating a mood or special frame of mind that seemed to speak of God, Christ's love, and the need to be saved, with the mood the result of technique rather than of intellectual argument. A much more serious charge is that "frequently Moody's methods largely determined the special emphases to be found in his theological statements." Ostensible examples of this are Moody's doctrine of work, his use of the word "power," his acceptance of premillennialism, and his understanding of love and the atonement. These were all concepts conditioned by the needs of evangelism, that is, bringing about the conversion experience. "The need to save souls seemed normative in all phases of Moody's thought and work. And the conversion experience, while not without theological content and significance, was principally a function of technique." Revivals were to be worked up, not prayed down. The man-made elements of revival had come to dominate.[30]

It must be added, however, that Findlay does not leave Moody wholly at the mercy of his critics on these points, for he indicates that technique was not the sole basis of Moody's appeal. Furthermore, Moody's sermons are credited with containing bits of information that reveal a man who knew intimately and profoundly what it was to be grasped by the love of God as revealed in Jesus Christ. In fact, Findlay credits Moody with opposing superficial religious sentiments, yet ironically and unwittingly, Moody's techniques were producing these effects.[31]

Although Findlay has the insight and fairness to give due credit to Moody's personal faith and understanding of the Christian message, his analysis and critique of the role of Moody's evangelistic techniques sounds very much like an echo of earlier and less sympathetic writers. For instance, Sidney Mead correctly observes that revivalists are strongly tempted to stress tangible results and to justify whatever means will produce them. Will it help or hinder the salvation of the prospective convert? Mead then asserts:

> This pragmatic emphasis on results reached a peak in the eminently persuasive albeit muddled thinking of Dwight L. Moody who reputedly said he was an Arminian up to the Cross but Calvinist beyond—and who declared forthrightly that "it makes no difference how you get a man to God, provided you get him there."[32]

Mead's judgment on Moody is similar to William McLoughlin's; even the statement of Moody that Mead alludes to is taken not from the original source but from McLoughlin's book on Billy Sunday.[33]

In his various treatments of American Evangelicalism and revivalism, McLoughlin presents a consistent view of the nature of revivalism

30. Findlay, *Dwight L. Moody*, pp. 261, 260, 301, 203-4.
31. Ibid., pp. 261, 259; cf. pp. 203-4.
32. Mead, *Lively Experiment*, p. 124.
33. William G. McLoughlin, *Billy Sunday Was His Real Name* (Chicago: U. Chicago, 1955), p. 158.

in general and of Moody in particular. His basic thesis is that earlier in the nineteenth century, evangelist Charles G. Finney had established the theory of modern revivalism that revivals could be produced at will by the proper use of means, that the end did justify the means for subsequent revivalists (including Moody), and that Moody took Finney's theory and made professional revivalism a big business enterprise conducted according to the principles of corporate business. Moody applied these principles to urban evangelism for the first time, so that "it became possible to promote city-wide interdenominational revivals at will."[34] Bernard Weisberger is in essential agreement with McLoughlin's interpretation, emphasizing the "superdevelopment" of "machine-made" revivals under Moody.[35]

The evaluation of such interpretations of Moody's method and message is fraught with difficulties and dangers. It is impossible, for instance, to separate one's interpretation or evaluation from one's personal faith commitment. Furthermore, the above views not only involve Moody, but Finney who came before Moody and those who came after Moody, such as Billy Sunday. The difficulties of evaluation are compounded by the fact that the above charges against Moody are not all of the same order, although there is superficial verbal similarity. For instance, it is one thing to say that the nature of Moody's evangelistic message in the quest for souls influenced what he would preach; it is quite another thing to charge that the expediencies of evangelism actually shaped his understanding of theology, or to suggest that he accepted certain doctrines, such as premillennialism, because they were more effective in making converts or motivating Christian witness. And this in turn raises what is perhaps the greatest difficulty.

The very nature of the criticisms presumes that present-day interpreters can have such an insight into Moody's mind as to be able to discern motives and tendencies of which Moody himself may have been largely unaware. This is not intended to suggest that such efforts are altogether illegitimate, but such interpretations must be regarded as tentative and subject to being checked in the light of what external evidence is available. This is especially important in the case in question, for documentation from primary sources supporting this interpre-

34. Ibid.; McLoughlin, *Modern Revivalism*, pp. 166-67; McLoughlin, ed., *The American Evangelicals, 1800-1900: An Anthology*, p. 171.
35. Weisberger, *They Gathered at the River*, pp. 220-23, 231.

tation is usually conspicuous by its absence, whereas evidence for a contrary interpretation is either unknown or bypassed in the interests of a preconceived theory.

One mainstay of McLoughlin's argument is a statement Moody allegedly made in 1877: "It makes no difference how you get a man to God, provided you get him there."[36] This statement as it stands is so at odds with views which Moody consistently expressed and which can readily be documented that even if it were not available in the primary source, it could not be accepted at face value. One would either have to question the accuracy of the newspaper reporter, withhold judgment because the statement is not seen in context, or regard the statement as an off-the-cuff remark not intended in the sense that McLoughlin and others have taken it.

But the source of the quotation is available so that one is not left to pure conjecture on the matter. The source of the alleged quotation is a reporter's account and personal analysis of the meetings that were being conducted in the Boston Tabernacle. He wrote, "He has one answer which he makes to all objections as to the propriety of the course which he is pursuing: 'It makes no difference how you get a man to God, provided you get him there.' " The reporter then cited charges that had been brought against Moody to which Moody had supposedly given this answer. The charges included Moody's illiteracy, "undue influence by means of animal magnetism," and religious excitement which was said to be driving people crazy. The reporter concluded, "For every objection he has an answer, and for every act a scriptural authority."

Several observations are in order. First, it is not certain that Moody made the statement attributed to him. The nature of the article suggests that the reporter may have put a conveniently stylized statement into Moody's mouth. It is an analysis, not a verbatim report, nor even a rather full summary of Moody's words. Second, assuming the statement was made by Moody, the reporter does not place it within the context of Moody's original statement. Third, the context that the reporter provided for the statement does not justify the inferences which McLoughlin has drawn from it. And finally, even the reporter's concluding observation suggests that it was not the end which justified the

36. McLoughlin, *Billy Sunday Was His Real Name*, p. 158; "Moody and Sankey," *Boston Daily Advertiser*, Feb. 3, 1877, p. 4.

means for Moody; it was Scripture. This report in the *Boston Daily Advertiser* cannot support the case McLoughlin builds on it.

Elsewhere McLoughlin quotes William Hoyt Coleman, an observer of Moody's meetings in New York in 1876, to support his case. The excised quote reads, "The Hippodrome work is a vast business enterprise, organized and conducted by businessmen, who put their money into it on business principles, for the purpose of saving souls."[37] Aside from the fact that this quotation does not prove that Moody thought business technique could save souls, it is, to say the least, interesting that McLoughlin did not go on to quote the observer's next sentence. The next sentence reads, "But through all the machinery vibrates the power without which it would be useless—the power of the Holy Ghost."[38] Finally, the use of business techniques by Moody does not in itself argue that technique became or even tended to become the controlling consideration for Moody. It may have been a danger to which he was prone; it may have been a trap into which later revivalists fell; but the significance of use of techniques is precisely the thing that needs to be discovered. The use of technique is the question, not the evidence.

Rather than attempt to answer the individual criticisms of Moody cited above, we shall examine the positive evidence that can be brought to bear on these questions. That examination must begin by taking another look at Charles Finney.

In the winter of 1834-35 Charles G. Finney gave a series of lectures on revivals that gave systematic expression to trends and viewpoints that had been growing in American revivalism since the time of Jonathan Edwards. The Calvinistic viewpoint had been that revivals, coming from the working of the Holy Spirit, were supernatural and that they came at the time of God's sovereign appointment. This view was gradually eroded by the Arminianizing of American evangelical theology through the eighteenth and early nineteenth centuries, so that they came to be regarded less as sovereign workings of the Spirit and more as man-made. Finney's lecture series has achieved fame because he defined so clearly and systematically the pragmatic approach to producing revivals and conversions.

The first of these lectures sets the philosophic tone for all that fol-

37. McLoughlin, *Modern Revivalism*, p. 166.
38. Cited by W. R. Moody, *Moody* (1900), p. 281.

lows. His first major point in that lecture was that a revival of religion is not a miracle. "The laws of matter and mind remain in force. They are neither suspended nor set aside in a revival." It is not a miracle in the sense that a revival is something above the powers of nature, nor is it dependent on a miracle in any sense. The point Finney was driving for and quickly reached was that a revival "is a purely philsophical result of the right use of the constituted means—as much so as any other effect produced by the application of means." It comes as naturally as a farmer's crop comes from the use of appropriate means. Even conversion itself was not a miracle. The lectures then went on to elaborate the appropriate means and the proper use of the appropriate means. Success *would* attend the proper use of the appropriate means, which meant that if a minister was not successful he was either not called to preach, was badly educated, or too lazy and wicked to do his duty. His degree of success in winning souls "invariably decides the amount of wisdom he has exercised in the discharge of his office."[39] In his *Memoirs* Finney later recalled that he had said:

> Show me a more excellent way. Show me the fruits of your ministry; and if they so far exceed mine as to give me evidence that you have found a more excellent way, I will adopt your views. But do you expect me to abandon my own views and practices, and adopt yours, when you yourselves cannot deny that, whatever errors I may have fallen into, or whatever imperfections there may be in my preaching, in style, and in everything else, yet the results justify my methods?[40]

Thus the pragmatic test of success came to be the test of what was right, and since the new measures of Finney were judged to be successful in winning converts and reviving churches, they were justified. However, in fairness to Finney, it must be added that Finney did not feel that he had excluded the agency of the Spirit in conversion nor eliminated the minister's dependence on God for his success.[41] In fact, it can be argued that Finney did not intend to say that revivals are manmade and merely the result of the right use of proper means; rather, he was opposing a passivistic approach to evangelism that simply waited for the Spirit to move. In this connection it is also significant that Fin-

39. Charles G. Finney, *Lectures on Revivals of Religion* (New York: Revell, reprint from 1868), pp. 12-13, 134, 174-78.
40. Charles G. Finney, *Memoirs* (New York: Revell, 1876, 1903), p. 83.
41. Finney, *Lectures on Revivals of Religion*, pp. 16, 175-76, 300.

ney spoke highly in his memoirs of the revival of 1857-58, the so-called prayer revival in which laymen, including D. L. Moody, played the most prominent part. This was apparently a spontaneous movement across America, a revival without revivalists using Finney's new measures.[42] It should also be noted that for Finney, regeneration was not simply the result of the use of means, for the Spirit is active in regeneration, as brought out in his *Systematic Theology*.[43]

However, even if Finney has not been fairly represented by recent treatments of revivalism, it does seem valid to say that by setting up the pragmatic test of success as the justification for his new measures, Finney has in effect given a programatic outline for the production of man-made revivals by the proper use of the appropriate means. We will let others debate the question of Finney's intention; but whatever his intentions, the conclusion that the end justifies the means is not simply implied, it is stated in so many words by Finney. And the right use of means *will* bring revival. However, is Moody the true successor of Finney? Is Moody the creative institutional architect who builds on Finney's sturdy foundation, as McLoughlin claims? Was Finney the prophet of means which Moody employed, as John Wesley White maintains? Did Moody complete the "reduction of evangelism to a matter of technique and personality," as Weisberger insists?[44] In short, did technique triumph over theology in D. L. Moody? Or, did Moody's theology lead him to a particular use of technique?

The question can be approached first from the angle of Moody's relationship to Finney. When evidence for any direct or indirect relationship between the men is sought, one draws a complete blank. Though this is an argument from silence, it may very well be significant silence. Finney was alive until 1875, plenty of time for Moody to have consulted with the great revivalist if he had felt he could have benefited by that. It must be remembered that this was Moody's method of instructing himself. He traveled to Great Britain three times before 1873 to consult with and learn from the great evangelical leaders there. So far as I have been able to discover, there is no evidence that Moody had

42. Finney, *Memoirs*, pp. 441-47.
43. Charles G. Finney, *Lectures on Systematic Theology*, ed. J. H. Fairchild (New York: George H. Doran, 1878), pp. 287-300.
44. McLoughlin, *Modern Revivalism*, pp. 164-65; White, "The Influence of North American Evangelism in Great Britain between 1830 and 1914 on the Origin and Development of the Ecumenical Movement," 2:1; Weisberger, *They Gathered at the River*, p. 176.

read any of Finney's published works. This is not conclusive, but Moody did occasionally express indebtedness to the writings of such men as Charles Spurgeon and C. H. Mackintosh. Yet there is not a word about Finney.

Furthermore, it should be remembered that Moody's roots as a new convert were firmly imbedded in the revival of 1857-58, a revival which was not the result of the right use of right means by professional revivalists or ministers, and a revival in which Finney played no significant part. Though Finney had nothing negatively critical to say of the revival, he did describe it as having "some very peculiarly interesting features."[45] Finney then mentioned the lay leadership of the revival and the fact that the ministers had been put in the shade. Did Finney find it peculiar that there could be a revival without the new measures, a revival that appeared to be spontaneous?[46] In any case, this revival was the spiritual milieu in which Moody moved as a young Christian in Chicago. These considerations seem to have special significance when seen in the light of how Moody conducted his meetings.

In the midst of meetings in New Bedford, Massachusetts, in 1895, Moody expressly repudiated the idea that "new measures" were what the churches needed to revive them. It is true that he did not define these new measures in Finney's terms, but rather as new choirs, new organs, and new churches. But it is significant and very characteristic of him to insist that measures and techniques would not bring the revival he earnestly desired. It would come only when Christians were renewed with power or filled by the Spirit. "What we need specially is to be filled with the Spirit so we shall know how to use the word." Significantly, he closed that portion of his sermon with this statement: "It is not our work to make them [skeptics] believe in it [the Bible]; that is the work of the Spirit."[47]

It is also significant that from the beginning to the end of his career as an evangelist, Moody eschewed both in word and in practice the type of emotionalism and high pressure that can be so readily used by evangelists to manipulate crowds, if they so choose, in order to produce "conversions." In fact, it was this absence of emotionalism and manip-

45. Finney, *Memoirs,* p. 442.
46. It should be noted that secular historians would deny that this was a spontaneous revival, seeing it instead as a natural response to the commercial crash and panic of 1857; cf. Weisberger, *They Gathered at the River,* pp. 148-49.
47. "Power—In and Upon," *Journal* (New Bedford, Mass.), Oct. 8, 1895.

ulation that commended the work of Moody and Sankey to the Scots. As early as January, 1874, the following report appeared in *The Christian* about the work of these two men who had been relatively unknown a few months earlier:

> One of the first things that would strike a stranger who came to examine this work of grace, was the *absence of excitement* even at the time of greatest interest. There were, doubtless, crowded churches and halls, most earnest preaching, fervent, hearty singing, and many moved to tears of penitence; but there were no articulate wailings, no prostrations, no sudden outbursts of rapture, of which we have heard in former revivals. We account for this by the fact that the Spirit of God has done more, and man less, in this work than in any similar awakening since the days of the Reformation.[48]

R. W. Dale, the leading Congregational minister of England, had a similar assessment of the Moody-Sankey meetings. He candidly attempted to explain the interest of the people in the meetings and their apparent success. He attributed it fundamentally to the power of God, but then went on to speak of concurrent circumstances. Among those circumstances were the preliminary prayer meetings, reports of previous meetings in the religious and secular press, the dull ache in the hearts of people for God, the number of people who had relatives in America, the contagious joy of new converts, the expectations of people in evangelical churches, handbills, and the attractiveness of the services, including the music and the power and naturalness of Moody himself.

But, significantly, Dale repudiated the suggestion that the interest was due to hysterical religious services. "Nor were the services at all 'hysterical;' the first sign of hysterical excitement was instantly repressed by Mr. Moody, and although I attended a very large number of the meetings, I saw nothing of the kind again."[49] Moody refused to tolerate such excitements as had been characteristic of so much earlier revivalism, sometimes even dismissing the meeting abruptly when there were such outbreaks.[50] Though Moody insisted that religious meetings

---

48. "The Awakening in Edinburgh," *The Christian*, Jan. 29, 1874, p. 3; cf. Findlay, *Dwight L. Moody*, p. 220.

49. *Addresses and Lectures of D. L. Moody, with a Narrative of the Awakening in Liverpool and London* (New York: Anson D. F. Randolph, 1875), pp. 26-35, a reprint of R. W. Dale's account of the Birmingham meetings that originally appeared in the *Congregationalist*, Mar. 1875.

50. W. R. Moody, *Moody* (1930), p. 187.

should be enthusiastic in the sense of being interesting and alive, he expressed his own view that revival and conversion were not merely emotional experiences and that emotional extremes should therefore be avoided.[51]

However, this is not to suggest that Moody did not believe in the use of means, as Dale's description above suggests. Moody was exacting in the preparations which he insisted be made for and maintained throughout the meetings. L. A. Gotwald, a Lutheran pastor and professor, described in 1879 such preparations and arrangements as union of purpose among pastors and churches, prayer, publicity in the papers and by word of mouth, appointment of committees, selection of ushers, formation of a large and select choir, and the acquisition of a "suitable auditorium, large, airy, well-ventilated, properly heated, easily accessible, attractive, comfortable, adapted so that the truth spoken may be most easily and impressively heard." Gotwald then described the conduct of the services which were decorous yet arranged to be interesting and adapted to intensify religious sentiments. He also spoke of "rigid enforcement of the strictest possible order."[52]

Moody himself often spoke of using "vigorous means." Advertisement was chief among these means. "This is the age of advertisement, and you have to watch your chance." Moody preferred not to advertise his topic, but if he saw he was losing his audience, "then I begin to push, begin to advertise." "I would have anything rather than empty pews. I will not preach to empty pews if I can help myself." He said that God doesn't call men to preach to empty pews. "I don't think it is beneath a man's dignity to go out and ask people to come in."[53] In terms of the methodology of evangelism, Moody was an innovator.

The question, then, is not whether Moody believed in the use of innovative means. The real question relates to the significance of the use of means to Moody. Previous studies already cited tend to jump from the fact that Moody used means to the conclusion that Moody thought that the right use of means would produce revival and conversions, much as they understand Finney to have said. But such was neither Moody's

---

51. *New Sermons*, pp. 13, 115-16, 642.

52. L. A. Gotwald, "Human Conditions of a Good Prayer Meeting," *Quarterly Review of the Lutheran Church and Lutheran Quarterly Review* 9 (Jan. 1879): 54-56.

53. *New Sermons*, pp. 33-34; "Questions Answered by Mr. Moody, at General Conference, Tuesday Afternoon, August 16, 1898," typed manuscript, Moodyana; D. L. Moody, *Thou Fool: And Eleven Other Sermons Never Before Published* (New York: Christian Herald, 1911), p. 78, cited as *Thou Fool; To All People*, p. 181.

practice nor his expressed view. As one looks at his statements on advertisement, Moody's rationale is perfectly obvious. "It's my business to let it be known that I am going to preach." The world knows enough to advertise theaters and places of amusement. "Why shouldn't we give the Gospel a chance? If people don't know about the meetings why not advertise them?"[54]

But even this, Moody insisted, had to be done in a legitimate manner. Commenting in 1899 on the Spirit's work of conviction and conversion, he had occasion to refer to advertisement of sensational sermon subjects as a means of bringing in people. "I abominate this trying to catch people by a sensational subject," said Moody. "I was going by a big fashionable church in the fashionable part of the city, and there was a great sign out Sunday night saying the preacher was going to preach on 'The Under Dog.' I colored to the very roots of my hair." "We don't need to stoop to those things; but let it be known that there is going to be a live evangelistic address every Sunday night."[55]

Actually, those who attempt to sustain the thesis that Moody simply took Finney's methods and united them with business principles so as to produce man-made or machine-made revivals and converts almost totally misrepresent Moody's concepts and practice. Moody held to what might be called a proclamation evangelism in which he was to use every legitimate means to attract hearers to the meetings and maintain their comfort and interest while there. He preached the Gospel as he understood it, stripped of as much debatable and divisive extraneous material as possible. Emotions were to be subdued. Feelings would not substitute for belief. A person was to be brought to Christ "coolly, calmly, and intelligently."[56]

Those who claim that for Moody the end justified the means and that success in evangelism was of paramount importance also have forgotten that Moody was a premillennialist.[57] Though this might seem an irrelevant point, in actuality it is a very significant factor that distinguishes Moody from Finney, who was postmillennial. Premillennialists did not necessarily expect a large number of conversions when the

54. "Questions and Answers General Conference, Wednesday Morning, August 2, 1899," pp. 8-9 of typed manuscript, Moodyana.
55. Ibid.
56. *New Sermons*, pp. 343, 348, 384, 593; cf. D. L. Moody, *Great Joy: Comprising Sermons and Prayer-Meeting Talks* (New York: E. B. Treat, 1877), p. 343, cited as *Great Joy; Glad Tidings*, p. 229; Shanks, *D. L. Moody at Home*, pp. 86 ff.
57. For a fuller treatment of Moody's premillennialism see chap. 9.

Gospel was preached. Evangelism was thought of as dispersing the Gospel message, not necessarily in the sense of converting the world. Even the slogan of the Student Volunteer Movement, "the evangelization of the world in this generation," was understood in this sense, reflecting the early influence of Moody and other premillenarians on the movement.[58] Given Moody's premillennialism, it would be very surprising to find him fitting the caricature drawn of him by recent historians.

When one turns to Moody's expressed attitudes on success in evangelism, they do not fit the caricature either and are consistent with his premillennialism. Moody took the example of Noah who preached 120 years without visible results, yet without getting discouraged, as a guiding principle for himself. In fact, his comments on Noah provide the key to his view of evangelism. Moody said in New York:

> I made up my mind then, that, God helping me, I would never get discouraged. I would do the best I could, and leave the results with God, and it has been a wonderful help to me. And so let me say to the Christians of New York that we must expect good results, let us not look on the dark side, but keep on praying, and in the fulness of time the blessing of God will come.

Significantly, within a few minutes, Moody was also telling his congregation that if New York was to see a revival, it would not be in the Hippodrome, but out among the people. "We musn't [sic] go around professionally if we want to see any result."[59] This is the key to understanding Moody, "I would do the best I could, and leave the results with God." It was for this reason that Moody never took credit for conversions, and did not even keep a record of the number of converts. A. P. Fitt, Moody's son-in-law who served as his confidential secretary through most of the 1890s, said:

> Mr. Moody never counted converts, or traded on the spiritual successes he gained. He deprecated the boastful use of statistics. People used to ask him what were the most notable conversions he had achieved, and the greatest meetings he ever conducted. They could not draw him out on such matters.[60]

58. Sandeen, *Roots of Fundamentalism*, pp. 184-85.
59. *Glad Tidings*, pp. 34-35, 37; cf. W. R. Moody, *Moody* (1930), pp. 114-15.
60. Arthur Percy Fitt, "D. L. Moody as I Knew Him," typed manuscript of address delivered at Biblical Seminary, New York City, Dec. 19, 1936, Moodyana.

R. W. Dale in 1875 wrote that Moody disapproved of the newspapers publishing the number of converts. Moody himself once observed that "it makes me creep all over to hear a man tell how many he has converted."[61] This facet of Moody's practice is too well known to need further documentation, though the significance of it seems to be lost on many who have written on Moody.

The fact is, Moody did not believe that the end justifies the means. Finney and many of his imitators had used the "anxious bench" whereby potential converts had been brought to the front and seated beneath the piercing glare of Finney's eyes and subjected to the unseen group pressures to be converted. Moody had none of this. Instead there was an "inquiry room" where those whose concern had been aroused by the message could come for further information and counseling in a quiet setting. It was Moody's desire that they not be subjected to high pressure during that time. He did not make final pleas for converts in the mass meeting; it was always to come to the inquiry room. It was this novel use of the inquiry room as a means of nurturing seeking souls that probably first attracted young Henry Drummond to Moody.[62]

A college student in Northfield in 1887 asked Moody if he would advise having the unconverted make a public commitment to Christ by standing. Moody replied, "I never would get a man to take a position beyond the leading of the Spirit, or beyond his own conviction."[63] Moody went on to emphasize the caution needed in public meetings lest people be led by an enthusiastic mood rather than by the Spirit of God. Sometimes, he warned, it takes days rather than minutes or hours. For the same reason Moody rejected gimmicks as a means of catching people and scare tactics as a way of getting people into the Kingdom of God. Jesus would not have done it that way. Besides, he said, "We cannot scare people into repentance; they must be born in, not scared in."

Moody said that some were critical of him for not preaching the terrors of religion. His response was that if he wanted to do that he

---

61. *Addresses and Lectures of D. L. Moody, with a Narrative of the Awakening in Liverpool and London*, p. 34; D. L. Moody, *Sermons and Addresses, Question Drawer, and Other Proceedings of the Christian Convention Held in Chicago, September 18th to 20th, 1883. Under the Direction of D. L. Moody* (Chicago: Fairbanks, Palmer, 1884), p. 954, cited as *Sermons and Addresses, Question Drawer*.

62. George Adam Smith, *The Life of Henry Drummond* (New York: Hodder & Stoughton, 1898), p. 67; cf. Findlay, *Dwight L. Moody*, pp. 262-63.

63. Shanks, ed., *A College of Colleges* (1887), pp. 259-60.

would hold the terrors of hell over their heads, "but I don't believe in preaching that way. If I did get some in that way they would soon get out. . . . That is not the way to win men." On another occasion he said, "The only work that is going to stand for eternity is the work done by the Holy Ghost, and not by any one of us. We may be used as his instruments, but the work that will stand to eternity is that done by the Holy Ghost." Later in the same sermon he asserted that conviction of sin does not come from the preacher but from the Holy Spirit. "If He does not do it they won't be converted."[64]

Of course it must be emphasized that Moody saw God working through instruments; that was why he would do the best he could and use aggressive means in proclaiming the Gospel. Indeed, he could warn people that if God did not work it would be their fault, not God's. God works through others and His instruments must be ready. God works in partnership. The one who asks for a blessing must have an active disposition to help. But human effort is put at God's disposal, with never a hint that man himself achieves the results; yet the person is culpable who does not give his work to God.[65]

Though Moody could use rhetoric in admonishing Christians to get to work, that might sometimes suggest that they could themselves produce the revival they wanted, these occasions were relatively few and were not incompatible with Moody's major emphasis. Only when taken out of the larger context of what Moody said and practiced, and only when magnified to a prominence that they do not actually have in the total collection of Moody's recorded sermons and statements, can such statements be taken to imply that Moody thought a revival could be produced at will. Moody expressly repudiated "the idea that a man can start a revival and stop one." When asked how he began services for revival purposes, he replied, "I don't like the word 'revival'; we cannot tell whether we are going to have a revival or not. That depends upon whether God comes." Even advertising would not produce conversions. "If the Holy Spirit comes upon us, we can do it." In short, revivals and conversions are miraculous or supernatural. "It is super-

64. *Glad Tidings*, pp. 122, 269, 273, 281; *New Sermons*, p. 258; *Wondrous Love*, p. 237. By way of contrast, Finney said, "God calls the sinner to repent, he threatens him, he draws the glittering sword, he persuades him, he uses motives, and the sinner is distressed to agony, for he sees himself driven to the dreadful alternative of giving up his sins or going to hell" (Finney, *Lectures on Revivals of Religion*, p. 329).

65. *New Sermons*, pp. 9-10, 25, 30; cf. "Questions and Answers, General Conference, Wednesday Morning, August 2, 1899," pp. 11-12 of typed manuscript, Moodyana.

natural. That is what conversion is. I don't believe a man will ever see the kingdom of God that is not converted; and it will be supernatural. A supernatural conversion."[66] This is a most "un-Finney" approach, if one accepts the currently popular interpretation of Finney; and it is certainly not the *emphasis* to be found in Finney's *Lectures on Revival of Religion*.

A twofold emphasis marked the early sermons in Moody's crusades. The individual's responsibility to become involved in the work of spreading the Gospel, while certainly one of those two themes, has been so overemphasized in recent literature on the subject as to obscure the other parallel theme, man's dependence on God in the work. The first sermons preached in London, New York, and Boston in 1875 and 1876 may be taken as examples. In the first sermon in each of these locations the theme that comes through loud and clear is, "It is not our strength we want." Don't rest on man, God must do the work.[67] The significance of this fact should not be passed over.

Moody's evangelism was a proclamation evangelism which by his own admission demanded work from God's people and should employ vigorous means to bring the people to the message, or vice versa. But it did not presume that man could produce the results by his own efforts; it did not presume that there necessarily would be results. And this was the viewpoint that Moody advocated and practiced from the middle '70s to the late '90s. In 1876-77 he said, "I can not convert men; I can only proclaim the Gospel." In one of the earliest volumes of sermons approved for publication by Moody himself, *Secret Power* (1881), he declared, "It is not our work to make them [skeptics and infidels] believe it; that is the work of the Spirit. Our work is to give them the Word of God; not to preach our theories and ideas about it, but just to deliver the message as God gives it to us." On January 21, 1897, in Tremont Temple, Boston, Moody was still saying, "It's a good thing to give them [the self-righteous] the Word of God. *I* am not responsible for their conviction. *I* cannot convict them; but I can give them the Word of God."[68]

66. *New Sermons*, pp. 118, 574; Daniels, *Moody: His Words, Work, and Workers* (1879 ed.), p. 538; *To All People*, pp. 197-200; cf. *Glad Tidings*, pp. 14-19.
67. *London Discourses*, pp. 1-2, 5; D. L. Moody, *The Faithful Saying* (London: Morgan & Scott, 1877), p. 5; *To All People*, pp. 21-22.
68. *New Sermons*, p. 298; D. L. Moody, *Secret Power; or, The Secret of Success in Christian Life and Christian Work* (Chicago: Revell, 1881), p. 37; D. L. Moody, "Conviction of Sin," *The Christian Herald*, Oct. 25, 1911, p. 1060.

This chapter has investigated the questions surrounding Moody's attitude toward theology and the relationship between technique and theology. From this discussion has emerged the emphasis Moody put on evangelism as proclamation. This theme not only helps put the questions dealt with in this chapter into proper perspective, it also directs attention to the heart of Moody's understanding of Christian theology. He was no systematic theologian, but he did preach a certain understanding of the Gospel. To the extent that he had an articulated theology, it was fundamentally a proclamation theology.

3

RUINED BY THE FALL

IF IT IS TRUE that D. L. Moody's basic concern was the proclamation of the Gospel, it follows that one cannot accurately or fairly grasp Moody's understanding of theology without first discovering his understanding of the Gospel itself. From that vantage point the rest of his theology may be viewed, for both what he says and does not say have significance as related to this basic concern. Therefore, rather than organizing a compendium of Moody's theology according to the traditional schemes of systematic theology, my aim has been to be true to the genius of Moody's understanding of theology by first setting forth his understanding of the Gospel and then by relating all else to that. Although any systematic discussion of his unsystematic statements runs the risk of pouring him into a mold, the risks are at least minimized by this approach.

Even the search for a unifying scheme of Moody's understanding of the Gospel can be quite frustrating, especially if the search is confined to some systematic statement from Moody himself. Diligence is not unrewarded in this case, though, for tucked away in the introduction to a little book first published in 1877 is the key to Moody's understanding of the Gospel. The volume, entitled *The Way and the Word,* is something of an enigma. The cover to the 60,000th copy indicates it is by D. L. Moody, whereas the 86,000th copy softens the identification to "Prepared by D. L. Moody."[1] The introduction and the contents of the book suggest that the first part of the book is written by an anonymous Englishman, whereas the last part of the book is the substance of one of

1. D. L. Moody, *The Way and the Word* (Chicago: Revell, 1877).

87

Moody's messages. Be that as it may, the introduction was written by Moody, and therein he defines the Gospel as teaching "three great Bible truths: man *ruined* by the fall; *redeemed* by the blood; and *regenerated* by the Holy Spirit."[2] Although none of Moody's extant sermons are organized with exactly this outline, examination reveals that the formula conveniently summarizes his understanding of the basics of the Gospel.

This conclusion is supported by W. H. Daniels in his discussion of Moody's theology, also published in 1877. Having commented that perhaps it had never entered Moody's mind to arrange his theology into a system, he observed that its exceeding simplicity makes the task an easy one. According to Daniels, Moody was accustomed to say:

> "There are three R's in the Bible: Ruin by sin, Redemption by Christ, and Regeneration by the Holy Ghost." According to this triad of topics, he lays out all his campaigns. Outside of them, in the region of speculative, historic, or inferential theology, he does not go; not even into the realm of the Church, its institution, orders, and sacraments.
>
> His system of theology is bounded by his work as an evangelist.
>
> "I have in all about seven hundred sermons," said he; "but there are only about three hundred of them that are fit to convert sinners with."
>
> By this rule of fitness he tests all the ideas which present themselves to his mind. If there be salvation in them he adopts and uses them; if not, he casts them aside.[3]

Although this scheme is not spelled out in so many words in the surviving sermons of Moody, it is implied in them whether taken singly or as a whole. Furthermore, it appears that Moody acquired it from Henry Moorhouse, for in the latter's private memorandum book this entry is found shortly after his conversion: "My creed is this: Ruin by the Fall; Redemption by the Cross; and Regeneration by the Holy Spirit." Moorhouse, who had influenced Moody's understanding of God's love and his use of the Bible, quite possibly gave Moody this outline of the Gospel, and perhaps profoundly influenced Moody's very understanding of the Gospel as summarized in this triad. This must remain conjecture in the absence of further evidence, but in view of the known indebtedness of Moody to Moorhouse and their close rela-

2. Ibid., p. iii.
3. Daniels, *Moody: His Words, Work, and Workers*, p. 256.

tionship, this is certainly a plausible explanation.[4] Following this outline that Moody may have picked up from Moorhouse, we now direct
attention specifically to Moody's understanding of the Gospel.

The presupposition of all of Moody's preaching to the unsaved was
that humanity had been ruined by the Fall. This in turn involved two
basic concepts, namely, sin and its harmful effects, that is, fall and
ruin. As in all areas of Moody's theology, whether implicit or explicit,
it must be remembered that Moody was not a speculative theologian and
systematizer. Consequently, some questions are not addressed and
others are only indirectly alluded to by Moody.

Furthermore, the student of Moody should not only be prepared to
find blanks but also inconsistencies in what he does say. It is especially
important to emphasize this with reference to his hamartiology, for the
profound significance of this doctrine for the rest of theology will tempt
the researcher to fill in blanks which cannot be filled in and to impose
consistency where consistency does not exist. Nevertheless, Moody's
preaching does present a certain view of man and sin—the present
human condition and future prospect—which is the presupposition,
sometimes expressed and sometimes not, of his preaching of redemption and regeneration. Or, as Moody both preached and practiced, the
first thing that must be done in bringing a person to salvation is to convince him that he is a fallen, lost sinner.[5]

THE PRESENT HUMAN CONDITION

Summed up in a sentence, Moody understood man to be both sinful
and sinner, with this condition traceable to Adam. Both by the inherited nature from Adam and by deed emanating from this nature,
men are characterized by sin, without exception. It is this that consti-
tutes the need of mankind for both redemption and regeneration. A
sketch of one page of Moody's sermon on the "Brazen Serpent" (John
3:14-15) is almost sufficient to sum up his typical ways of expressing
his view of the human condition. Moody expounded the account of
Jesus' dialogue with Nicodemus. Nicodemus was a nobleman, a coun-
selor, one of the chief rulers of the Jews, a man whose integrity and honor

---

4. Needham, *Recollections of Henry Moorhouse, Evangelist*, p. 100; cf. pp. 109-10, 123,
125, 127, 151, 160, 188, 197-99 for the influence of Moorhouse on Moody and the contacts
and working relationships between the two. Moody frequently acknowledged his indebtedness to Moorhouse.
5. *New Sermons*, pp. 63, 369, 381.

could not be excelled, yet he needed to be regenerated; for, "that which is born of the flesh is flesh," and it will always remain so until it crumbles away in the grave. "We may try to patch up our old Adam nature, but it is of no use." "God has said that it is bad." Moody himself received a human nature from his parents, "and it was a very bad nature too," as was the nature that they had received from their forefathers. "We might trace it right back to Adam." Even the new birth does not renew the Adam nature; it is a new nature that is created, setting up a conflict between the flesh and the Spirit in the regenerated. "You may say the earth is a vast hospital. Every man and woman coming into it needs a physician. If you search, you will find everyone wounded. By nature we are sinners."[6]

At other times Moody would speak of mankind as being under Satan's power, and at still other times as captives who were bound and blind. "We are born under Satan's power. In sin my mother conceived me. By nature man is born away from God." "Our natural hearts are as black and deceitful as hell." "Children are not born good. Men may talk of natural goodness, but I don't find it."

> The first man born into the world became a murderer; he became the killer of his own brother; and all the way down through the ages man had been piling up sins against God and against himself. It didn't take the Bible to prove that man was entirely depraved. All experience of every age proved it. There was nothing good in man.

Maybe it did not take the Bible to prove man's depravity for Moody, but he did find that to be the consistent teaching of the Bible. "We are wicked by nature; there is nothing good in us; the Bible teaches us that all the way through." David was right when he said, "There is none that doeth good; no, not one." "He was right. We are all evil in our nature. It is the old Adam. I tell you man without God is a failure, and a tremendous failure. There's nothing good in him."[7]

In expanding the thought of the sinfulness of humanity, it was common for Moody to speak of the acts of sin such as ingratitude to parents, drunkenness, acts of sexual immorality, theater attendance, worldly

---

6. Ibid., p. 128. Nussbaum says that it made little difference to Moody whether the sin problem began for the entire race with Adam or for each man when he personally sins; he also claims that for Moody sin was not inherent in man's nature, but in man's actions ("D. L. Moody and the Church," pp. 23-24). Excerpts from this one page and citations to follow show this interpretation to be inaccurate.

7. *New Sermons*, pp. 144, 150, 222-23, 227, 381, 627, 686; *Glad Tidings*, pp. 485-86.

amusements, Sabbath-breaking, etc. But such deeds were the inevitable expressions of a fallen nature, what Moody commonly called the Adam nature. He could even say on occasions, "If you don't actually do any sin, yet if you neglect Christ, and neglect salvation as a gift from God, you must perish." However, this was not Moody's emphasis, and on other occasions he would sound as though a man who had not sinned (an actual impossibility) would not need a saviour.[8]

Moody's point in proclaiming that man had been ruined by the Fall was that man was in need of a salvation that only God could provide. He could do nothing to change his nature inherited from Adam, a nature that at its core and in its entirety was corrupt. His deeds were the predictable expression of that nature. Consequently, man has not only the problem of corruption, but of condemnation. The twin motifs of corruption and condemnation pervade the whole body of extant Moody literature. The purpose of the Law was to show humanity its great failure; man is condemned by the Law. "The law was never given to save men by. . . . It was given to show man his lost and ruined condition. It was given to measure men by their fruits. Before God saves a man he first stops his mouth."[9]

Daniel 5:27 was a verse which Moody often preached upon: "Thou art weighed in the balances, and art found wanting." "Weighed and wanting" became the title for both a sermon and a book of sermons on the Ten Commandments in which man is weighed in the balances of God, the Law, and found wanting.[10] Just as the corruption of human nature constituted man's need of regeneration by the Spirit, so also man's condemnation by the Law of God constituted man's need of redemption by the blood, a theme that Moody expressed in terms of substitutionary atonement.

Since Moody's purpose in proclaiming man's ruin by the Fall was to bring his audiences to an awareness of their need of redemption and regeneration, he did not strive for a consistent system, and he discussed problems associated with the doctrine of sin only as they affected his work as an evangelist. The problems Moody did discuss were usually of the nature of excuses that unbelievers might throw at him as objections to his message and appeals. For instance, he addressed himself

8. *New Sermons*, p. 243; but cf. *Glad Tidings*, p. 79.
9. *Glad Tidings*, p. 411.
10. "Weighed in the Balances of the Law," *New Sermons*, pp. 420-28; D. L. Moody, *Weighed and Wanting: Addresses on the Ten Commandments* (Chicago: BICA, 1898).

to the excuse that said, "What a piece of injustice it is in God to condemn us because Adam sinned six thousand years ago; because somebody else sinned we are to be punished." Moody's answer to this objection was not that man is not culpable for the Adam nature or for what the Adam nature does. It was rather to assert that "you are lost because you are spurning the remedy." "If you men and women are lost it is because we have spurned the remedy, not because we are the sons of Adam and have inherited his nature." In other words, God is absolved of the charge of injustice for holding man responsible for the Adam nature and its deeds in that God provided the remedy that is available to all. That settled the problem for Moody.[11]

Moody also referred to those who "murmur because God permitted sin to come into the world." Moody had no answer to the problem of the origin of sin itself, other than to say it was a great mystery. But typical of his proclamation theology, he shifted the focus of attention away from the mystery of the origin of sin to the mystery of redemption—"it was a greater mystery how God came to bear the brunt of it Himself," a formula he had taken from Andrew Bonar of Scotland. Why talk about the origin of sins? "If I see a man tumble into the river and going to drown, it would do no good for me to sit down and bow my head and indulge in deep thought and reasoning how he came to get in there. The great question would be how he was to be got out?"[12]

Another objection to which Moody addressed himself was the claim that man could not believe if he was blinded by Satan or totally depraved, an objection that is not unrelated to another excuse Moody often heard: "I can't believe because I am not elect." Moody's replies tended to be superficial and inconsistent. At times he spoke as though regeneration or some type of common grace preceded faith. At other times he spoke as though one still had the ability resident within to believe apart from grace. Moody either had not thought these things out or could not resolve the theological problem. His more consistent manner of speaking suggests that in spite of ruin by the Fall, man is able to accept the remedy on his own. In fact, that is why it is just of God to punish man for Adam's sin. Moody frequently spoke of man's sin and being lost, and yet within the same context insisted on man's ability to believe, to accept the remedy. Typical, though especially

11. *New Sermons*, pp. 129-33.
12. *Glad Tidings*, pp. 99-100; cf. *New Sermons*, p. 701; *London Discourses*, pp. 51-52.

striking by the proximity of the two ideas, is the following statement: "You are under the power of the devil. You can believe it [the gospel] if you will."[13] The idea that you can if you will was Moody's standard answer to the objections raised by the doctrines of election and total depravity. This is no answer to the problem, though, for it either fails to explain how completely sinful man can have the ability or insight to make a positive decision to believe, or it only appears to answer the question when in reality the question has been pushed one step further back.

But Moody probably would not have been bothered by these inconsistencies or unresolved problems. His understanding of the Gospel as a proclamation would probably have dictated his reply in spite of problems that unbelievers or systematic theologians might raise. The Bible proclaims that I am ruined by the Fall, but it also proclaims that there is a remedy. It offers that remedy to all, and it is being offered to you now. You can accept, you can believe if you will. "What we want to do is each one of us just to take God at His word. He has offered salvation to every soul here; tell Him you will reach out your hand to-night and accept faith in Him."[14]

In spite of Arminian tendencies in Moody's assertions that man could believe if he chose to, Moody's view of man and sin was out of step with the *Zeitgeist* apart from the evangelical circles in which he moved. By the last quarter of the nineteenth century in America, converging streams of thought flowing from the Enlightenment, Romanticism, and positivism tended to bring into disrepute the Calvinistic doctrine of human depravity and the literal interpretation of the Genesis 3 account of the Fall.

The evolutionary philosophy of Herbert Spencer, so very popular in America, and Charles Darwin's *Origin of the Species* (1859) and *Descent of Man* (1871) not only called into question the biblical account of the creation, including that of man, but they also challenged the biblical idea that mankind had fallen. Instead, according to the popularizers of evolutionary theories, humanity had not only evolved upward physically from the brute, but there was also an upward evolution intellectually, morally, and religiously. Man had not fallen; he was rising.

13. *New Sermons*, p. 144. More detailed discussion of these questions are in chaps. 5 and 6, especially p. 135. See *New Sermons*, pp. 242-43, for a simplistic attempt at an *ordo salutis*.
14. Ibid., p. 144.

In most cases, this did away with original sin, and whatever concept of sin may have remained tended to be associated with remnants of man's brute beginnings which were being progressively overcome by the process of natural selection in the evolutionary climb. These conclusions of scientific and social evolutionism were not incompatible with the Romanticism of the earlier part of the century which preached progress and humanity's essential goodness and likeness to God.

Even the general Arminianizing of American theology, especially through the influence of Nathaniel William Taylor (1786-1856), prepared some to adapt to if not adopt the evolutionary viewpoint by locating the essence of sin in the act rather than in nature and by progressively ascribing more and more power to man's abilities. Though he was moving away from what many of the time would have regarded as Evangelicalism, Horace Bushnell was in the stream of Arminian and romantic New England theology. His famous book, *Christian Nurture*, argued that conversions were not necessarily sudden and that it was a disservice to children to try to impress them with their sinfulness in order to bring them to a climactic and sudden conversion. Sin inhered in act and not in nature. Rather, conversion was a lifelong process of bringing out the goodness of human nature. Though Bushnell himself did not adopt the evolutionary view, those who followed in his train, such as Theodore Munger, Henry Ward Beecher, and Lyman Abbott, did become exponents of accommodating the doctrines of creation, man, sin, and salvation to the evolutionary viewpoint. This adjustment practically became a dogma in American theological liberalism in its attempt to rescue the faith for the modern mind.[15]

Though Moody was out of step with the optimistic views of man that were gaining favor, he was not unaware of what was going on around him. Even his dearly loved Henry Drummond had steadily moved in the direction of what is perhaps best called evangelical liberalism after the years of working with Moody in the first British campaign (1873-75). In fact, Drummond authored one of the most famous contemporary attempts to reconcile evolution with Christian doctrine, *The Ascent*

---

15. Horace Bushnell, *Christian Nurture*, introduction by Luther A. Weigle (New Haven: Yale U., 1967); see further, Sydney E. Ahlstrom, *A Religious History of the American People* (New Haven: Yale U., 1972), pp. 420-21, 609-14, 763-83; Carter, *The Spiritual Crisis of the Gilded Age*, pp. 45-61 (chap. 3, "Of Sin and Freedom"); Paul F. Boller, Jr., *American Thought in Transition: The Impact of Evolutionary Naturalism, 1865-1900*, The Rand McNally Series on the History of American Thought and Culture (Chicago: Rand McNally, 1969), pp. 22-69.

of Man. Though Moody was loyal to Drummond as a devoted friend and a genuine Christian, he would have nothing to do with the new theology and was deeply grieved over the direction in which Drummond had moved.[16] In saying that Moody was aware of these trends, it is not being suggested that he had a sophisticated understanding of them. There is no evidence to suggest that he did, and neither training, interests, nor abilities would have inclined him to investigate such questions. But he could not escape the spirit of the times; and as he saw it, that spirit was incompatible with the Bible in general and his understanding of the Gospel in particular. In this, he was undoubtedly right.

Even as early as the middle 1870s, allusions in Moody's sermons suggest this awareness. Christ "didn't come to preach up the greatness and goodness of man—you have enough of that kind of preaching in the churches." Moody then alluded to men of literary skill who preached sermons on science. No, Christ came to show men the way out of their sins, to proclaim liberty to every burdened, captive sinner if he only comes to him.[17] One can only conjecture who might have been in Moody's mind—perhaps Henry Ward Beecher of Brooklyn's Plymouth Congregational Church or Phillips Brooks of Boston's Trinity Episcopal Church, men known both for their pulpit oratory and progressive theology and men who could hardly have been unknown to Moody.

These early sermons even contain references to men of science who go "down into the bowels of the earth, digging away at some carcass, and trying to make it talk against the voice of God."[18] Moody seems also to have been aware of Bushnell, or at least of his influence. His repeated assertions that man does not start from the cradle to heaven, but from the cross, and his emphasis on the suddenness of conversion seem to be most naturally regarded as directed against the viewpoint expressed in *Christian Nurture.*

Some have suggested that Moody mellowed in his evaluation of liberal theology in his latter years, a claim examined in chapter 10. However, at this point it can be asserted that his sermons as published in books and newspapers do not support this claim. With reference to man's state in sin and contemporary views of man and sin, a sermon on "Regeneration" preached by Moody in Northfield on August 18, 1898,

16. Henry Drummond, *The Ascent of Man* (New York: James Pott, 1894).
17. *New Sermons*, p. 200.
18. Ibid., pp. 220, 292, 398-99.

could hardly be a clearer expression of his unchanged views in spite of the currents of the times. He decried the fact that among religiously educated people not having spiritual discernment there was the view that "if a man is brought up in a good community and has good surroundings, that he don't need to be born again, . . . that the natural life will be all right, and that he can be educated into the kingdom of God."

Moody did not "believe one word of it"; there was only one way into the Kingdom of God, and that was to be born of the Spirit. People are not naturally good. "We are a bad lot, the whole of us, by nature. . . . It is astonishing how the devil does blind us and make us think we are so naturally good." "Don't talk to me about people being naturally good and angelic. We are naturally bad, the whole crowd of us." The fact that sin leaped into the world full-blown and that the whole race had been "bad all the way down" constituted the necessity of the new birth. Moody even said that "man lost the image of God," although he gave no explanation of the precise meaning of that moot theological point. But he did make clear what he thought of the social reform movements that had gained momentum in the 1880s and 1890s and which were to come forth as the Social Gospel after the turn of the century. He declared in 1898 that he was sick and tired of hearing of reform. Man did not need to be patched up; he needed to be regenerated.[19]

THE FUTURE HUMAN DESTINY

The corollary of Moody's view of human sin is that after death comes judgment. The corrupt Adam nature cannot stand in the presence of God, and man stands condemned by the Law of God. Hell is the dread alternative to heaven. However, this was not a theme that Moody enjoyed preaching upon, and his failure to preach on hell as frequently or in the same vivid pictures as previous evangelists has led to unwarranted conclusions both by Moody's critics and friends since the early days of his evangelistic campaigns. At the height of the tour of Scotland there came into the possession of the Edinburgh committee a letter from a John Mackay, residing in Chicago, intended to discredit Moody as being unorthodox. Moody and his followers were said to have made

19. "Regeneration, Address delivered by Mr. D. L. Moody, General Conference, Thursday Evening, August 18, 1898," typed manuscript, pp. 1-6, Moodyana.

the Chicago YMCA "a very hot-bed of rationalism." Among other things, Mackay accused Moody of denying eternal punishment.[20]

Moody was exonerated of the charge to the satisfaction of the Scottish churchmen, though Moody still did not emphasize hellfire preaching. This probably explains why George Adam Smith thought that Moody did not preach salvation from hell but from sin, and why Augustus Fry makes the statement that Moody never preached on hell.[21] But a Canadian critic who regarded Moody's message as subversive of the very foundations of modern thought had a much more accurate assessment of Moody's view of eternal punishment. He wrote:

> They do not dwell much, we are told, on the terrors of future punishment; but their audiences know full well what is the *ultima ratio* of every argument and appeal; every "unconverted" person in these assemblies is made thoroughly to understand that he is suspended by only the frailest and most uncertain of cords over the abyss. From this terrible position the only rescue possible is by an act of faith. All natural striving after goodness and truth is of no avail.[22]

"Laon" [a pseudonym], though thoroughly unsympathetic to Moody, had the insight to see that though Moody did not dwell on the terrors of hell, the existence of hell and the futility of the efforts of the unconverted to escape were an integral part of the rationale behind all of Moody's preaching.

Moody would have agreed without equivocation. Christ had come to save from hell, Moody told a London audience in 1875. "If I believed there was no hell, I am sure I would be off to-morrow for America." He would give up going from town to town spending day and night "urging men to escape the damnation of hell."[23] Though Moody did not follow Finney's advice to preach up the terrors of judgment, his sermons contain frequent incidental references to hell, the wrath of God, and future judgment.[24] Even the most casual reader of a cross section of Moody's sermons could hardly miss this.[25]

20. A typed copy of this letter is in Moodyana and also in John V. Farwell, *Early Recollections of Dwight L. Moody* (Chicago: Winona Pub., 1907), pp. 90-94. It was Farwell who exonerated Moody from the Chicago end of the line.
21. Smith, *The Life of Henry Drummond*, p. 98; Fry, "D. L. Moody: The Formative Years, 1856-1873," p. 2.
22. Laon, "Messrs. Moody and Sankey and Revivalism," *Canadian Monthly* 7 (June 1875): 510; cf. the critique of Gamaliel Bradford, *D. L. Moody: A Worker in Souls*, pp. 81-82.
23. *Wondrous Love*, p. 127.
24. Finney, *Lectures on Revivals of Religion*, pp. 329, 343.
25. For a beginning, examine *New Sermons*, pp. 223, 241, 257-58, 374, 405; *Glad Tidings*, pp. 240-45; *London Discourses*, p. 123; *Great Joy*, p. 359; *Bible Characters*, p. 40.

Moody's older son felt that in later life his father seldom referred to future punishment, although he does not suggest he had given up the doctrine. Since there is not a broad cross section of Moody's sermons in print as preached in later life, this assertion is difficult to confirm or refute, but Moody's message of deliverance from future penalty through the work of Christ remained unchanged. As late as 1897 he repudiated the suggestion that he believed all the punishment a person would have was in this world and reaffirmed his belief in future punishment. To emphasize the point he said, "I believe it [future punishment]; I stand on that platform, and expect to die holding the truth, that same truth. I don't care anything about your 'New Theology' or 'New Doctrines.' You can't go back on Christ's say so." At the time he was preaching in Boston's Tremont Temple and expressed the hope that after being in Boston for two months, no one would think that he did not believe in future retribution. He did not want anyone to rise up in judgment and say he had not warned him.[26]

This is the approach to the subject of future punishment that Moody had taken at least since the mid-1870s. Though this was the case and though he frequently referred to it incidentally, Moody never dwelt on the horrors of hell in lurid detail. Sermons devoted exclusively to the subject were preached infrequently and somewhat grudgingly. Through all his years of evangelistic preaching he had one basic sermon on hell built on the text of Luke 16:25, "Son, Remember." Even this sermon did not dwell on the physical torments of hell, but rather asserted that the "worm that dieth not" that made hell so terrible was the memory of bypassed opportunities. The same Christ who told about heaven had told about hell. And Moody felt that as a faithful messenger he had to present all sides of the truth as he found it.[27]

But Moody would have preferred to stay away from the subject. Occasionally his statements introducing the sermon on hell suggest that he preached it just often enough to assure his auditors of his orthodoxy.[28] He was convinced that the preaching of the love of God was more fundamental to the Gospel message than the preaching of the terrors of hell. People had to be warned of future prospects, but fear

26. "Sermon of D. L. Moody, Tremont Temple, Thursday a.m., February 11, 1897," typed manuscript, pp. 2-3, Moodyana.
27. *London Discourses*, pp. 107-8, or *Wondrous Love*, pp. 125-27; *Glad Tidings*, pp. 252-55; *Signs of Our Times*, June 3, 1875, pp. 412-15; *New Sermons*, pp. 334-38.
28. In addition to the above references, cf. *New Sermons*, p. 255.

was not the way to bring them to God. Moody answered those who criticized him for not preaching up the terrors of religion by saying that he did not want to scare people into the Kingdom of God. Scaring people into heaven by holding hell over their heads would only produce slaves, but heaven does not have any slaves, only sons. "Terror never brought a man in yet." Fear may make people fall on their knees so that they appear to be converted, but "they ain't, they're only scared. There's no repentance there, and as soon as the storm is over, and they get on shore, they are the same as ever." "Mark you, my friends, I believe in eternal damnation; I believe in the pit that burns, in the fire that's never quenched, in the worm that never dies, but I believe that the magnet that goes down to the bottom of the pit is the love of Jesus."[29]

R. W. Dale told of asking Moody if he ever used the element of terror in his preaching. Moody replied that he normally preached one sermon each on heaven and hell in the course of a visit to a town, but that a "man's heart ought to be very tender" when speaking of the doom of the impenitent. Moody then expressed shock at the way in which some preachers threatened unbelievers with the wrath to come as though they had a kind of satisfaction in thinking of the sufferings of the lost.[30]

But if Moody did not preach on hell frequently, the theme of death ushering one into a final accounting constantly recurs in his sermons. The theme is not theologically or exegetically developed by Moody, but rather is presented as a reality which no one can escape. For Moody himself and for Christians in general, death offered a joyous prospect, though death itself was not an event that Moody looked forward to.[31] But Moody was convinced that for the unbeliever, death offered only an eternity of damnation. The issue of immediate moment was to be ready for death when it came. Moody's sermons abound with heart-rending tales, many drawn from his Civil War experience, of those who died either prepared or unprepared to meet God. So frequent are these illustrations that no less an admirer of Moody than Wilbur M. Smith suggested to me in a telephone conversation that Moody's preoccupa-

29. Ibid., pp. 257-58; *Great Joy*, p. 359; cf. Daniels, *Moody: His Words, Work, and Workers* (1879 ed.), p. 581.
30. R. W. Dale in *Addresses and Lectures of D. L. Moody*, pp. 32-33.
31. *Thou Fool*, pp. 195-97; "Ninety-First Psalm. Address delivered by Mr. D. L. Moody, Young Women's Conference, Saturday Evening, July 15, 1899," typed manuscript, pp. 13-15, Moodyana.

tion with deathbed stories might indicate an unbalanced emphasis or a morbid personal preoccupation with death.

The frequency of such stories certainly raises this as a legitimate question; however, the nature of the case makes a definitive diagnosis of Moody's mental health with reference to death impossible. Not the least of the problems is, who is to say what is a healthy outlook on death? But it is possible to take a closer look at the sermons for what they might show. One fact becomes immediately apparent. Moody did not dwell on the morbid details of the death scenes he narrated. One does not read the descriptions with a sense of horror or revulsion. But they are heartrending accounts which still have the power to bring tears even when read on the printed page. Moody's skill as a master storyteller is most evident in his recitations of deathbed scenes and accounts of prodigal sons.

It also becomes evident that Moody had had the reality of death impressed upon him early in life and consistently through life, which might as plausibly suggest his conviction that this was a reality most people preferred to ignore, as that he had a personal problem. His autobiographical statements tell a great deal in this connection. His first memory was the death of his father. Moody testified that his father's sudden death made an impression on him he would never forget. Nor was his first touch of the face of a cold corpse an experience he could erase from his mind. He remembered how the village bell had tolled for the dead when he was a lad, and the solemnity imparted when the tolling indicated that a youth had died, rather than someone seventy or eighty years of age. Even the thud of the sexton shoveling the dirt into the grave had sounded like a death knell to his soul. He recalled serving as a pallbearer for a deceased classmate, and said, "I did not get over it for days and days." At such times he had been afraid to go to bed alone, for he was afraid of death.

Childhood impressions of the reality of death were reinforced by scenes of death to which he was exposed during the Civil War in his work with the Christian Commission. He later recalled, "I could hear the groans of dying men, and I helped bear away some of the wounded, and I saw the scene in all its terrible reality." Moody himself had been twice at the point of death with the whole panorama of his life flashing before him in an instant. Moody remembered one summer in Chicago when so many children from his Sunday school died that he became calloused to death. But such was not his normal experience, for he was a very sensitive person who felt keenly the reality, tragedy, sorrow, and finality of death. These early impressions had been frequently and repeatedly reinforced, and with his native abilities as a speaker he was able to communicate the pathos of death with telling effect.[32]

His rationale for speaking often of death is quite clear. He himself had been delivered from the fear of death through his own faith, and he wanted to share this freedom from fear with others.[33] But just as significantly, Moody's references to death were a warning to be prepared. It was not that Moody wanted to scare people into the Kingdom, a tactic that would have been inconsistent with his concept of what it meant to become a Christian. Why then did he speak about death, he once asked himself rhetorically?

> I will tell you why it is. It is because nine out of every ten die unexpectedly; it is because nine out of every ten die wholly unprepared. They may have been warned, death may have come very near, it might have entered their house, . . . yet they're unprepared. . . . I am speaking to some who may be in eternity tomorrow. I come to tell you to be prepared.[34]

There were not many things one could be sure of in life. But one could be sure of death and "after that the judgment. You can be sure of that." "Are you ready?" "We are on a journey toward judgment."[35] His audiences needed to be awakened to the gravity of the decisions they were making. Who could say with certainty that tomorrow was his? For those who died unprepared, hell as the place of judgment was the dread alternative to heaven—the place where one forever remembered the lost opportunties of life—the inevitable destiny of those who, ruined by the Fall, had not accepted the remedy.

32. *Thou Fool*, p. 195; *Glad Tidings*, pp. 69, 213, 253; *Great Redemption*, pp. 309-10; *New Sermons*, pp. 43, 181, 206, 335; *Wondrous Love*, p. 120.
33. Ibid.
34. *New Sermons*, p. 467.
35. Ibid., p. 469; cf. Moody's sermon delivered on the occasion of the death of his close friend, P. P. Bliss, in *Great Joy*, pp. 519-28.

4

REDEEMED BY THE BLOOD

IN MOODY'S UNDERSTANDING of the Gospel, ruin by the Fall meant that the remedy of which mankind stood in need should be adequate to deal with the corruption of human nature and the condemnation incurred by the Law of God. Moody's proclamation was, "We don't start, as some people suppose, from the cradle to heaven. We start from the cross. We have got a fallen nature that is taking us hellward. We must be born of the Spirit, and sheltered by the blood, and then we become pilgrims for heaven."[1] Calvary was the only way of escape. "If the Word of God don't teach that it don't teach anything." The whole Bible was to be understood in the light of Calvary, and in preaching, Moody was accustomed to tracing what he called the scarlet thread through both the Old and New Testaments. Moody often said that the man who talks against the blood throws out the Bible.[2] In short, man was redeemed by the blood, and that was the theme of the Bible.

The Bible itself was the source of this way of speaking of salvation. The practice of animal sacrifices in the Old Testament involved the shedding of blood. Moody, like other Evangelicals, saw these sacrifices as foreshadowing the death of Christ, and he, like they, frequently used New Testament phraseology referring to the blood of Christ. The "blood" functioned as a code word referring to Christ's death and its saving benefits. The New Testament ascribed saving powers to the blood, including justification (Ro 5:9); redemption (Eph 1:7; 1 Pe 1:18-19); remission of sins (Heb 9:22); and cleansing (1 Jn 1:7, 9; Rev 7:14). Moody frequently used this language in his sermons.

1. *Wondrous Love*, p. 54; cf. *New Sermons*, p. 150.
2. *New Sermons*, pp. 338, 347-48; *Wondrous Love*, p. 73; *Great Joy*, p. 242.

The Gospel songs used in his meetings were also full of these allusions; on one occasion Moody referred to Sankey's "solos upon the redeeming blood." For example, in the book *Gospel Hymns No. 2*, compiled by P. P. Bliss and Ira D. Sankey for use in Moody's meetings, there are 132 songs. Of these, twenty-six, or 20 percent of the total, contain explicit references to the blood of Christ or His bleeding. If references to the cross or Calvary were included, the number would be even higher. Some are very general references to the "bleeding Saviour" or "His precious bleeding side." But they usually identify the blood as the purchase price or for its powers of cleansing, saving, redeeming, or justification.[3]

Moody was always reluctant to pin a theological label on himself, so that it becomes particularly significant when he did so. In 1899 in Detroit, Moody declared that if his theology was not 6,000 years old he would pitch it into the Mississippi. "I believe that sin is the same today as then, and that its remedy is the same. I'm an Abelite."[4] Moody's point was that the way of salvation had been by blood sacrifice throughout the whole of human history, and sometimes he would even attach this significance to the provision of animal skins for Adam and Eve as coverings; this first gracious provision of God for fallen mankind involved the shedding of blood. Redemption by the blood was at the very center of Moody's conception of the Gospel and his understanding of the Bible. Without the blood, there was no message to preach.

Yet this does not tell the whole story, for what significance did Moody attach to the blood? What was the significance of Christ's death on the cross? If it is the remedy, how? Why? In theological terminology, what was the nature of the atonement? In his recent thesis, Stan Nussbaum described the early Moody, that is, prior to his contact with Henry Moorhouse, as hyper-Anselmic, although Moody himself said that there was a time when he did not believe in the doctrine of substitution.[5] Supposedly Moody moved away from the Anselmic view as a result of his newly acquired appreciation of God's love as manifested on the cross. Consequently, Findlay, who has the only serious discus-

3. P. P. Bliss and Ira D. Sankey, *Gospel Hymns No. 2* (Cincinnati: John Church, 1876), Numbers 5, 6, 7, 9, 13, 26, 30, 35, 39, 40, 48, 61, 65, 68, 72, 76, 77, 93, 99, 100, 103, 107, 110, 111, 116, 119; *New Sermons*, p. 150.
4. "To Stir up the Churches and Convert Christians," *Detroit Journal*, Apr. 1899. This newspaper clipping in Moodyana is not dated.
5. Nussbaum, "D. L. Moody and the Church," p. 26.

sion of Moody's view of the atonement, considers Moody essentially to have been an exponent of the moral-influence theory of the atonement.[6] This conclusion, however, represents a serious misunderstanding of the theories of the atonement and of Moody's own statements on the subject.

Findlay correctly places the moral-influence theory of the atonement in opposition to the Anselmic theory. He quotes B. B. Warfield to the effect that in this theory the stress is laid on the manifestation of God's love for sinners in the total mission and work of Christ, which, when perceived by sinners, breaks down their opposition to God. Findlay then describes the penal theory of the atonement as expounded by Calvinistic supporters of Anselmic themes. This penal theory is seen as having its primary effect on God the Father in that Christ's death relieves the sinner from the wrath of God and releases him from the demands of the Law, with only a secondary effect on man. The Anselmic viewpoint is said to view God as principally stern, wrathful, and righteous, whereas the Abelardian or moral-influence viewpoint softens the image to one of loving-kindness and tenderness, a God who melts the human heart by the sacrifice of His Son on the cross.

Findlay also mentions the governmental theory of the atonement that had originated with the Dutch jurist, Hugo Grotius, and had been adopted by many of the New England theologians in the eighteenth and nineteenth centuries as well as by some Arminians and the English Congregationalist, R. W. Dale. But Findlay correctly recognizes that Moody's view does not correspond to the governmental theory; consequently, further discussion of that view is unnecessary here.[7]

But otherwise his analysis is in serious error. Findlay sees the essential difference between the penal and moral-influence theories of the atonement to be that the former views God as a stern, wrathful judge and that the latter views God as tender and loving; he then concludes that Moody held the moral-influence theory since Moody was, in fact, convinced of the love of God as revealed by Christ's death on the cross. Is the love of God really the *crux interpretum?*

The types of theory in question can also be designated as objective

6. Findlay, *Dwight L. Moody*, pp. 231-37.
7. Ibid., pp. 232-33, 236. Findlay states that in the nineteenth century, the governmental theory was the standard evangelical expression of the significance of the atonement. While this may have been the case with many written evangelical expressions of theology, I would suggest that this may not have been the case in popular evangelical preaching. This would be a worthy area for research.

(penal) and subjective (moral influence).[8] It was Anselm in the twelfth century who made the first attempt to present a harmonius and consistent theory of the atonement from the objective viewpoint. In his work *Cur Deus Homo* he asked the question, "Why a God-Man?" and then sought to give a rationale explaining why Christ must unite in one person the two natures, deity and humanity. Why could not the purpose of the incarnation have been met just as well by God alone or man alone?

Anselm's answer was that only in this way could an atonement be rendered for *man's* sin which was satisfactory to *God*. His reasoning was that sin consists in the creature withholding from God the honor which is His due. By his disobedience, man has robbed God of that honor which is His due. Since God must preserve the honor of His majesty, either the honor withheld must be satisfied or punishment must follow. By either means the honor would be vindicated. Either satisfaction or punishment must follow every sin. God has not chosen the way of punishment, but, rather, the way of satisfaction. That creates a new problem, for it will not suffice to restore what has been withheld; more ought to be restored than was withheld. Furthermore, even the smallest sin weighs more than all of creation. Consequently, the satis-

8. It should be noted that in the history of Christian thought there have been other views of the atonement. These have been subjected to different schemes of classification and interpretation. Wolfhart Pannenberg identifies seven soteriological motifs in the history of Christology. Gustaf Aulén identified three main types of the idea of the atonement. Aulén's lectures before the University of Uppsala in 1930 (translated into English in *Christus Victor*) argued that there was a third idea of the atonement in addition to the so-called objective (Anselmian) and subjective (Abelardian) theories. This third view he called the classic idea of the atonement. This view also was objective, Aulén said, but it had "a distinct character of its own, quite different from the other two types." "Its central theme is the idea of the Atonement as a Divine conflict and victory; Christ—Christus Victor—fights against and triumphs over the evil powers of the world, the 'tyrants' under which mankind is in bondage and suffering, and in Him God reconciles the world to Himself." He contended that this was the dominant idea of the New Testament and the ruling idea of the atonement in the first 1,000 years of Christian history. In the Middle Ages it lost its supremacy, but was more vigorously and profoundly expressed than ever before in Martin Luther. Protestant Orthodoxy reverted to an Anselmic view, and in the polemics of the Enlightenment, the classic view was again eclipsed. Aulén's work has a certain corrective value, but its adequacy has been challenged historically, theologically, and biblically. In any event, Aulén's treatment does not help clarify Moody's doctrine of the atonement. Cf. Wolfhart Pannenberg, *Jesus— God and Man*, trans. Lewis L. Wilkins and Duane A. Priebe (Philadelphia: Westminster, 1968), pp. 39-47, 274-80; Gustaf Aulén, *Christus Victor: An Historical Study of the Three Main Types of the Idea of the Atonement*, trans. A. G. Hebert (London: SPCK, 1965), especially pp. 1-15, 143-59. For critiques of Aulén's interpretation, see Paul Althaus, *The Theology of Martin Luther*, trans. Robert C. Schultz (Philadelphia: Fortress, 1966), pp. 218-23; G. C. Berkouwer, *The Work of Christ*, trans. Cornelius Lambregtse (Grand Rapids: Eerdmans, 1965), pp. 327-42; Leon Morris, *The Cross in the New Testament* (Grand Rapids: Eerdmans, 1965), pp. 288, 373-74, 381-82; John McIntyre, *St. Anselm and His Critics: A Reinterpretation of the Cur Deus Homo* (Edinburgh: Oliver & Boyd, 1954), pp. 197-200.

faction required is so great that man cannot render it; indeed, whatever good man may do he already is under obligation to give to God, so that it cannot even be considered as satisfaction.

But at the same time, man must render the satisfaction since it is his obligation. The nature of the satisfaction is such that only God can render it. Thus, it is necessary that the God-man render the satisfaction. Only the surrender of his life in death will suffice, since his obedience in fulfilling God's will through life is the obligation of every rational being. In this manner the incarnation and sufferings of the God-man give the necessary satisfaction to the divine honor, a satisfaction that man must render but which is of such a character that only God can perform it. Such is the answer to the question, "Why a God-man?" as given by Anselm.

Two observations are in order before we leave Anselm. Anselm did not neglect the love of God nor the exemplary value of Christ's life and death. It was God's love that was Anselm's starting point. God's mercy is the source of salvation; the atonement was an overflowing of divine grace. God made the necessary satisfaction, thus showing His compassion and love for man. Furthermore, Christ's death as a manifestation of love for man and obedience to God stimulates a responsive love for God and imitation of Christ's obedience.[9]

Protestant theology of the sixteenth and seventeenth centuries is generally classified as Anselmic, though it should be mentioned that there were modifications and changes of emphasis. Calvin and Luther were appreciative of the Anselmic view in that it recognized the magnitude of human sin, provided a rationale for the incarnation and death of the Son inherent within the very being of God, and attributed to Christ's work an objective value with reference to man's standing before God. In fact, the finished work of Christ was the warrant for rejecting the Roman Catholic sacramental system. Through Christ's atonement, the price of man's redemption has been paid once for all so that nothing remains but to appropriate its benefits through faith. Christ's work in atonement provided the objective basis of justification by faith.

9. McIntyre, *St. Anselm and His Critics: A Reinterpretation of the Cur Deus Homo*, pp. 76, 104, 154-86, 203-4; George Huntston Williams, *Anselm: Communion and Atonement* (St. Louis: Concordia, 1960), p. 52; Joseph M. Colleran, trans. and ed., *Why God Became Man and The Virgin Conception and Original Sin by Anselm of Canterbury* (Albany, N. Y.: Magi Books, 1969), pp. 47, 66, 68, 161-62 (using the divisions of *Cur Deus Homo*, see bk. 1, chaps. 1, 4; bk. 2, chaps. 11, 18-20).

But in Reformation theology, especially by Calvin, it was not the honor of God which needed to be satisfied, thus providing the rationale for the atonement; it was the holiness of God. While God is gracious and desires to forgive sin, this grace can only be exercised in consistency with His holiness; justice requires that punishment be rendered proportionate to the sin. Hence, Christ's death has penal significance as satisfying the demands of God's law, the expression of His holiness. God graciously provided the Substitute, the Son, making it possible to forgive sin in a way consistent with His justice. In Reformation theology, emphasis was placed not only on the theme of deliverance from the guilt of sin, but also on deliverance from all that is evil. In addition, while satisfaction of divine justice constituted the fundamental and objective significance of the atonement, being at the same time the highest possible manifestation of God's holiness and love, the subjective moral influence of the atonement was not negated.

Abelard (1079-1142) developed the moral-influence theory of the atonement in opposition to the theory that Anselm had developed. Abelard argued that God could not take pleasure in the death of His Son as the means of His being reconciled to the world. Was it proper that God should accept the blood of the innocent as a ransom? How can a greater sin be the basis of forgiving a lesser sin? Thus Abelard rejected Anselm's view that God is satisfied or reconciled by the death of Christ. Abelard did labor under the necessity of trying to maintain his orthodoxy, and so at times he said that there was a satisfaction made by Christ that is imputed to man. But in spite of these claims to orthodoxy, the center of Abelard's doctrine of the atonement was the exemplary value toward man of Christ's work. Christ's death was efficacious by its subjective influence on the mind of the sinner. He did not try to bring his assertions of his orthodoxy into harmony with an otherwise manward understanding of the doctrine. Such an attempt would have failed, and perhaps he realized it. Some have questioned how serious he was in his claims to orthodoxy on this point.[10]

Instead Abelard found the positive value of the atonement to be that in Christ God's love was revealed. Christ assumed human nature and as Teacher and Example remained faithful unto death. God's love thus

---

10. J. G. Sikes, *Peter Abailard* (Cambridge: U. Press, 1932), pp. 204-11; A. Victor Murray, *Abelard and St. Bernard: A Study in Twelfth Century "Modernism"* (Manchester: Manchester U., 1967), pp. 117-39.

exemplified awakens faith and love in the human heart which is then the ground of the gracious forgiveness of sins. The significance of Christ's death is that it is an example or moral influence designed to awaken a responsive love in the human heart which is the ground of forgiveness. Rather than accomplishing anything objective with reference to God, Christ's life and death are aimed at a subjective response within the human heart, which in turn secures God's favor. God's favor is thus only mediately the effect of Christ's death.

Abelard's formulation is the classic response to the Anselmic type of theory, though later expressions of the moral-influence view might vary according to the emphasis placed on Jesus' teaching, example, life of faith, or manifestation of God's love in His total ministry and epitomized in His death. But the fundamental rationale is the same in them all. Christ's death has no immediate and objective significance with reference to satisfying the offended honor or the broken law of a holy God. Rather, His life and death have an exemplary value, a moral influence, intended to awaken within man a responsive love and faith that become the immediate ground of God's gracious forgiveness. Through the centuries since Abelard this view has not lacked defenders. Following the Reformation the Socinians were vocal and persuasive advocates of this view, as were many later rationalists. In Moody's nineteenth-century America, Unitarians and Universalists attached this significance to Christ's death, as did Horace Bushnell, who is often called the "Father of American Liberalism."[11]

At the beginning of this discussion of the distinction between moral influence and Anselmic or penal theories of the atonement, I suggested that Findlay's identification of Moody as preaching a moral-influence theory was in part due to a failure to see the essential difference between the two views. He understood the love of God to be the *crux interpretum,* suggesting that in the former view God was loving and in the

11. In addition to works already cited, the above discussion of these two views of the atonement will be found to be in essential agreement with the following discussions of the atonement, each of which is written by an author from a somewhat different theological tradition: Benjamin Breckinridge Warfield, *Studies in Theology* (New York: Oxford U., 1932), pp. 261-80 (reprint of his article on "Atonement" in *The New Schaff-Herzog Encyclopedia of Religious Knowledge*); W. Adams Brown, "Expiation and Atonement (Christian)," *Encyclopaedia of Religion and Ethics,* ed. James Hastings (New York: Scribner's Sons, 1914-27), 5:641-50; Reinhold Seeberg, *Text-Book of the History of Doctrines,* trans. Charles E. Hay (Grand Rapids: Baker, 1966), 2:66-73, 266-72, 400-401; Vernon C. Grounds, "Atonement," *Baker's Dictionary of Theology,* ed. Everett F. Harrison (Grand Rapids: Baker, 1960), pp. 71-78; Pannenberg, *Jesus—God and Man,* pp. 42, 277-80.

later He was only a stern and wrathful judge. In view of Moody's strong and consistent emphasis on God's love and the drawing power of God's love, Findlay had no choice but to conclude that Moody was preaching a moral-influence theory of the atonement.

However, it should now be evident that: (1) the moral-influence theory has no room for an immediate satisfactory or penal significance of the atonement toward God, themes which, it will be shown, Moody consistently and frequently emphasized; (2) Anselmic-type views can, in fact, place much emphasis on the love of God as supremely and perfectly revealed in Christ's death on the cross as a penal, substitutionary sacrifice; and (3) the Anselmic or penal views do not necessarily rule out a secondary moral influence that the revelation of God's love manifested in Christ's life and death might have in drawing sinners to God.

Findlay's mistaken identification of Moody as preaching a moral-influence view of the atonement rather than a penal view is based on a misapprehension of the essential nature of the two views. This prompted him practically to ignore the motifs that are inconsistent with a moral influence view and are, rather, indications of an understanding that is at least implicitly penal.

Inasmuch as the death of Christ on the cross stood at the heart of Moody's understanding of the Gospel, his statements in this connection were so numerous that the choice of a starting point becomes quite arbitrary. It would not seem too far amiss, though, to begin with a survey of Moody's two sermons on the blood of Christ. In reality the two sermons are one sermon, preached in two parts on successive evenings. The first sermon traced the line of blood through the Old Testament, and the second did the same thing through the New Testament. The evidence indicates that Moody preached them frequently, and they are included in several of the volumes with titles referring to either the blood or the scarlet thread. The version contained in *New Sermons, Addresses and Prayers* serves as the text for this survey[12]

Moody began that sermon by quoting the prohibition given to Adam (Gen 2:17) that he should not eat of the tree of the knowledge of good and evil. This is significant in that it provided for Moody the basis for his discussion of the blood in the Old Testament. "There can not be a

---

12. *New Sermons*, pp. 146-64. In the following survey, page numbers will be placed in the text in parentheses when helpful.

law without a penalty," so that the penalty of death resulted from Adam's disobedience (p. 146). But the very first thing that God did was to deal with Adam in grace, for God made Adam and Eve coats of skin before driving them out of paradise. While God dealt in government (punishment of the broken law), he also dealt in grace (the coverings of skin). "Adam broke the divine law, and so he had to suffer the penalty; but He gave him the grace to be redeemed by." Moody attached significance not just to the gracious provision of the skins for covering, but also to the fact that animals had to be killed to obtain the skins. This became a paradigm for Moody, for he said, "Here we find the first glimpse of the doctrine of substitution—the substitution of the just for the unjust—the great doctrine of the atonement and substitution foreshadowed in Genesis" (p. 147).

Moody did not have far to go to find this principle illustrated again, this time in the sacrifices which Cain and Abel brought to God (Gen 4). Cain's sacrifice was unacceptable to God in that it was a bloodless sacrifice. And Moody added as an aside that men and women were to be found in the churches of that day with their own good deeds and righteousness, "ignoring the blood completely," coming in their own way as Cain had. But the one with the blood, Abel, had the sacrifice acceptable to God. By the same token Noah came forth from the ark (Gen 8) and "put blood between him and his sins."

Likewise the last-minute sacrificial substitute for Abraham's son Isaac on Mount Moriah exhibited the principle. Abraham's faith response to God's command so pleased God that He "lifted the curtain of time to let him look down into the future and see the Son of God offered bearing the sins of the world." However, on that occasion "there was no voice heard [Abraham, spare thine only son] on Calvary to save the Son of Man" (pp. 148-50). From the book of Genesis, Moody's conclusion was that all the patriarchs went to heaven through the blood atonement. At that point Moody jumped to chapter 12 of Exodus (institution of the Passover), identifying it as the "most important chapter in the Word of God," and interpreting it as another prefiguring of Calvary. To be safe within the house, the blood of the lamb had to be on the front door. Natural birth in the house was not enough.

At this point in the sermon Moody began to elaborate on the significance of the blood as he understood it. He referred to people who say "preach anything but the death, preach the life of Christ. You may preach that and you'll never save a soul. It is not Christ's sympathy— His life—we preach, it is His death." Some might think this is absurd, just as the Egyptians who saw the blood upon the lintels and doorposts. Nevertheless, "this blood was to be a substitute for death. . . . It was death that kept death out of the dwelling. . . . If you have not a substitute you will die. Death has passed upon all of us. Why? Because of our sin. If we have not a substitute, we have no hope" (p. 161). Salvation does not depend on man's deeds, righteousness, or life. "It depends upon whether or not we are sheltered behind the blood." Moody then confessed, "There was a time when I didn't believe in the substitution and in the blood, and my prayers went no higher than my head; but when I came to God by Jesus Christ—by way of the blood—it was different" (p. 152).

Moody followed this with references to the Aaronic priesthood and its functions of sacrifice as described in Exodus and Leviticus, emphasizing that atonement involving substitution is the only thing that will bring God and sinner together. He took this as an occasion to explain why God demanded atonement by blood to those who objected that this was either a mysterious thing or who detested the idea of a God who would demand blood; he was apparently referring to Unitarians and Universalists who attacked his views at this very point. Moody's reply to the demand "why?" was:

> God is not an unjust God. He don't [sic] demand it without giving us a reason. . . . "The life of the flesh is in the blood." Take the blood out of me and I am a dead man. Life has been forfeited, the law has been broken, and the penalty must come upon us, and this blood He gives us is life. . . . You and I have lost life by the fall, and what we want is to get back that life we lost, and we have it offered to us by the atonement of Christ. . . . Let us thank God we have a refuge, a substitute for the sin we are groaning under (pp. 153-54).

Finally, Moody referred to Isaiah 53, the chapter that he had called his creed in London in 1875. This chapter he understood to be prophetic of the sufferings of Christ, a prophecy made 700 years before it took place "that He would die and be a substitute for you and me, that we might live." This doctrine was his only hope of eternal life. "Take the doctrine of substitution out of my Bible, and I would not take

it home with me tonight" (p. 154). So ended the first installment of
Moody's sermon on the blood.

The next night he preached on the blood in the New Testament. His
closing remarks the night before had included the comment that it was
a scarlet thread that bound the two Testaments together. As he began
this sermon he answered the challenge, "Where did Jesus ever teach
the perilous and barbarous doctrine that men were to be redeemed by
the shedding of His blood?" Having quoted the words of institution of
the Lord's Supper (Mt 26:28), Moody insisted:

> If Christ did not teach it, and also the Apostles—if Christ did not
> preach it, then I have read my Bible, all these years, wrong. I haven't
> got the key to the Scriptures; it is a sealed book to me, and if I don't
> preach it—if I give it up, I've nothing left to preach. . . . I tell you the
> moment a man breaks away from this doctrine of the blood, religion
> becomes a sham, because the whole teaching of this book is of one
> story, and this is that Christ came into the world and died for our sins
> (pp. 156-57).

Moody then alluded to several New Testament passages containing
references to the blood and again gave the reason why, in his view,
blood needed to be shed for man's salvation. "The law had been broken
and the penalty of death had come upon us, and it required life to
redeem us. . . . Christ has bought me by His blood. I am no longer my
own. I am His. He has ransomed me" (p. 158).

In this second installment of the sermon on the blood, Moody spent
as much time in the book of Hebrews as any other New Testament
portion, emphasizing there the high-priesthood of Christ whereby with
one sacrifice He had put away the sin of the world. "It was love that
prompted God to send His Son to save us and shed His blood." Without the blood there is no hope (pp. 159-60). For this reason, in the
closing portion of the sermon Moody again warned against those who
leave out the blood, even going so far as to exhort his auditors to flee
from the ministry of a man who omits the blood as one would flee from
Sodom (p. 161).

Although he does not debate the theoretical aspects of the atonement
as an Anselm or an Abelard, with his rambling style and his biblical
allusions and terminology, Moody revealed his basic understanding of

what it meant to be redeemed by the blood. Concepts expressing this understanding can be found in the sermon on the blood and other evidences from the 1870s and 1880s.

Just as Moody himself began the first of the two installments with reference to the Fall of man, it is appropriate to point out that the condition of mankind which demands redemption is man's ruin by the Fall, as chapter 3 has adequately indicated. The law of God has been broken, and consequently man is under the penalty of the law, that is, death, understood as spiritual as well as physical death. This had been predicted as the punishment for sin, and it had happened. The Mosaic Law had not been given as a way of salvation as such, but further to show man his guilt and his failure.[13] It is because Christ kept the law, never breaking it, that he is qualified to die for the sins of man. It is God's grace that provided the Substitute to bear the penalty. "Christ died for us, that's the end of the law."[14]

The motif of substitution is relevant to the penalty of condemnation to which man is subject for having broken the law of God. As used by Moody, it is essentially a penal concept, though other themes are intermingled. Often man's sin would be described as a debt that man could not pay, a debt to God which He offers to pay. The only hope for man is Christ who settled the claim for all time. "That is the doctrine of the Bible, the glorious doctrine of substitution. Christ paid the penalty, Christ died in our stead."[15] Though He had never transgressed the law, the sins of the world were put upon Him as the Substitute. It was this that produced reconciliation between God and man, and to take Him as Saviour and Redeemer is to take Him as Substitute.[16] By His death, sins are taken away, because, "Christ was judged for me. He was condemned for me—and by His death on the tree, ransomed me." Moody often illustrated this by reference to the practice of frontiersmen when a prairie fire was sweeping toward them. They would set a back fire, and then get inside the burned spot. Thus when the prairie fire reached them they were secure and safe. "There is one spot on earth that the Lamb of God has cleared for mankind, and that is Calvary." There "Christ tasted death for every man, and all we have

13. *New Sermons*, p. 107; *Glad Tidings*, pp. 410-16.
14. *Glad Tidings*, pp. 416-17.
15. Ibid., pp. 80-82; *New Sermons*, p. 210.
16. *New Sermons*, pp. 181, 183, 188.

to do is take this truth." It was there that the fury of the wrath of God had swept over.[17]

Moody also frequently spoke of the substitutionary value of Christ's death as the price of redemption that "bought us back from the sentence of justice."[18] At other times he spoke of Calvary as the place where the sins of the lost world were placed on the One who had never transgressed the law.[19] But however stated, the fundamental concept that Moody had in mind in substitution was that the one who came to Christ would never come into judgment because Christ had been judged for him. "There is no sense in the sacred history of the atonement unless our sins have been transferred to another and put away." "If he didn't [sic] settle the claims of sin, what did He come into judgment for? What does the Cross mean if it was not for judgment?" Consistent with this are Moody's uses of the word "satisfaction" to express the fact that as the result of Christ's death God is not angry with mankind; He is reconciled because He is satisfied.[20] Thus it is the atonement that brings God and man together.

As described to this point, the key words descriptive of Moody's doctrine of the atonement have been penalty, substitution, and satisfaction. To this must now be added "love," just as he had closed his two-part sermon on the blood by citing the love which prompted God to send His Son and shed His blood. Though it was God's holiness and justice which required that a broken law be punished, it is love alone, "sheer love which gave Christ for us." Indeed, "if you want to know how much God loves you, you must go to Calvary to find out." It followed that to preach the blood was to preach God's goodness; Calvary could not even be understood apart from grace.[21] Justice and mercy meet on Calvary. "I want to say, My God is full of mercy! But don't be so blind as to believe that God is not just, and that he has not got a government. . . . We have sinned, and death must come, or justice must take its course. Glory to God . . . because He sent His Son."[22] It is not merely

17. Ibid., pp. 207-8; cf. *Wondrous Love*, p. 199; *London Discourses*, pp. 67-68; *Glad Tidings*, p. 71.

18. *New Sermons*, p. 264; cf. *Wondrous Love*, p. 219; "Moody's Ministrations," *Daily Inter-Ocean* (Chicago), Nov. 9, 1876.

19. "Services of the Fifth Sunday," *Boston Journal*, c. Feb. 1877, newspaper clipping, Moodyana.

20. *Glad Tidings*, pp. 70, 362, 371; cf. *Wondrous Love*, pp. 45, 50-52, 57-58, 191; *Great Redemption*, pp. 311-12; *New Sermons*, p. 121; *London Discourses*, pp. 143-45; "Convention of Ministers of the Gospel," *Daily Express* (Dublin), Nov. 25, 1874.

21. *New Sermons*, pp. 167, 173, 348, 255; cf. pp. 168-69, 174.

22. *Wondrous Love*, pp. 58-59.

the love of the Son that is manifest in the incarnation. Moody appealed to John 3:16 and argued that it was the Father's love for fallen humanity that sent the Son to be punished in its place. The magnitude of that love for mankind can be appreciated only when one remembers that it was His own Son the Father sent, and what surpasses the love of a father for his son? Moody confessed that in the first years following his conversion he had more love for Christ than for God the Father, because he looked upon Christ as the Mediator between himself and the "stern Judge" whose wrath had to be appeased. But, said Moody, "After I became a father and woke up to the realization of what it cost God to have His Son die, I began to see that God was to be loved just as much as His Son was." It took more love for the Father to give His Son to die than it would to die Himself.

What then happened to the anger of God in Moody's understanding? He subsumed it under God's love. "It is because God loves the sinner that He gets angry with him" for taking a wrong course. God's anger "is one of the very strongest evidences and expressions of God's love." It would not be love to overlook the judicial or penal consequences of man's sin. But God is not merely a stern judge. Justice itself is an evidence of love. Even more than that, it was God's unchangeable, everlasting, and unfailing love that delivered humanity from the penal sentence of justice. Consequently, Moody regarded it as a terrible thing to despise God's provision of salvation in the blood of Christ, whether by not accepting the free gift of the Gospel or by preaching against the blood in the pulpit. It is significant that Moody, the advocate of Christian love and interdenominational cooperation, nevertheless advised that no cooperation was possible with "Cainites." To despise the blood was to despise God's love.[23]

Moody also testified that he came to a new appreciation of God's love when he came under the influence of Henry Moorhouse. Moody frequently told the story of how Moorhouse had opened his eyes to the truth that while God hates sin, He loves the sinner. Using the text of John 3:16 in Moody's church in Chicago in 1868, Moorhouse had preached night after night from Genesis to Revelation that God loved the sinner. Moody's understanding of the Bible and God was transformed through this and subsequent contacts with Moorhouse.[24] The

23. *Glad Tidings*, pp. 242-51. This sermon on "Love" is a good example of Moody's understanding of that attribute of God.

24. Moody's own account of this can be found in *New Sermons*, pp. 176-78; cf. pp. 45-46.

March 19, 1868, issue of *The Advance* (Chicago) reported that Moorhouse had left the city on March 14. As early as April 30, 1868, the following report of Moody speaking in the Chicago Noon Prayer Meeting (YMCA) is found in *The Advance:*

> Said Mr. Moody, "I used to think that Christ loved me more than God, because he gave his life for me; but since God gave me a child I don't think so. . . . To save her life I would willingly lay down my own. And yet, God so loved the world that he gave his only begotten son that whosoever believeth in him shall not perish, but have everlasting life."[25]

The contact with Moorhouse reinforced a conviction that had apparently been developing in Moody's mind since the birth of his first child in 1863. It was the love of God which sent the Son to Calvary to die as man's Substitute, thus meeting the penal demands of the law. This was the supreme manifestation of God's love, and this love manifested in redemption by the blood was the pervasive theme of Moody's message.

It should be evident from the above discussion that Moody's view of the atonement had more affinities with the penal theory of the atonement than with the moral-influence theory. The themes of broken law, consequent punishment, divine wrath, debt, substitution, and satisfaction imply this understanding. Though Moody's emphasis on the love of God might superficially suggest that he held to a moral-influence theory, closer examination indicates that his profound appreciation of the love of God revealed on the cross presupposes an essentially penal theory. This conclusion should not be taken to imply that Moody had worked out the theory in the fashion of a systematic theologian. William Moody reported that his father had told him:

> In the atonement you never lose sight of the fact of the oneness of the Father and the suffering Christ. The mystery of the atonement is the mystery of the Trinity, you cannot understand the sacrifice of Christ and its relation to God until you understand the Trinity itself.[26]

How accurate William's memory was in recalling the incident is a matter of conjecture; but assuming that the recollection was substantially

---

25. "Notes of the Chicago Noon Prayer Meeting," *The Advance* (Chicago), Apr. 30, 1868.
26. W. R. Moody, *Moody* (1930), pp. 440-41.

correct, it does not suggest so much that Moody was indifferent to theories of the atonement as it does that Moody himself was not a theorizer and that he felt that ultimately the atonement was a mystery.[27]

It should be added that Moody did use other biblical motifs to describe Christ's work on the cross. Most notable of these are deliverance and cleansing. The atonement was preached as deliverance from the slavery of sin and Satan, and the blood was said to cleanse from sin.[28] These and similar themes do not hold the place of prominence that the penal ideas do, nor are they inconsistent with Moody's penal understanding of the atonement. Furthermore, such motifs drawn from his understanding of the biblical materials generally describe more the effects of Christ's work on the cross than the nature of that work.

A good test of the conclusion that Moody's understanding of the atonement was essentially penal is to see what his contemporaries said of him, especially those who might have been inclined to be his critics. It is noteworthy that Calvinists, who have generally accepted the penal theory, did not criticize Moody on his preaching of the cross. Even John Mackay, the Calvinist who in February, 1874, wrote to the ministers in Scotland a caustic and accusatory letter against Moody, did not cite Moody for deficient views of the nature of Christ's work.[29] Other avowed Calvinists, who expressed opposition to Moody's preaching on other ponts, found no fault here; two examples may be cited: A. Williams, Vicar of Kingston, and J. K. Popham, minister of the Particular Baptist Chapel in Liverpool.[30]

By the same token, C. H. Spurgeon, the Calvinistic Baptist preacher of London, while not uncritical of Moody's views of election, nevertheless supported Moody's cause and preached a sermon entitled "Messrs. Moody and Sankey Defended: or, A Vindication of the Doctrine of Justification by Faith." The immediate occasion of the sermon was to defend Moody against those who criticized him for preaching justification by faith. In sum, his defense was that Moody's doctrine of justification was the Gospel as understood by "the general consent of Protestant

27. Cf. *New Sermons*, p. 596, where Moody in essence says to never mind the philosophy of the atonement, just accept the pardon.
28. Ibid., pp. 68, 150, 162-63, 170, 219-26, 302, 338.
29. See pp. 95-96.
30. A. Williams, *Weak Points in Mr. Moody's Teaching* (London: William MacIntosh, 1875); J. K. Popham, *Moody and Sankey's Errors versus The Scriptures of Truth* (Liverpool: J. K. Popham, 1875).

Christendom," a doctrine that was based on the finished work of Christ
in His substitutionary atonement.[31]

Consistent with the fact that Calvinists did not criticize Moody's
preaching of the atonement is the fact that Unitarians and Universalists
did criticize him most severely at this very point. W. H. Ryder, pastor
of St. Paul's Universalist Church in Chicago, censured him for preaching a blood atonement and neglecting the needed emphasis on morality.
"The Bible puts an emphasis upon the state of the heart, and not upon
the blood of Christ," he wrote. Ryder continued, "Christ died to save
sinners—to reconcile man to God; not God to man."[32] Similarly, H. H.
Barber in the March, 1877, *Unitarian Review*, within a Unitarian exposition of the moral-influence theory, wrote:

> We judge their theology to be extremely narrow and unintelligent,
> their use of Scripture crudely literalistic, often fantastic and coarsely
> familiar, and their conception of Christianity commercial and mechan-
> ical [apparently a reference to their Anselmic tendencies] to the last
> degree. High spiritual views of religion, or any apprehension of the
> worthiest aspirations and most generous sentiments of the human soul,
> seem to be entirely foreign to their preaching, and the one end towards
> which all their persuasions seek to move men is that of future safety
> from perdition, to be secured by implicit faith in the merits of Christ's
> sacrifice literally made over to the believer. The coarse materialistic
> interpretations of the selfish sacrificial scheme which these men put in
> the place of Christ's gospel of grace and truth are often extremely
> offensive.

Barber concluded that Moody's view of the atonement was pagan rather
than Christian. Barber arrived at this conclusion on the basis of reports
that had been received from Great Britain, admittedly secondhand.
Perhaps he had read a similar critique given by the English Unitarian
minister, John Cuckson.[33] The pastor of All Saints Unitarian Church

---

31. C. H. Spurgeon, "Messrs. Moody and Sankey Defended: or, A Vindication of the Doctrine of Justification by Faith," *The Metropolitan Tabernacle Pulpit: Sermons Preached and
Revised by C. H. Spurgeon During the Year, 1875* (Pasadena, Tex.: Pilgrim, 1971, reprint),
21:337-38, 345.

32. W. H. Ryder, *An Open Letter from W. H. Ryder, D.D., to D. L. Moody, Esq., The
Evangelist* (Boston: Universalist, 1877), pp. 4-6.

33. H. H. Barber, "The American Revivalists in England," *Unitarian Review* 4 (Aug.
1875); 186-87, 190-91; John Cuckson, *Religious Excitement, A Sermon on the Moody &
Sankey Revival, Preached in the Unitarian Church, Newhall Hill* (Birmingham: A. J. Buncher, 1875), pp. 4, 6, 8.

of Colorado Springs, responding to Moody's preaching in that city in the 1890s, probably 1899, likewise expressed typical Unitarian objections to Moody's emphasis on blood, substitution, and debt in exposition of the significance of Christ's death.[34]

Fish's observations are significant for another reason, that is, they indicate that Moody's preaching of the atonement had not changed since the middle and late 1870s. Other evidence clearly confirms this. On November 2, 1892, Moody preached to 6,000 people in Dublin, Ireland, a sermon entitled "The Blood-Stained Way." This sermon was as clear an exposition of the penal view of the atonement as Moody had given at any earlier time. The themes are familiar by now: Cainites versus Abelites; Christ's death saves, not His life; God can only be approached through the blood; blood is necessary because it meets the demand of death; no sin can be forgiven without being punished; the blood is the scarlet thread that holds the Bible together from Genesis through Revelation; the doctrine of substitution satisfies the justice of God; and the shedding of Christ's blood is *the* evidence of God's mercy.[35] Similar statements are available in Moody's sermons preached in Boston's Tremont Temple on February 11 and 24, 1897. In the former case, speaking of the atonement, he affirmed that there was no Law without penalty and that the broken Law must be satisfied. In the latter case he defined the Gospel as Christ dying in the sinner's place, entering into judgment and dying for the sinner.[36] The same emphasis is to be found in a sermon on the atonement preached in Pueblo, Colorado, in 1898. In addition to the usual emphasis of the innocent suffering for the guilty, Moody repudiated those who said that Christ was a martyr who died for his principles.[37] The last formal address delivered by Moody in the Northfield Auditorium, on August 12, 1899, summed up why he had nothing to fear in time or eternity—it was his "standing in Christ." "For a man whose life is hid with Christ in God, judgment

34. William H. Fish, Jr., *Mr. Moody's Theories and the Gospel of Christ* (Colorado Springs: n.p., c. 1899), pp. 1-7. An interesting sidelight to Moody's relations with Unitarians is his account of returning to the Northfield Unitarian Church after his conversion to the evangelical faith, and there preaching on the atonement. Cf. John Hall and George H. Stuart, *The American Evangelists, D. L. Moody and Ira D. Sankey, In Great Britain and Ireland* (New York: Dodd & Mead, 1875), pp. 419-21, cited as *The American Evangelists*.
35. D. L. Moody, *A Friendly Message to Irishmen From America*, reprinted from the *Irish Daily Independent*, Nov. 3, 1892, pp. 1-14.
36. D. L. Moody, "Sermon of D. L. Moody, Tremont Temple, Thursday A.M., Feb. 11, 1897," typed manuscript, pp. 1-2, Moodyana; *Thou Fool*, p. 197.
37. Newspaper clipping, "It Is Between God and Man," only identified as Pueblo, Colo., 1898, Moodyana.

is already passed; he will not come into judgment. Christ was judged for me, and judgment is behind me."[38]

If "Abelites" affirmed the necessity of a substitutionary blood atonement, "Cainites" were those who did not accept the doctrine.[39] This dichotomy in Moody's thinking between Abelites and Cainites can be traced as far back as his preaching in Edinburgh in late 1873 and through his sermons to 1899.[40] He also seems to have identified the Cainites with what would now be called theological liberalism and with what he often referred to as "preachers of moral essays." Findlay correctly insists that Moody was not a "thoroughgoing advocate of 'liberal' theology." But his conclusion that Moody espoused the moral-influence theory of the atonement along with those who were laying the foundations of liberal theology in the United States (such as Bushnell) has no basis in fact, and betrays a misunderstanding of the two theories in question and a failure to examine and account for all the evidence to the contrary that is readily available in Moody's sermons.[41]

38. *Moody's Latest Sermons*, p. 25.
39. See pp. 102-3.
40. Hall and Stuart, *The American Evangelists*, pp. 416-17; *Wondrous Love*, pp. 47-51, 71; *New Haven Daily Palladium*, Apr. 18, 1878; "To Stir up the Churches and Convert Christians," *Detroit Journal*, Apr. 1899 (this clipping is in Moodyana, but the day of the month is not given).
41. Findlay, *Dwight L. Moody*, pp. 231-36.

5

REGENERATED BY THE SPIRIT

CHRIST by His substitutionary death satisfied the penalty of the broken Law and bore the wrath of God in man's place, but the effect of the Fall on human nature must be cared for differently, according to Moody's preaching. By nature, people are sinners, corrupt and without natural goodness.[1] This nature can never come into God's sight, which means that the unregenerated person cannot enter heaven. Such people would be utterly miserable in heaven, and their presence would cause another war in heaven. There must be a new birth before one can come into the presence of God. Those bound for hell not only must be "sheltered by the blood," they also must be "born of the Spirit."[2] In three different places in Moody's handwritten notes on the "New Birth" this formula is found: atonement, something done for us; regeneration, Holy Spirit's work in us.[3] The atonement as something for man pertains to the objective, legal standing before God; regeneration as the Holy Spirit working in man pertains to a subjective change in the nature of man before he can come into heaven.

Regeneration held a place of at least equal emphasis with the atonement in Moody's preaching, though not always being designated by that name. Synonymous designations were conversion, new birth, born again, born of the Spirit, and born from above. It is the power of the Spirit that not only convicts people, but also in the regenerative event gives them a new nature by the new birth. Of necessity this is the case since fallen mankind is not only corrupt but dead. Life must come from

1. *New Sermons,* pp. 128, 627; see pp. 89-91.
2. Ibid., pp. 128, 168; *Wondrous Love,* p. 54.
3. "New Birth" sermon envelope and notes, Moodyana. Normally these notes are so sketchy as to be of little value.

God.[4] This theme kept creeping into sermons that did not even immediately pertain to regeneration.

According to records kept by Moody and a personal secretary, he preached the "New Birth" sermon 184 times between October 23, 1881, and November 2, 1899. Though the record does not go back beyond 1881, the sermon in one form or another is in nearly every significant book of sermons before that date; and there is record of its having been preached on a Friday evening in late 1873 in the Free Assembly Hall, Edinburgh.[5] It is also one of the most frequently occurring sermons as one looks through the file of newspaper clippings in the Moodyana Collection at Moody Bible Institute. That Moody never conducted an evangelistic mission without preaching on the new birth, or incorporating the substance of the sermon into other sermons, would seem to be a justified conjecture on the basis of the available evidence.[6]

Moody often began the "New Birth" sermon with a listing of what the new birth was not, a listing which he felt represented the common misunderstandings. The list would vary from time to time, but the list he gave in Chicago in 1876-1877 is representative. It included going to church, baptism, confirmation, the other ordinances, prayers, reading the Bible, and "trying to do the best I can."[7] Moody regarded these as mere forms and futile human efforts. One should not let such false assurances divert him from the most important question in life, "Have I been born of the Spirit?" Repudiating such human efforts, Moody strongly emphasized the divine monergism in salvation. God was alone in creation. Christ went to Calvary alone. "And when we get to the third chapter of John we find that the work of regeneration is the work of God alone. The Ethiopian can not change his spots [sic; probably a reporter's error, as other versions quote the biblical allusion correctly]; we are born in sin, and the change of heart must come from God." Dead souls can be brought to life only by the Spirit. "God alone is the

---

4. Findlay, Dwight L. Moody, p. 237 has a good brief discussion of the Spirit's work in conversion.

5. "The Work of Grace in Edinburgh," The Christian Jan. 1, 1874, p. 10; "New Birth" sermon envelope, Moodyana.

6. Cf. the comments of Wilbur M. Smith in his The Best of D. L. Moody (Chicago: Moody, 1971), p. 89.

7. New Sermons, pp. 121-22; other typical versions of the sermon are to be found in the following volumes of Moody sermons (the list is not complete): Glad Tidings, pp. 86-108; London Discourses, pp. 42-50; Wondrous Love, pp. 29-44; To All People, pp. 416-28; Holding the Fort, pp. 81-97; The Way to God and How to Find It (Chicago: Revell, 1884), pp. 22-40.

author of life. If you have the new birth, it must be God's work."[8] As noted in chapter 2, this emphasis is not in the tradition of the preaching of Charles Finney. Even if it is granted that recent interpreters of Finney, such as William McLoughlin, may not have truly represented Finney, it is difficult to imagine Moody saying with Finney, "Conversion is not itself a miracle." Indeed, Moody emphasized to a Boston audience, "Every conversion, I believe, is supernatural."[9]

The result of the new birth is a "new heart," a "second nature" that exists alongside the old Adam nature.[10] Beyond that point Moody was unable to explain the new birth. He said that he could not explain how it was done; he even claimed to have read a great many books and sermons trying to explain the philosophy of it, but in his judgment they all failed. He personally was content to let the matter remain in the realm of mystery, appealing to his personal experience as testimony of the reality of regeneration. As Christ had reasoned with Nicodemus, one is convinced of the reality of the mysterious wind by its effects. To Moody this seemed eminently reasonable, though he suspected that the unregenerate mind would not be satisfied with that explanation. All Moody could positively say was that regeneration is the impartation of God's life by the Spirit, but not simply the old nature made over; "he receives God's nature."[11]

To this point in the "New Birth" sermon Moody has emphasized the sinful condition of man and the sole activity of God in regeneration in a manner that is remarkably Calvinistic in tone. In fact, he defended the necessity of the new birth with the challenge, "Has not the God of Heaven a right to say how a man shall come into His Kingdom, and who shall come?" A statement most un-Arminian in tone! With this emphasis on man's need and God's sole and sovereign agency in regeneration, Moody closed the sermon. But he was not done and he picked it up at that point the next night, reemphasizing that the new birth is not simply reformation or making up your mind to lead a better life.

In 1878-79 in Baltimore Moody explained the difference between reformation and regeneration. "When a man tries to better himself, that is reform. Regeneration is letting God do it all." Moody had pre-

8. *New Sermons*, pp. 122, cf. 276; *Wondrous Love*, pp. 40-41.

9. Finney, *Lectures on Revivals of Religion*, p. 134; McLoughlin, *Modern Revivalism*, pp. 66-75; D. L. Moody, *To All People*, p. 199; cf. pp. 90-93.

10. This point becomes significant when Moody's relationship to nineteenth-century perfectionism is discussed; see pp. 156-60.

11. *New Sermons*, pp. 123-25; *Wondrous Love*, pp. 30-31, 37.

faced that distinction by expressing skepticism about the alleged intellectual advances of man and the development of man.[12] Nor was it sufficient to change only the outer man (reformation); the inner man must be renewed (regeneration). A fountain must be made sweet at its source. Apart from the new nature, the source of a person's actions is the old Adam nature, a concept that he then elaborated and which has been discussed above (pp. 90-93). All in all, Moody's message of man's need of a supernatural work of regeneration was out of step with the liberal theological trends of the times, especially as represented by the avante garde Unitarians and Universalists. In their judgment, man as a reasonable animal knowing the reasonableness of God's law, could cultivate his own character through education and training to assure salvation, without any miraculous help from God. Indeed, there was no hell to fear nor depravity to overcome according to the more "advanced" thinkers.[13] Given the intellectual climate of Boston where such views were especially at home, it is no wonder Moody said that in no city had he encountered such strong opposition to the doctrine of sudden conversion as from the "enlightened Bostonians."[14] Moody's emphasis on depraved humanity's absolute dependence on a supernatural regeneration by the Spirit is in apparent contrast both to Finneyite revivalism and liberal optimism. He even sounded quite Calvinistic at times, a fact that did not escape even his sympathetic Methodist supporters, much less a "Campbellite" critic or an enlightened Bostonian lampooner.[15]

Yet at the very point in the "New Birth" sermon where Moody sounded most Calvinistic he suddenly changed to an "Arminian" key. "By nature we are sinners," but there is a "universal remedy."

---

12. *New Sermons*, pp. 124, 127-28; *Wondrous Love*, p. 35; "Overcoming Evil," *Baltimore Sun*, newspaper clipping in Moodyana, identified by date only with 1879-80, though it should probably read 1878-79.

13. McLoughlin, *The American Evangelicals, 1800-1900: An Anthology*, p. 9; Barber, "The American Revivalists in England," *Unitarian Review* 4 (Aug. 1875): 186-91; Laon [pseud.], "Messrs. Moody and Sankey and Revivalism," *Canadian Monthly* 7 (June 1875): 510-13; I. A. M. Cumming, *Tabernacle Sketches* (Boston: Times Pub., 1877), p. 38; "Shall the Church Rely on Revivalism or on Christian Nurture?" *New Englander* 38 (Nov. 1879): 800-806.

14. *New Sermons*, pp. 590, 597; *To All People*, p. 465.

15. J. H. Crespi, "Moody and Sankey," *Southern Review* 19 (Jan. 1876): 196-97; Daniels, *D. L. Moody and His Work*, pp. 107, 249; Walsh, *Moody versus Christ and His Apostles: A Vindication of the Truth of the Gospel*, p. 63; I. A. M. Cumming, *Tabernacle Sketches*, the entire book being a lampoon, complete with cartoons, of Moody with frequent allusions to his Calvinism and orthodoxy.

We have not got to pick a man here and there—that man in the gallery there, or that woman yonder, and say, "You can be saved." It is for all, all! Some one may say, "That is Universalism." Call it what you like. God has offered the blessing to every wounded one, to everyone who groans under the curse of the flesh, and thus I can prove that any man born on the earth has got a Saviour. "Ye must be born again," and "He must be lifted up." He has done His part—He has given us the remedy, and we must lift Him up.

Moody expanded this into a theodicy. He held man responsible for the old Adam nature and its acts by saying that if man is lost, it is because he has rejected the remedy that God has offered. "He is free to all." If a person dies in unbelief, "Whose fault is it?"[16]

Moody's simultaneous emphasis on the sole work of God in salvation, particularly in atonement and regeneration, raised problems that were by no means new or unique.[17] Boiled down to the simplest terms for the case of Moody: how can man who is corrupt from the sole of his foot to the crown of his head, and thus wholly dependent upon God for salvation, still have the power to accept or reject the remedy for his condition? On the one hand God is said to have done everything He could toward salvation, yet on the other hand man is dead with no life or power until he is born of the Spirit. But the remedy is free to all. Does man still have an inherent ability to look to God in faith? Is there some sort of common grace, or even a work of regeneration, that enables man to turn from sin to God? Moody's statements on these questions were inconsistent and the inconsistencies are most obvious, as one focuses on man's need of regeneration. This fact did not escape the notice of Moody's critics on both sides of the fence. The "Campbellite" (Arminian in orientation), John Walsh, criticized Moody for saying man could do nothing and God had done everything; you need not wait for God to do more. It is a "Babylonish dialect," "confusion worse confounded." The Particular Baptist (Calvinist in orientation), J. K. Popham, objected:

> What is this! a *dead* soul *walking* to Christ for life! The *act* and *motion* of life the cause of that life! No mention of the eternal and ever blessed Spirit's gracious work on the soul, no; but the dead sin-

---

16. *New Sermons*, pp. 129-34.
17. See pp. 29-31 for discussion of Arminianism and Calvinism, and chap. 6 for detailed discussion of Moody's Calvinist-Arminian tendencies.

ner's ceasing from certain specified work, and commencing another, or
rather others, "coming and taking." Regeneration, then, is a dead soul,
performing the most active functions of life.

The inconsistencies disturbed those looking for a consistent system of
theology.[18]

But the inconsistencies and problems apparently did not disturb
Moody. On some occasions Moody would say that with the gift and
the command comes the ability from God to take and to do; on other
occasions the standard answer was, you can if you will. Sometimes he
sounded as though no gracious operation was necessary before a person
could turn to God, sometimes he sounded as though it was necessary for
there to be some gracious influence. Even his statements that God gives
the power to accept contain the inconsistency of dead people having
the power to accept or reject the power to accept. Moody probably
would not have known what an *ordo salutis* was, but on at least one
occasion he gave one of sorts which revealed his unresolved problems.

> If you would be saved, call upon God first, and then God will give
> you help, and by His power you can turn away from sin, and from your
> evil thoughts, and will get pardon. But you haven't power to give up
> your evil courses until you call upon God, and until He gives you
> strength. After you have called upon the Lord, you must receive Him
> when He comes; you must make room for Him.[19]

But perhaps one should not be too hard on Moody at this point, for
what theological system has been wholly adequate in bringing God's
sovereignty and human responsibility together in a logically consistent
system without betraying either one or the other? Moody understood
the Bible to present an unresolved dialectic. At the one pole stood mankind in its corruption and deadness, entirely dependent on God's work
of grace in salvation, the case in point here being regeneration by the
Spirit. At the other pole stood the biblical evidence for universal provision and the calls to mankind implying responsibility and ability to accept the remedy given. This was the Gospel as Moody understood and
proclaimed it. His sense of human responsibility prompted him to use
aggressive methods to bring the Gospel to the people; his keen aware-

18. Walsh, *Moody versus Christ and His Apostles: A Vindication of the Truth of the Gospel*, pp. 63-64; Popham, *Moody and Sankey Errors versus The Scriptures of Truth*, p. 5.
19. *New Sermons*, p. 242.

ness that salvation was a work of God saved him from high-pressure tactics and allowed him to leave the results with God once the message of the Gospel had been delivered. Consequently, Moody does not fit the caricature of professional revivalists from Finney on that has become commonplace in so many recent studies.[20]

Although the "New Birth" sermon in *New Sermons, Addresses and Prayers* (pp. 121-35) referred to here contains no reference to this concept, there is one other feature of Moody's understanding of regeneration or conversion that must be discussed because of the opposition it raised. That is the suddenness of conversion. Usually the idea of sudden conversion was prominent in Moody's preaching of regeneration, new birth, or conversion, and whole sermons would be devoted to the proposition that salvation or regeneration is instantaneous. Arguments for and examples of instantaneous conversion are numerous throughout Moody's sermons.[21] However, his discussions of instantaneous conversion are neither profound nor detailed. What then was implied in the concept that aroused such opposition? What was Moody's point?

In the first place, he implied that there was no middle ground between being a Christian and not being a Christian. There were simply two classes of people, those who believe and those who don't; and Moody's mission was to call on those who did not believe to get into the other class.[22] But the deeper significance of the concept related to the sinful condition of mankind and the nature of salvation. Sinful man cannot gain his own salvation by giving up his sins, by working, by education, or by nurturing any presumed human goodness. Salvation is a free gift. One does not have to give up sins first—one cannot. Simply take the gift, and Christ takes the sins. While the Christian life involves growth, conversion takes place at a certain minute and is instantaneous, to be compared to Noah walking into the door of the ark and into safety, or to a slave fleeing to Canada. "One minute he is a slave, and in an instant he is a free man." Instantaneous conversion was related to Moody's denial that one starts from the cradle to heaven.

---

20. See pp. 71-86.
21. "Regeneration is Instantaneous," *New Sermons*, pp. 362-68; cf. pp. 65, 243, 590-97; *New Sermons* (Goodspeed ed.), pp. 387, 392-93; *Glad Tidings*, pp. 82, 227; *Great Joy*, pp. 257-64; Goss, *Echoes*, pp. 116-17.
22. *New Sermons* (Goodspeed ed.), pp. 392-93.

It was an affirmation of human depravity and that God alone could save.[23] Thus, "sudden conversion" served as a convenient focal point for those not in sympathy with Moody's views. One sermon on instantaneous regeneration began with a reference to the large number of letters he had received wondering how he could teach such a "pernicious doctrine," and later in the sermon he said that "in England they were at me all the time about this sudden conversion. They said it was a life-work from the cradle down to the grave."[24] In Boston he declared that he did not think any city had given "so much downright opposition to this doctrine" as there had been there.[25]

Who these objectors were is not revealed by Moody, but one does not have to look far to discover who they might have been. Those in the Unitarian-Universalist tradition were quite likely among their number.[26] Likewise, those influenced by Horace Bushnell's concept of Christian nurture would not have looked favorably on Moody's denial of salvation from the cradle and of education of dead men into the Kingdom, nor his insistence that in an instant one is regenerated, moving from the effects of sin into the benefits of the new nature. Bushnell had depreciated the value of revivalism and crisis conversions, insisting that conversions were not always miraculous and that a child might grow up without ever knowing himself to be other than a Christian.[27] Many of Moody's barbs against those who denied sudden conversions would seem to be especially appropriate, from Moody's perspective, if directed against Bushnell's Christian Nurture and those influenced by it.

But that is not all, for at the opposite end of the theological spectrum the English Particular Baptist Popham did not like the doctrine of sudden conversion any better than some of the other doctrines of Moody. He was not specific on this score, but there are clues that suggest it did not accord with "the deep experimental religion of our Puritan fathers." Popham may have had in mind the Puritan doctrine of seeking, wherein there were certain steps to salvation, and the Puritan doctrine of

23. *Glad Tidings*, pp. 82, 226-27, 275-76; *New Sermons*, pp. 243, 276, 362-65, 586.
24. *New Sermons*, pp. 362, 366; cf. *Great Joy*, pp. 257, 263.
25. *To All People*, p. 465; cf. *New Sermons*, p. 590.
26. Cf. I. M. Atwood, "Revivals and the Unchurched," *Universalist Quarterly* 33 (Jan. 1876): 87-97.
27. Bushnell, *Christian Nurture*, pp. 3-73; cf. the following article for a Bushnell-type criticism of Moody's type of evangelism, "Shall the Church Rely on Revivalism or on Christian Nurture?" *New Englander* 38 (Nov. 1879): 800-806. See also McLoughlin, *Modern Revivalism*, pp. 149-52.

assurance, wherein assurance comes to the believer through an actively working faith in constant dependence on God's promises.[28]

The "Campbellites" had reason to object to the doctrine of sudden conversion as well, and for reasons not dissimilar to the probable reasons of Popham, though with a special twist of their own. John Walsh specifically repudiated the doctrine, insisting that salvation was not by faith alone and therefore was not instantaneous. One must not only have faith, but must also repent, be taught, be discipled, and be baptized. Since obedience could not be separated from faith and since baptism was a part of the new birth, salvation was not by faith alone and conversion was not instantaneous.[29]

It is natural that those who differed with Moody on the nature of man's need, on salvation simply received as a gift, and on assurance, would find his preaching of sudden conversion or regeneration to be a "pernicious doctrine." Moody continued to preach it, although with the passage of time he moderated his statements on the subject. As early as the 1876-1877 meetings in Boston he was saying that it was not necessary to know where or how one was converted, only to know that one was in fact converted. In the same sermon he even said that with some, conversion is like the flashing of a meteor, while with others it is "like the rising of the sun, gradually." But even so, he still insisted that "this is not a matter of education, it is the work of God."[30]

At the student summer conference in Northfield in 1888, Moody was asked if all conversions had to be sudden or instantaneous. Moody answered no and cited the case of children especially. And then he explained with almost the exact words he had used over ten years earlier in Boston; but he concluded, "That doesn't change the fact that there must be a time when we are born into God's kingdom."[31]

28. Popham, *Moody and Sankey's Errors versus The Scriptures of Truth*, pp. 9-10; cf. Conrad Cherry, *The Theology of Jonathan Edwards: A Reappraisal* (Garden City, N. Y.: Doubleday, 1966), pp. 143-58, and John H. Gerstner, *Steps to Salvation* (Philadelphia: Westminster, 1960), especially chap. 9, pp. 71-88.

29. Walsh, *Moody versus Christ and His Apostles: A Vindication of the Truth of the Gospel*, pp. 23-42; Almer M. Collins, *The Contradictions of Orthodoxy; or "What Shall I Do to be Saved?" as Answered by Several Representative Orthodox Clergymen of Chicago* (Chicago: Central Book Concern, 1880), pp. 26, 28-29, 49-57, 156, 160. Neither one of these men identifies himself as a "Campbellite," but one must remember that the followers of Alexander Campbell, also called Disciples of Christ, repudiated all denominational labels and insisted on being known only as Christians. We have used the designation "Campbellite," not as a term of reproach, but because its meaning is more specific. These two books contain the typical "Campbellite" doctrines.

30. *New Sermons*, pp. 583, 586; cf. *To All People*, pp. 417, 422.

31. Shanks, ed., *College Students at Northfield* (1888), p. 204.

Addressing personal workers on January 18, 1897, in Boston's Tremont Temple on the subject of dealing with inquirers, Moody warned that no two cases of conversion are exactly alike, and again used the simile of a morning sunrise—you can't always tell when light began to dispel darkness.[32] Similarly, on the afternoon of August 18, 1898, in Northfield, Moody was asked about sudden conversion and he gave his stock answer, emphasizing that it was not the where or the when that was important, but the fact. Children may be so trained that they will be converted so early they can't remember when they were converted. Nevertheless, conversion should still be the thing the church aims for, and Moody expressed pity for the church that was afraid of the word. Moody probably had in mind the turning away from individual salvation to a Social Gospel which was taking place in so many pulpits by that time.

That night he preached the famous "New Birth" sermon. The usual themes were there—inborn depravity, the absolute necessity of the new birth, and the futility of trying to bring people into the Kingdom by education or good surroundings. But his essentially unchanged message of regeneration by the Spirit contained an emphasis that did reflect a change taking place in American Christendom. He warned:

> The trouble with people is that they are trying to make that stream good while the fountain is bad. And that is why I am so opposed to all the work being put on the old man, trying to straighten out the old man and make him upright when he is bad from the crown of his head to the sole of his foot. It isn't patching up the old man, but it is hewing down that tree and putting a new graft in. It is entirely changed, a new creation. I have heard of reform, reform, until I am tired and sick of the whole thing. It is regeneration by the power of the Holy Ghost that we need.[33]

32. *Thou Fool*, p. 90.
33. "Questions and Answers at the General Conference, Thursday afternoon, August 18, 1898"; "Regeneration. Address delivered by Mr. Moody, General Conference, Thursday Evening, August 18, 1898," pp. 1-6. Both are typed manuscripts in Moodyana. Cf. D. L. Moody, *Thou Fool*, pp. 143 ff., W. R. Moody, *Moody* (1930), pp. 310-11. Cf. pp. 94-96.

6

TAKING THE REMEDY

THE GOSPEL OF *redemption* and *regeneration* was the God-given remedy for man in his *ruined* condition. Moody's understanding of this triad has been the focus of the three preceding chapters, with only a brief reference to the problem of the relationship between regeneration and the appropriation of salvation as reflected in his preaching. Now that problem must be brought into sharper focus. To whom were the benefits of the Gospel extended? Did fallen mankind have the ability to appropriate these benefits? How might they be personally appropriated? In short, who may become a Christian and how?

Since the aim of this book is to examine the message of Moody the evangelist in its own terms so far as is possible, rather than forcing an extraneous system upon it, in this chapter Moody's concepts of faith, repentance, will, election, and assurance are considered. It was in this order, more or less, that Moody tended to discuss them, and it most fairly and accurately represents his approach.[1]

FAITH

Fundamental as a presupposition to the understanding of Moody's concept of faith is his view of the finished work of Christ on the cross in atonement and the Spirit's work of regeneration in the heart. Both represent in their own way God's gift of salvation, the divine provision of the remedy fallen man needs.[2] Within this context, faith is essentially trust in God and His provision; it is the hand that takes the gift offered. Salvation is earned neither by forsaking sins nor by performing good

1. See a sermon simply entitled, "Preach the Gospel," *Great Redemption*, especially pp. 313-19, in which these themes appear. Though not elaborated as fully as in other places, the themes occur in that sermon in basically the order followed in this chapter, thus providing a convenient model.
2. Ibid., pp. 311-13, 316.

works. "It is a gift . . . and the way to be saved is not to delay, but to come and take—t-a-k-e, take."[3]

Taking was really the third of three elements of faith. Moody defined faith as "dependence upon the veracity of another," with that dependence being composed of three things, knowledge, assent, and laying hold. It is the kind of relationship that people have toward one another and which they commonly exercise in daily life. Saving faith looks to God and takes Him at His word. "Faith is just the hand that reaches out and gets the blessing. Faith sees a thing in God's hand. Faith says I will have it." The ultimate object of faith for Moody was God Himself, for one's trust was not to be put in churches, creeds, doctrines, ministers, sacraments, etc. Or as Moody summarized, not in "some institution of man," but in God.[4] He regarded a merely intellectual faith as a dead faith. Faith was to be in a person, not merely a creed.

Moody was careful to emphasize, though, that this did not imply that intellectual content was unimportant. Faith was not some "leap into the dark" without giving a person "evidence or something to believe." "Do not suppose for a moment that it does not make any difference what you believe in or what your faith is, so you are only sincere." Indeed, it is folly to say any creed is good enough just so long as you believe it, and what a pity it is that there are so many who don't know what they believe. Faith comes through reading the Word of God, which provides the intellectual content of faith and which may be formulated into creeds or doctrines. But Moody would warn:

It isn't a mere creed or doctrine. Doctrines are all right in their places, but when you put them in the place of faith or salvation, they become a sin. If Dr. Horton should ask me up to his house to dinner tomorrow, the street would be a very good thing to take me to his house, but if I didn't go into the house, I wouldn't get any dinner. Now a creed is the road or street. It is very good as far as it goes, but if it doesn't take us to Christ, it is worthless. "He that hath the Son hath life." Faith in a person, and that person is Jesus Christ. It isn't a creed about Him, but it is Himself.[5]

3. *Glad Tidings*, pp. 82-83; cf. *Thou Fool*, p. 179, and *A Friendly Message to Irishmen from America*, reprinted from the *Irish Independent* newspaper, Nov. 3, 1892, p. 8.
4. *New Sermons*, pp. 136, 138; *Glad Tidings*, pp. 170, 176.
5. *New Sermons*, pp. 138-41; *Glad Tidings*, pp. 172-73; "The Moody Meetings" (" 'Faith' Was the Text for the Day"), *News* (Providence, R.I.), Jan. 22, 1894; cf. "Moody Talks on Faith," *Journal* (New Bedford, Mass.), an undated newspaper clipping in Moodyana.

This understanding of faith and its proper object led Moody to sub-ordinate the emotional element that had been present in so much earlier revivalism. In fact, feelings were not a necessary part of faith. "Feeling has nothing to do with it. Never mind feelings, take God at His Word."[6] By the same token, works have nothing to contribute to salvation, though they should be the inevitable result of salvation.[7]

REPENTANCE

Repentance occupied a subsidiary place in Moody's preaching. Moody even admitted this fact and mentioned the criticism that had been directed against him in Chicago in the mid-1870s for not touching upon it more frequently.[8] Moody's emphasis was on the goodness rather than the severity of God, so that he did not feel as comfortable or as successful when preaching repentance. On those occasions when Moody did preach on repentance, he defined it in a way that would be consistent with his understanding of faith. He was apparently aware of the Greek *metanoia* and spoke of repentance as a "change of mind," a "right about face," a turning around and facing God. Repentance, then, seems to have been the negative side of faith, or perhaps more accurately, conversion.[9]

In January, 1884, R. W. Dale wrote to Henry Wace, who with C. A. Buchheim had translated and edited *First Principles of the Reformation or the Ninety-five Theses and the Three Primary Works of Martin Luther.* Dale had recently read one of Wace's introductory essays in this 1883 work. He told Wace that Moody's preaching in 1875 had reminded him of Luther. Like Luther, Moody exulted in the "free grace of God" that "leads to repentance—to a complete change of life." Dale also compared the criticism that Moody's preaching provoked in 1875 to the criticisms that had been made of Luther. However, Dale now complained that in Moody's more recent meetings in Britain (in Birmingham, 1883) Moody's emphasis and tone had shifted since his preaching there some eight years earlier. He wrote to Dr. Wace:

He insisted very much on Repentance—and on Repentance in the

---

6. *Glad Tidings*, p. 228; cf. D. L. Moody, *Bible Readings Delivered in San Francisco and Oakland* (San Francisco: Bacon, 1881), p. 35.

7. *A Friendly Message to Irishmen from America*, p. 8. For sermons on "Faith" from 1875 and 1897 presenting the same understanding of faith as described above, see *London Discourses*, pp. 148-56 and *Thou Fool*, pp. 127-42.

8. *New Sermons*, p. 255.

9. *Great Redemption*, p. 89; *The Way to God and How to Find It*, pp. 74-75.

sense in which the word is now used by "Evangelical" as well as other divines, as though it were a doing of penance instead of a metanoia— a self torture, a voluntary sorrow, a putting on of spiritual hair-shirts.[10]

Dale conjectured that this shift in emphasis might account for the less than sensational results that attended this second tour of Britain. He also wrote to Moody about the matter, and Moody replied that Dale's observations had "set him a-thinking."

It has been difficult for me to evaluate Dale's contention because very little material from Britain in this period is available in this country. The volume *The Way to God and How to Find It,* published in 1884, does contain a sermon on "Repentance." It does not evidence the shift of emphasis and change of tone cited by Dale, and it corresponds very closely with a sermon delivered in Cleveland in 1879.[11] In both sermons repentance is defined as a change of mind, and Moody took pains to avoid the impression that repentance is some sort of penance or wearing of "spiritual hair shirts." However, this is inconclusive, for though *The Way to God and How to Find It* appeared in the period in question, the sermon may have been preached before the alleged shift took place.

However, two other bits of evidence seem to support Dale's criticism of Moody in January, 1884. Moody's personal records indicate that he preached his sermon on "Repentance" on at least fifty-one different occasions between 1875 and 1888. Thirty-three of these were in the British Isles between 1881 and 1884. This accords well with Dale's comment, "He insisted very much on Repentance." In 1883 Moody briefly returned to Chicago where he led a Christian convention. In at least one sermon delivered there he strongly emphasized parting with sin in order to get into the Kingdom of God. Later, when one participant asked him if "he would preach the law or only the love of God," Moody replied, "I preach more law than I did a few years ago."[12] However, Moody's records indicate that the sermon on repentance was preached infrequently after 1884, and it seldom appears in books published after 1884.

Similarly, the theme of forsaking sin in order to be saved is essentially absent from the scores of sermon books and newspaper reports

10. A. W. W. Dale, *The Life of R. W. Dale of Birmingham* (London: Hodder & Stoughton, 1898), p. 530.
11. *Great Redemption,* pp. 84-100.
12. Typed sheet with year and places where the sermon was preached, Moodyana; *Sermons and Addresses, Question Drawer,* pp. 877-78, 919.

after 1884 examined for this investigation. This suggests that repentance came to be especially emphasized in the British tour of 1881-84, but after that it fell into the background, perhaps as a result of Moody's rethinking the matter in the light of R. W. Dale's observations to him. If Dale was correct in his analysis, it was apparently a temporary aberration. This conclusion is also supported by the fact that Moody's sermons on "Faith" reflect a consistent viewpoint from the mid-1870s to the late 1890s, a viewpoint that would have been quite inconsistent with the shift alleged by Dale. Again, if Dale was correct in his analysis, perhaps his word to Moody caused Moody to see that what he was preaching on repentance was inconsistent with what he was preaching on faith.

WILL

We have already noticed that Moody insisted that God could not be criticized for holding depraved man responsible for the Adam nature and its actions, in that God had made His universal remedy available in the atonement and regeneration to all. The Holy Spirit also is trying to give peace and happiness to everyone.[13] Nothing remains to hinder a person from being saved. The provision is universal and universally open to all. "The water of life is offered freely to everyone." As Moody so frequently contended in his sermon on "Excuses," not even election could be cited as a legitimate excuse. As a matter of fact, God wants everybody saved, and Moody had a whole sermon to prove the point.[14]

What then determines who will be saved? That question brings attention to one of the most obviously Arminian points in Moody's message, for he pressed for decisions on the basis that "you can if you will." "Whosoever will." "If you will, you will; if you won't, you won't." "Every creature can be saved if he will." Though the English grammar of the sentences cited would allow the word "will" to be understood as an auxiliary verb expressing the future tense, the contexts of these statements make it clear that Moody did not use the word this way. He spoke in this manner, referring to the power of volition, a power which everyone had. It was almost synonymous with "decide" or "determine." "Nine-tenths of the battle of becoming a Christian is to make up your mind." For example, "No soul in this audience will go down to the

13. *New Sermons*, pp. 70-71, 129, 134.
14. Ibid., pp. 170, 194-95, 297-98, 301.

dark cavern if he is willing to obey God. And now the question comes
to you all, Will you obey Him?" The will itself was a battleground.
Those who rejected the invitation "don't want to give up their will."
He said that the door of salvation hangs on one hinge, the will, and the
surrender of the will was the turning point in conversion. Everyone is
a free agent, choosing life or death; Moody set before his audiences the
choice, urged them to seek the life in the Kingdom of God, and concluded, "You can do it if you will."[15]

At times Moody spoke as though this were an inherent natural ability
which all people had, though his statements more frequently suggest
that it was a divinely given ability. He insisted that God does not command what man cannot do, and he asked if God would offer the Gospel
to everyone and not give the power to take it. He was sure that with the
command and offer came the power to do and to take. On this basis,
Moody would argue in his sermon on "Excuses" that inability was no
excuse. Moody was using an appeal and argument that had been frequently used by others before him reflecting the Arminian trends of
American Evangelicalism (Charles Finney, Lyman Beecher, Nathaniel
Taylor); indeed, it was not an argument new with American theology,
being found also in Arminius, Erasmus, and Pelagius.[16] At this point,
he could hardly sound more Arminian. What did he think, then, of the
doctrine of election?

ELECTION

Closely aligned with Moody's preaching of the will's ability to decide
for God and accept the remedy for sin were his allusions to the matter
of election. The word "allusion" is used deliberately, for it can hardly
be said that Moody discussed this doctrine in any depth. References to
election in his sermons come only in the contexts of discussions of excuses that sinners might use to avoid the decision that Moody was
pressing upon them. As early as the Chicago Noon Prayer Meeting on

15. Ibid., pp. 96, 113, 144, 208-9, 236, 252, 257, 260-62, 307-9, 332, 383, 430, 590; *Glad Tid-
ings*, pp. 83, 338-39; Shanks, *D. L. Moody at Home: His Home and Home Work*, pp. 69-70;
Wondrous Love, pp. 144-45; *London Discourses*, pp. 52-53, 136; D. L. Moody, *Sovereign
Grace: Its Source, Its Nature and Its Effects* (Chicago: Moody, 1891), pp. 91-93, cited as
Sovereign Grace; Thou Fool, p. 179.
16. *Glad Tidings*, pp. 75, 77; *Great Redemption*, pp. 94-95; D. L. Moody, *Men of the Bible*
(Chicago: Moody, 1898), p. 45; cf. *Sovereign Grace*, pp. 91-93; 103-4; Daniels, *Moody: His
Words, Work, and Workers*, p. 239; McLoughlin, *The American Evangelicals, 1800-1900: An
Anthology*, pp. 8, 71; Finney, *Lectures on Revivals of Religion*, pp. 195-97, 334. See pp.
29-31 for discussion of Arminianism and Calvinism.

July 27, 1868, Moody was warning the participants, "You need not, my friends, stumble over that doctrine into hell." His explanation at that time was that some forty or fifty years after His ascension, Christ "was afraid that someone would feel that he was not invited, and so he told John upon the isle of Patmos to repeat the invitation." That invitation was "whosoever will" (Rev 22:17).

He was still using this very explanation in the meetings in Tremont Temple in 1897. Every sermon on "Excuses" I have examined dealt with the matter of election; the earliest of these sermons was preached in London in 1875 and the last was the very last sermon he preached, in Kansas City on November 16, 1899.[17] In all of them Moody's treatment of the problem was consistent. Positively he reaffirmed the "whosoever will's," and negatively he denied that election had anything to do with the unbeliever. By this he simply meant that the Bible never addresses discussions of election to the unbeliever; they are not *apropos* to the unbeliever. The Gospel invitation alone is addressed to them, and would God offer a gift if He did not give the power to receive it? Speaking to the unconverted, Moody's consistent theme was, "You have no more to do with the doctrine of election than you have with the Government of China."[18] Brief though his discussion was, Moody's approach is most significant.

James Findlay's statement that Moody repudiated the doctrine is much too strong. He never did that. He simply said that it was not addressed to the unbeliever. And Moody did not take the standard route of explaining away the offense of election by saying that God elected those whom He foreknew would believe of their own free will.

But if the unbeliever had nothing to do with election, the believer did; and Moody affirmed his belief in it, though he made no attempts to harmonize it with the preaching of human responsibility and ability, other than the approach just indicated. In London in 1875 he affirmed, "I do believe in election; but I have no business to preach that doctrine to the world at large. . . . After you have received salvation, we can talk about election. It's a doctrine for Christians, for the Church, not for the unconverted world." Twenty-two years later in Boston Moody com-

17. "Notes of the Chicago Noon Prayer Meeting," *The Advance* (Chicago), Aug. 6, 1868; *Thou Fool*, pp. 176-77. George T. B. Davis, *Dwight L. Moody: The Man and His Mission* (Chicago: Monarch, 1900), pp. 167 ff.
18. *London Discourses*, pp. 92-93; *New Sermons*, pp. 194-95; *Glad Tidings*, pp. 338-39; *Thou Fool*, pp. 176-77; *Sovereign Grace*, pp. 91-93.

pared the matter to a sign outside Tremont Temple inviting whosoever will to come in; but once inside "I look up and see on the wall, 'D. L. Moody was elected from the foundations of the world to be saved.' . . . It is a very sweet doctrine to the Child of God and very precious, but not to an unbeliever."[19]

Moody really came to no resolution of the problem of election. The universal offer of salvation and the ability of the will were put in one compartment, and election was put in another compartment. In view of the emphasis that Moody put on the former, one is tempted to conclude that it undercut any real meaning for the latter. While that may have been the effect on many of Moody's listeners, it is not a satisfactory explanation of Moody's faith. There have already been indications that his faith was content to let certain tensions between Arminian and Calvinistic themes remain unresolved—depravity and human responsibility, divine monergism in salvation and the necessity and possibility of individual faith, regeneration and calling upon God, and now, election and the ability of the will. On this very point Moody said, "I don't try to reconcile God's sovereignty and man's free agency."[20]

That there was still real content in the doctrine of election for Moody is indicated in the very fact that it was *not* appropriately addressed to unbelievers, but rather, to believers. As such it was a "sweet" and "precious" doctrine. Moody did not indicate in what sense this was true, but it may be conjectured that it expressed the believer's confidence that his salvation was not from himself or of his own effort. Consequently, the believer could rest in assurance of faith, knowing that his salvation was entirely of God, not subject to loss by human failure.

ASSURANCE

The doctrine of assurance was the corollary of Moody's understanding of salvation as explained to this point. Since God's remedy for sin is available to everyone to be simply taken by the hand of faith, the believer's salvation is certain and irrevocable. Although assurance was

19. *Wondrous Love*, pp. 144-45; *Thou Fool*, p. 177. There is a certain verbal similarity between Moody's statements that the unbeliever has nothing to do with election and Charles Finney's statements on the matter. However, Moody never developed the elaborate explanation of election that Finney did in his *Lectures on Systematic Theology*, pp. 481-99; cf. *Lectures on Revivals of Religion*, pp. 195-97, 334.

20. *Bible Readings Delivered in San Francisco and Oakland*, p. 39.

not necessary to salvation, it was clearly the privilege of every believer who would simply take God at His word.

Moody's doctrine of assurance was consistent with his understanding of faith. Faith is knowledge of, assent to, and taking hold of God and His provision in salvation. If salvation is simply a gift provided in redemption and regeneration, and if faith is faith in a Person, taking Him at His word with reference to the gift, then the believing recipient may rest assured that salvation is in fact his. Since feelings were not faith and faith was not feeling, assurance was not dependent on how one felt. In fact, while feelings *might be* the concomitant of faith, it was dangerous to let feelings substitute for faith. For this reason, Moody did not allow wildfire emotionalism in his meetings; people should be brought to Christ coolly, calmly, and intelligently. Moody intended that the inquiry meetings following the sermon be models of order. And in these meetings he intended that people be shown that assurance of salvation comes by "taking God at His word."[21]

The nature of salvation as dependent on God's work received in faith also meant that continuance in salvation and assurance of salvation were not dependent on living in sinless perfection. Aside from the fact that that would make salvation dependent on man's work, such sinless perfection was an impossibility.[22] This did not mean that Moody granted license to the believer to live in sin, nor did it mean that he did not recognize that some professed believers fell by the wayside. But those who do not hold out are "spurious revivals & pretended conversions."[23] When preaching on "Assurance" to a crowd that filled Chicago's Auditorium to overflowing, Moody even referred the castaway passage (1 Co 9:27) to the believer who loses a prize, not to one who loses his salvation.[24] He has that already "as God's pure gift."

As it was grace that saved a person in the first place, it is grace that keeps one from falling, thus providing the basis of assurance. Though the predominant theme of this chapter has been Moody's Arminian emphasis on human responsibility and the ability of the will, his doctrine of assurance reflects the other side of the unresolved dialectic. At this point there is a distinctly Calvinistic tone. With justification

21. *Glad Tidings*, pp. 419-25, 229; *New Sermons*, pp. 348, 593; *Great Joy*, p. 343; Shanks, D. L. *Moody at Home: His Home and Home Work*, pp. 60 ff. Cf. p. 83.
22. *New Sermons*, p. 259. For a more detailed discussion of sinless perfection and Moody's repudiation of the doctrine, see pp. 156-60.
23. Sermon notes for "Elder Son," Moodyana; *Glad Tidings*, pp. 446-47.
24. Unidentified newspaper clipping dated Apr. 2, 1897, Moodyana.

the "Campbellite," John Walsh, chided Moody for holding to the doctrine of "once in grace always in grace"; and again one can understand why some of Moody's Methodist supporters had reservations about what they regarded as Calvinistic tendencies.[25]

A person who partakes of grace will not part with grace, and God's grace will keep one from falling. Grace excludes works, and as a person does not work to gain salvation, he does not work to keep it; he works because he has it.[26] The achievement of Christ's death was that He was judged for the sinner so that the one in Christ is perfectly safe. Sins are taken out of the way and the road to heaven is clear. Judgment is passed, and believers are saved by the merits of Christ. Moody declared that the doctrine of assurance was as clear in Scripture as the doctrine of justification by faith, and he explained the basis of assurance as being a forensic understanding of justification. God will not demand payment twice of the debt Christ paid for the believer. It is the standing in Christ that counts.[27]

It was not only the past work of Christ that assured the eternal destiny of the believer, for He continues to function as the believer's Keeper and Shepherd.[28] This was not too far removed from his conception of the Holy Spirit's ministry. To be a Christian is to have the Holy Spirit. By regeneration He produced a change called the new birth; referring to this new birth, Moody asserted that He will not unchild His children. Similarly, the Holy Spirit has sealed the children till the day of redemption, and "neither the devil nor man can break God's seal."[29]

Moody himself once summed up his understanding of assurance by saying that the Father, Son, and Holy Spirit are pledged to keep the believer. "Look at what He is, and at what He has done; not at what you are, and at what you have done. That is the way to get peace and rest." Assurance rests in God's word of promise, not in feelings.[30]

25. Walsh, *Moody versus Christ and His Apostles: A Vindication of the Truth of the Gospel*, p. 19.
26. *New Sermons*, pp. 101, 103, 105-6; cf. "Notes of the Chicago Noon Prayer Meeting," *The Advance* (Chicago), Jan. 9, 1868.
27. *New Sermons*, pp. 207-8, 284, 363-67, 580; *Moody's Latest Sermons*, pp. 25, 39; D. L. Moody, *The Full Assurance of Faith* (New York: Revell, 1885), pp. 22-23; *Glad Tidings*, pp. 363-67.
28. *New Sermons*, pp. 272-73, 383; *Glad Tidings*, p. 115.
29. *New Sermons*, pp. 284, 286; *Glad Tidings*, pp. 285-86; *The Full Assurance of Faith*, p. 25; "The Holy Spirit," *Daily Inter-Ocean* (Chicago), Nov. 11, 1896.
30. *The Full Assurance of Faith*, pp. 23, 27, 28; for other significant statements of Moody on assurance not cited above, see *New Sermons*, pp. 82, 354-56, 634-46, 690; *Glad Tidings*, pp. 227, 371-73, 392, 446-47.

Studies of American revivalism and of Dwight L. Moody have tended rather simplistically to categorize Moody as an Arminian. Even James Findlay, who does recognize that there are two sides to the question, places the major emphasis on the Arminianism in Moody's message and method, with minimal reference to the Calvinistic themes.[31] In placing Moody within the stream of Arminianizing tendencies and influences of American revivalism and Evangelicalism, it is all too easy to ignore the Calvinistic themes that were quite prominent in his preaching, themes which he did not explain away or put into the background so as to create a consistently Arminian theology.

It is also easy to forget that Moody was not simply the product of the Arminian influences in American Evangelicalism. While the obvious Arminian influences were all around Moody and playing upon him from the earliest days following his conversion to the evangelical faith, it should be remembered that more Calvinistic forces were also brought to play upon him—and that by his own choice.

Among the earliest and more influential of these was Charles H. Spurgeon, known for his Calvinism, although he rejected the "hyperism," as he called it, of some of his Baptist brethren. In chapter 1 it was noted that one of the principal reasons for Moody's trips to Great Britain in 1867 and following years was to learn from the British evangelical brethren. Spurgeon stood foremost among these in Moody's estimate. In 1884 Moody participated in Spurgeon's jubilee celebration at the Metropolitan Tabernacle and gave a brief testimonial to Spurgeon and the influence he had exercised on Moody. He recalled that in 1867 he had first made his way to the Tabernacle to hear Spurgeon. Why? "After I was converted, I began to read of a young man preaching in London with great power, and a desire seized me to hear him. . . . Everything I could get hold of in print that he ever said, I read."[32] Moody then testified that this influence from Spurgeon's printed sermons had come on him when he still "knew very little about religious things," and that he had been reading Spurgeon's sermons for twenty-five years.

31. Findlay, *Dwight L. Moody*, pp. 242-44; cf. McLoughlin, *Modern Revivalism*, pp. 246-52, and Weisberger, *They Gathered at the River*, pp. 43, 49, 62, 211-12.

32. Charles H. Spurgeon, *The Autobiography of Charles H. Spurgeon compiled from His Diary, Letters, and Records by His Wife and Private Secretary* (Philadelphia: American Baptist Pub. Soc., n.d.), 4:246-47; also in R. Shindler, *From the Usher's Desk to the Tabernacle Pulpit: The Life and Labours of Pastor C. H. Spurgeon* (London: Passmore & Alabaster, 1892), pp. 207-21.

Spurgeon had his own problems with Moody's Arminian tendencies, and this is commonly emphasized by those discussing the relationship between the two men. But he was able to support Moody's evangelistic efforts in London, and he even preached for Moody. In turn, Moody preached in the Tabernacle for Spurgeon and was invited to participate in the jubilee celebration, at which time a specially bound set of Spurgeon's books of sermons was to be presented to Moody. Letters from Spurgeon to the Moodys in 1884 were warm and cordial.[33]

The early influence of the Plymouth Brethren on Moody is well known and is more fully discussed later; they, too, were usually quite Calvinistic in their soteriology. As has already been mentioned, one of their number, Henry Moorhouse, had a very significant impact on Moody, and he, too, was Calvinistic.[34] Another Calvinist, not numbered among the Plymouth Brethren, who touched Moody was the Scotsman Andrew Bonar. Moody frequently alluded to Bonar in his messages, a practice that was otherwise unusual for him; and both men admitted to the influence Bonar had on Moody.[35]

It is not being suggested that Moody accepted the Calvinism of his mentors in every point, for such was obviously not the case. But it is significant that not one individual of thoroughly Arminian persuasion exerted the influence over Moody that Spurgeon, Moorhouse, and Bonar did. In other words, the unresolved tensions between Arminian and Calvinistic themes that are evident in Moody's sermons are a reflection of the Arminian American milieu of which Moody was a part and the Calvinistic influences of certain notable friends.

However, if the matter is allowed to rest here, perhaps this also would be too simplistic an explanation of the source of this unresolved tension in Moody's preaching. It must not be forgotten that the book he read and studied most was the Bible. There, also, one finds this unresolved tension. Findlay, in a statement of great insight into Moody's understanding, observes:

33. Spurgeon, *The Autobiography of Charles H. Spurgeon*, 4:169-70; in Moodyana there is a folder of Spurgeon notes and correspondence with copies of letters from Spurgeon to Mr. and Mrs. Moody dated Oct. 9; June 13, 1884; Oct. 12, 1881; Apr. 24; June 10, 1884; June 4, 1884; these letters give evidence of a cordial relationship between Spurgeon and the Moodys.
34. W. R. Moody, *Moody* (1930), pp. 102-11; Sandeen, *Roots of Fundamentalism*, pp. 73-75; Needham, *Recollections of Henry Moorhouse*, pp. 196-99.
35. W. R. Moody, *Moody* (1900), pp. 243-44, 257, 299; Marjory Bonar, ed., *Andrew A. Bonar: Diary and Life*, pp. 333-34, 528-35.

Moody . . . saw no ultimate contradiction in what he was preaching, because this was a truly Biblical approach to the question of salvation. After all, Saint Paul uttered words several times whose import is strikingly similar to the phrases used by the evangelist. "Work out your own salvation with fear and trembling," said the apostle, "for God is at work in you, both to will and to work for his good pleasure." Or, "God was in Christ, reconciling the world to himself. . . . We beseech you on behalf of Christ be reconciled to God." If Moody was confused, so was Paul. The Biblical message, in other words, is not reductionist, does not make the act of salvation an either-or proposition as both strict Arminians and Calvinists would have it.[36]

This is certainly preferable to Sidney Mead's reference to the "muddled thinking of Dwight L. Moody who reputedly said he was an Arminian up to the cross but Calvinist beyond."[37] That Moody said this may be true. But whose thinking is muddled on this point is another question.

---

36. Findlay, *Dwight L. Moody*, p. 243.
37. Mead, *The Lively Experiment*, p. 124; this reputed statement of Moody is often quoted, but I have yet to find it in a primary source, though it could well have come from Moody.

7

THE LIFE OF THE BELIEVER

MOODY HAS BEEN REFERRED TO as an evangelist and a revivalist, and his meetings as revivals and evangelistic campaigns.[1] Moody did not pretend that his own efforts alone would produce either spiritual awakening among Christians or conversion of unbelievers. But he directed his sermons toward both goals, and he referred to his work in both ways. A series of meetings would typically begin with messages directed toward reviving the Christians in attendance in order that they might become effective agents of evangelism. But well before the series was over, Moody would shift the emphasis in his messages to the unbelievers who were also in the audience. Just as regularly he would address some final words to the new converts before he moved on to the next city, giving them some basic counsel on the nurture of their newly found faith.

It can hardly be questioned that Moody's main emphasis was evangelism of the lost; however, he also had a great deal to say about the life of the Christian, and if there is a shift in the emphasis of Moody's preaching after his initial successes in the 1870s in the British Isles and America, it would be that he came to address his fellow Christians more and more. Such a shift of concern is reflected in the titles of books published with Moody's approval, as well as in the sermons themselves; this reflection also is seen in his changing approaches to evangelism, as

1. J. Edwin Orr, chronicler of "outpourings of the Spirit," would probably object to this practice. He insists on precise definition of "revival," "awakening," and "evangelism." In theory I agree, but in actual examination of these phenomena, it is impossible to consistently maintain precise distinctions. Moody's meetings are a case in point. Cf. J. Edwin Orr, *The Flaming Tongue: The Impact of Twentieth Century Revivals* (Chicago: Moody, 1973), pp. ix-x. Moody used the word "revival" of both renewal of believers and evangelism. Cf. *Bible Readings Delivered in San Francisco and Oakland*, pp. 56-60.

noted above.[2] The themes which he emphasized most frequently in his addresses to cold Christians and new converts were the Christian life as work and the Holy Spirit's ministry to the believer, especially baptism by the Spirit. Taken together, these two subject areas not only summarize Moody's view of the Christian life, but they also reflect concerns and debates within British and American Evangelicalism in the last quarter of the century.

WORK AND WORKS

Taking his cue from Moody's doctrine of assurance, that is, that one can be assured that salvation *is* his, Stan Nussbaum makes the incredible allegation that in Moody's view works need not result from salvation. Supposedly one only works to get rewards. While it is true that the very essence of Moody's salvation message was that works did not in any way contribute to the attainment of eternal life, it does not follow that Moody divorced works from salvation as the necessary result. In his 1877 meetings in Chicago while preaching on grace, he characteristically said:

> As I told you last night, by grace are you saved, and not by good deeds or good works. We work from the cross, not toward it; we work because we are saved, not to be saved. . . . You don't work for salvation, but work day and night after you have got it. Get it first before you do anything, but don't try to get it yourself.[3]

Toward the conclusion of his meetings in the Boston Tabernacle a few weeks later, Moody devoted an entire sermon to the matter of works. Beginning with a warning to the non-Christians present that they had nothing to do with works, Moody quickly addressed the Christians, with special attention to the new converts. What he told them can be boiled down to this: work, rightly understood, is of the essence of the believer's life. God never told an unbeliever to work, but He did tell believers to work. Those who had truly been born of the Spirit would be scattered after the meetings, but the work begun there would live on as long as anything in the world lasts. "We have in these three months only been getting ready for work, and now instead of coming here to hear, go out and be a doer of work."

2. See pp. 52-58. As examples of book titles reflecting his concern for the believer: *The Overcoming Life, Secret Power, Prevailing Prayer, Pleasure and Profit in Bible Study, To the Work! To the Work!*
3. Nussbaum, "D. L. Moody and the Church," pp. 30-32, 83; *New Sermons*, p. 101.

As Moody developed the implications of being a "doer of work," it meant first that the Christian would be characterized by a different lifestyle, one which he called "peculiar" (Titus 2:14). Moody only briefly explained what he meant by saying, "If the world can not tell the difference between us and other men, it is a pretty good sign that we have not been redeemed by the precious blood of Christ." One is tempted to suggest that he was alluding to the need for Christians to separate from "worldly" practices such as drinking, smoking, chewing, theater attendance, card-playing, horse racing, dancing, Sabbath-breaking, and reading Sunday newspapers. These he did frequently condemn, but in this sermon he probably refers to the fact that the believer is to be zealous of good works (the last phrase of Titus 2:14).

In fact, Moody went on to say that the church of his day was suffering more from professed Christians who had either gone to sleep or who had never waked up. "If we are living as Christ would have us live, we would be zealous of all good work." Consequently, Moody urged the new converts to join a church, for it was in a church that a Christian could work. And if the church does not provide enough opportunities for work, one should do as Moody himself had done in his early days in Chicago—make his own opportunities. Referring to the time when he started his own Sunday school class with eighteen pupils, he said, "If I am worth anything to the Christian Church to-day, it is as much due to that work as to anything else. . . . I used the little talent I had, and God kept giving me more talents, and so, let me say, find some work." A few minutes later he urged them to get to work at once and warned, "Laziness belongs to the old creation, not the new. There is not a lazy hair in the head of a true Christian. . . . If you are not careful to maintain good works, it is a good sign that you have not been born of God."

Moody did not leave it to chance that these newly converted Bostonians would understand what he meant by work. He urged them to "go down into the dark lanes and byways of the city" and witness by either word or song to women at the washboard or to have children's prayer meetings for "these little street Arabs." "Take care of them and look after them and teach them the love of Christ." Moody's experience in Chicago had made him keenly aware of the plight of children in the squalid slums of the cities. As Moody saw it, the fundamental solution was to lead them to the cross of Christ. "Are we going to let these boys go down to death? Are we going to let them fill our penitentiaries, and these daughters go into our houses of ill-fame? There is work for you. Take these children by the hand and lead them to the Cross of Christ."

Working also involved aiding "every society that is trying to give Christ to a dying, perishing world." Such aid involved giving money or words of comfort and cheer; but then Moody added, "Give it all the aid you can, with all that it means." Examples of such societies that Moody cited were tract societies, temperance reform clubs, and the Young Men's Christian Association. Any of these efforts that were preaching the Gospel of Christ were worthy of support. "Let us not be narrow and bigotted [sic]. But if they don't preach the Gospel of Jesus Christ, go for them; give them no quarter at all." Moody concluded his sermon with a final appeal to the new converts to give attention to two "W's", the Word and work. Feed on the Word and work by leading some soul to Christ.[4]

Moody's use of the word "work" overlapped with the secular concept of work as self-help.[5] He accepted the virtue of hard work generally; but specifically, work was the very genius of the Christian's life for God. To work was basically to witness, to attempt to win souls, and every Christian was responsible for this work. Indeed, there was no such thing as a lazy Christian. This concept is at the base of Moody's social ethic. Christian witness (work) was primary, for humanity's basic need was spiritual. This did not exclude the amelioration of human hardships and suffering. Moody both practiced and preached compassion for his fellowman on the individual level, and he frequently chided his fellow believers for showing too little of it. However, efforts at amelioration which were divorced from the primary goal of evangelism were off the mark.[6] Moody could say a good word for the social value of the YMCA or of temperance preaching and temperance clubs, but the moment he suspected that a social emphasis was displacing the spiritual, his tone radically changed. In the 1880s and 1890s there was normally a marked shift in his emphasis, reflecting his fear that reform was at least overshadowing and perhaps even replacing regeneration.[7]

4. *New Sermons*, pp. 573-81; cf. pp. 91, 634-44; *Great Joy*, p. 348.
5. Findlay has a very helpful discussion of the concept of work in nineteenth-century America and the relation of Moody's concept to it, *Dwight L. Moody*, pp. 83-84, 245-49.
6. *To the Work! To the Work!*, pp. 116-17, 120, 124; *New Sermons*, p. 401.
7. Cf. "Mr. Moody on Young Men's Christian Associations," *The Christian*, Mar. 19, 1874, p. 7; "Mr. Moody's Answers to Practical Questions," *The Christian*, May 7, 1874, p. 6; *Signs of Our Times*, May 12, 1875, p. 295; "The Revival Work," *Daily Courant* (Hartford, Conn.),

The basic need of man was regeneration, and therefore the highest form of Christian work was witnessing; all Christian work should have that in mind. This by no means meant that evangelism was limited to the clergy; Moody himself was an example of that fact. In some ways, lay people might be more effective in witnessing, if properly trained.

It was this that Moody had in mind in January, 1886, when he proposed the school for training "gap-men"; the school eventually came to reality as the Bible institute. The idea had been in Moody's mind at least since 1874 when he had written to *The Christian* expressing his conviction that some course of study was needed to train "more workers for Christ *outside* of the regular ministry." They would be specially trained for work among the "lapsed masses." "I believe there are many who would be glad to give part at least of their time to this work if they knew just *how* and *where* to work" (note the typical use of the word "work").

As early as September, 1883, Moody was proposing that a school to train men and women for standing in the gap be started in Chicago. In the summer of 1887 he explained the gap-men concept to the assembled college students at Northfield. Denying that he was opposed to seminary training, he nevertheless asserted that there was such a thing as educating a person away from the rank and file of people, creating a gap between clergy and laity. Moody was calling for bushwackers, irregulars to stand in that gap, "men that will go out and do work that the educated ministers can't do: get in among the people, and identify themselves with the people."

In a similar vein eleven years later, Moody proclaimed, "I don't believe our cities are going to be evangelized until we have laymen in to work. Let them preach!"[8] But quite aside from the training of gap-men

Feb. 6, 1878; Dwight L. Moody, "The Good Samaritan," *The Christian Herald*, Nov. 16, 1910 (sermon preached Jan. 15, 1897), p. 1048; "Questions answered by Mr. Moody, at General Conference, Tuesday Afternoon, August 16, 1898," typed manuscript, Moodyana; *Men of the Bible* (Chicago: Moody, 1898), p. 65.

8. "Mr. Moody on Practical Training for Christian Work," *The Christian*, June 11, 1874, pp. 6-7; for Moody's proposals for a training school in Chicago for "gap-men," see the *Chicago Tribune*, the *Daily InterOcean* (Chicago), and the *Daily News* (Chicago) for Jan. 23 and 25, 1886. Cf. *Sermons and Addresses, Questions Drawer*, pp. 920, 955; Shanks, ed., *A College of Colleges* (1887), pp. 212-13; *Thou Fool*, pp. 110-11, 116. Did the portent of labor troubles in Chicago prompt Moody to choose this time (Jan. 1886) to take definite steps to bring the school into existence? Haymarket was only four months away! Thirteen months later *The Christian Cynosure* (Feb. 24, 1887, p. 1) spoke of the confidence businessmen had in Moody's new venture in city evangelization. It was "the best, most direct, and most economical means of counteracting . . . rabid socialism"; "the Gospel is the only real remedy for these social and political evils."

(Moody included women in the concept, saying that they might be even more effective), there was something that everyone could do, and God expected everyone to do what he could.[9]

Though the highest form of work was Christian work which above all meant witnessing, all labor was sanctified in Moody's judgment. He consistently and frequently extolled the virtues of hard work, and his solution to the ills of society attendant to the mass immigrations and mushrooming industrialization and urbanization at the end of the century was hard work and honesty. Whatever truth there may have been in his individualistic approach, he failed to see that society was becoming more interdependent and that perhaps some societal and institutional reforms might be necessary. The problems of economic depression, poverty, and labor strife could be solved by honesty and hard work at the individual level.

Though it would be grossly unfair to rule out a priori the possibility of higher motivation (and there is reason to think there was such), it is little wonder that the captains of business and industry were readily enlisted to support Moody and his projects in the most tangible of ways—money. The list of such men included John Farwell, John Wanamaker, William Dodge, J. P. Morgan, Henry Field, George and J. F. Armour, and Cyrus McCormick.[10] What employer would not have delighted to hear Moody say to a group of newly converted men:

> You want to get these employers always under obligation to you. You must be such true men and be so helpful to your employers that they can not get along without you, and then you will work up, and your employer will increase your wages. If a man works in the interest of his employer, he will be sure to keep him and treat him well, but if he only works for money and don't take any interest in his employer's business, he will let him go at any time.[11]

Just as Moody doubted that there was any such thing as a lazy Christian in terms of Christian work, so also he asserted that a true Christian could not be lazy with reference to manual labor; in fact, he doubted that a lazy man could even become a Christian! He had never known a lazy man to be converted and had more hope for drunkards, thieves, and harlots than for a lazy man. It is not surprising, then, to hear

9. *To the Work! To the Work!*, pp. 105, 116.
10. Findlay, *Dwight L. Moody*, pp. 201-2.
11. *New Sermons*, p. 602.

Moody saying that Christians of wealth should give to the poor, but they should not give money or help to the lazy.

Giving material help to the poor was not Moody's major emphasis, though, for such efforts were only stop-gap measures. Poverty might come to a person as a means of driving a person to God, as had happened with the prodigal son. Consequently, those "in actual want, and struggling against poverty," should "press into the kingdom of God before doing anything else." "If men are in want it is because they are not in the kingdom of God. Don't come for the loaves and fishes, but seek Him for what He is." "No one ever saw a true child of God starving in the street; no one ever saw a child of God coming to the poor-house." After all, work was available to those who looked hard enough and were not too particular.[12]

Left at this, Moody's solution to the problem of poverty seems to be simplistic, unsympathetic, and one-sided. It is difficult to clear Moody of the first charge. He failed to appreciate the complexity of the problems arising from industrialization, urbanization, and immigration. Nor did he seem to understand that social structures and institutions could themselves perpetuate evils and injustices. To be content with calling for hard work, conversion, and individual charity toward those in distress was manifestly simplistic; and left at this, the problems tend to get worse.

But Moody was not unsympathetic. He knew well the conditions on Chicago's North Side, and both his early relief work and Sunday school work there stand as testimonials to his concern for those apparently trapped in these circumstances. This concern later surfaced with some frequency in his sermons and was behind the founding of the new school in Chicago in the 1880s. Moody himself well remembered what it was like to be in a strange city without a dollar, and he could feel with those who were in want. But his own experience had taught him that hard work could bring one up from the bottom; he really thought that this was the solution for all others: become a Christian and get to work.

Although Moody's solution was individualistic, it was not one-sided. Findlay says that Moody "never questioned in any ultimate sense the values of the ruthlessly acquisitive society that characterized America

12. Ibid., pp. 90, 248-49, 303-5, 603-5, 609; *Sovereign Grace*, p. 14; *Glad Tidings*, pp. 327-28; "Mr. Moody on Invitation to the Religious Life," undated newspaper clipping from the *Baltimore Sun*, Moodyana.

in his adult years, nor the men who governed that society."[13] If Findlay means that Moody did not question capitalism as a system, he is certainly correct. Nor did Moody seem to have realized that a perversion of the very work ethic he espoused was behind this "ruthlessly acquisitive society."

But if Findlay means that Moody did not question the values of the capitalists, he is wrong. The poor were not the only ones who needed regeneration. The individualistic solution based on spiritual need cut both ways. Moody censured the selfish acquisitiveness of the employers almost as severely as he condemned the laziness and dishonesty of the employees or the unemployed. Moody knew well the boomer spirit of Chicago and cited the "covetousness, the inordinate greed for gain" that had "fastened on the hand of Chicago, along with many another Western city." As would be expected, Moody primarily condemned the spiritual shipwreck that selfish materialism could bring. But he also condemned the deception and fraud that were being practiced. He even asked the employer, "Are you guilty of sweating your employees? Have you deprived the hireling of his wages? Have you paid starvation wages?"[14]

Henry May said that Moody "remained aloof from any discussion of the basic ills of society"; however, it must be remembered that in Moody's judgment the basic ill of society was the need of individual regeneration which would produce moral integrity.[15] "Nations are only collections of individuals, and what is true of a part, in regard to character, is always true of the whole." It had been individual sin that had planted slavery in this country, and both the nation and individuals reaped the consequences. The prison population was made up of individuals; what was needed was regeneration.

The same held for government. "You can't reform government without men who have been themselves reformed, and that reformation must be a regeneration through the power of the Holy Ghost." Why talk about sociological topics in the pulpit? "I say when we have got all the people to repent of their sins and live as God wants them to live, it'll be time to talk about sociological questions." It was unbelief that

13. Findlay, *Dwight L. Moody*, p. 278.

14. *New Sermons*, pp. 11, 86, 90, 443, 466, 468; *Bible Characters*, pp. 20-21, 43, 75-89; *Weighed and Wanting*, pp. 91-92; D. L. Moody, "When Jesus Comes Again," *The Christian Herald*, Dec. 21, 1910 (preached Feb. 2, 1897), p. 1208.

15. May, *Protestant Churches and Industrial America*, p. 83.

was the fundamental cause of social ills, and in the last several years of his life Moody seemed to become even more convinced of the impotency of human efforts and agencies of reform. He characterized such efforts as "patching over," "white-washing a pest house," and "trying to make that stream good while the fountain is bad." With great conviction he told a Boston audience in 1897, "What we want to have is a revival of righteousness, and we shall have 'good times.' "[16]

A discussion of Moody's understanding of work and the life of the believer inevitably leads to a consideration of Moody's social ethic. However, before leaving Moody's concept of work, one other facet deserves mention. James Findlay gives a very helpful survey of the attitudes of American Evangelicals toward work in the second half of the nineteenth century, carefully documenting his study with references from periodical literature.[17] Comparison of Moody's attitudes toward work with the mind-set of American Evangelicals in general reveals a very close correlation, which should not be at all surprising. However, within Moody's sermons there is evidence that he had not merely inherited the Puritan ethic of his New England forefathers nor uncritically adopted the activist attitudes of his fellow Evangelicals.

He frequently referred to those who engaged in Christian work out of mere duty, and he did so in a way that suggests his impatience with a rather prevalent attitude. "I am tired of the word duty," he said. "Tired of hearing duty, duty, duty. Men go to church because it is their duty. They go to prayer meeting because it is their duty." Moody's concept of work was a much more dynamic concept than mere duty. He would have been pleased to see the word banished from the Christian vocabulary.

16. Goss, *Echoes*, p. 224; *New Sermons*, p. 485; "In Temples of God," *Atlanta Journal*, Nov. 16, 1895; "Moody Speaks to a Host," newspaper clipping from an unidentified Chicago newspaper (probably Friday, Apr. 7, 1897), Moodyana; "To Stir up the Churches and Convert Christians," *Detroit Journal*, newspaper clipping simply dated Apr. 1899, Moodyana; "The Moody Meetings," *News* (Providence, R. I.), Jan. 22, 1894; a Moody letter to the *Record of Christian Work*, Nov. 1899, p. 623; "Overcoming Evil" and "Moody on Regeneration," unidentified newspaper clippings from the *Baltimore Sun*, Moodyana; "Regeneration." Address delivered by Mr. D. L. Moody, General Conference, Thursday Evening, August 18, 1898," pp. 5-6 of a typed manuscript, Moodyana; D. L. Moody, "A Sermon on Backsliders," *The Christian Herald*, Sept. 28, 1910, p. 860. For further discussion of Moody's social ethics, see Findlay, *Dwight L. Moody*, pp. 278-85; Dennis L. Olenik, "The Social Philosophy of Dwight L. Moody" (M.A. thesis, Northern Illinois University, 1964), pp. 10-43; Myron Raymond Chartier, *The Social Views of Dwight L. Moody and Their Relation to the Workingman of 1860-1900* (Hays, Kans.: Fort Hays Kansas State College, 1969), pp. 17-34. For a description of the events and conditions that had led many Protestant leaders to call for social reform, see Henry F. May, *Protestant Churches and Industrial America*, pp. 91-135.

17. Findlay, *Dwight L. Moody*, pp. 81-84, 274-75.

He warned new converts that if the inner life was not right, the outer life would not be right for long. The Word must come before work. Nor was this to be a mere mechanical ritual, for the Holy Spirit was needed to illumine the Word and to produce within the heart the one and only adequate motive of work, love. All work is for naught that does not come from the inner spring of love. The lack of success in the churches is the lack of love. The powerlessness of sermons is the absence of love. What atheist could not be won by love? Love is the badge of the Christian, but it is worn on the heart. The person who has it does not need to talk about it; he will simply show it in his life. "We cannot work for God without love." But, "the moment the love of God is shed in our hearts, my friends, we cannot help loving Him and working for Him." Findlay correctly observes, "The sure confirmation of that assertion appeared in his own career and in his personal attitudes toward his daily tasks."[18]

THE HOLY SPIRIT AND THE BELIEVER

If the Christian life is essentially a life of work spontaneously springing from the motive of love, it is the Holy Spirit who produces that love within and "empowers for service." The initial work of regeneration creating a new nature alongside the old Adam nature was the work of the Holy Spirit. Consequently, every truly converted person has the Spirit dwelling within from the moment of regeneration, the body having become the temple of the Holy Spirit. Furthermore, the Spirit who regenerates and indwells also seals and testifies, thus securing the believer until the day of redemption and giving assurance to the believer.[19]

But that was not the end of the matter for Moody, for he held that while the Holy Spirit established this permanent relationship with the believer at the point of conversion, something more from the Spirit was needed for effective Christian work. That "something more" was the "Holy Spirit upon us for service." One must proceed cautiously when examining Moody's statements on this matter, for it is all too easy to impose upon Moody's statements a meaning that he did not intend. The

18. Ibid., p. 249; *New Sermons*, pp. 277-78, 642-43; *Glad Tidings*, pp. 55-56, 60, 326-27; *Secret Power*, p. 17; *To the Work*, pp. 23-40; *Great Joy*, pp. 33-43, "Address delivered by Mr. D. L. Moody, General Conference, Saturday Evening, August 12, 1899," pp. 9-10 of a typed manuscript, Moodyana.
19. *New Sermons*, pp. 284-86; *Glad Tidings*, pp. 285-86; *Secret Power*, pp. 31-35, 44-46; *Thou Fool*, pp. 31-32; "Power in and Upon," *Journal* (New Bedford, Mass.), Oct. 8, 1895; "The Holy Spirit," *Daily Inter-Ocean* (Chicago), Nov. 11, 1896.

vocabulary he was using to describe this experience was being used by other American Evangelicals at the same time with different connotations, namely, the various strains of the perfectionist and/or holiness movements of the nineteenth century.

As an example, one can cite Findlay's description and analysis of Moody's 1871 experience of baptism by the Holy Spirit. Findlay repeatedly refers to it as Moody's second conversion experience.[20] This is terminology that Moody never used and which expresses a concept in direct contradiction to what he preached. There was one conversion or new birth by which a new nature was created and a permanent relationship established. Moody himself seldom went into the details of his 1871 experience, or at least existing sermons seldom give the details. But on those rare occasions when he did he described it as a filling, a baptism, or an anointing that came upon him when he was in a cold state. His selfish ambitions in preaching had been surrendered, and he then received power by which to do his work for Christ.[21]

In his frequent expositions of the topic to Christians, surrender to God's will with consequent empowering for service was the controlling theme and almost the exclusive emphasis. He used biblically derived terminology to refer to this divine enabling, such as anointing, unction, baptism by the Spirit, and filling. But the characteristically descriptive phrase, used synonymously with all of the above terms, was empowering for service. Some of Moody's contemporaries did not accept the necessity or validity of this kind of an experience, whereas others interpreted such experiences as an eradication of the old nature or as effecting an entire sanctification. Moody alluded to those who tried to straighten him out on the subject, but for Moody it had none of the latter connotations and was fundamentally a matter of receiving the power of the Holy Spirit for service and of leaving behind human ambition and fleshly efforts.[22]

The similarity of Moody's terminology to that of modern Pente-

20. Findlay, *Dwight L. Moody*, pp. 131-33; cf. pp. 113, 121, 219-22.
21. *Glad Tidings*, pp. 471-72; *New Sermons*, p. 274.
22. Extended discussions and incidental references to this concept abound in Moody's sermons and question-and-answer periods, reflecting not only the importance Moody put on the matter but also the interest which the topic had for Moody's contemporaries. The best and most readily accessible of Moody's discussions are in: *Thou Fool*, pp. 31-50; *Secret Power*, especially pp. 31-54; *To All People*, pp. 54-61; *College Students at Northfield* (1888, ed. Shanks), pp. 175-84, 205-6; *Glad Tidings*, pp. 284-92. These sources indicate that Moody's explanations did not significantly change between the mid-1870s and the late 1890s, in spite of his sympathies with the Keswick movement; see pp. 159-60.

costalism has led some to suggest that Moody was not only a forerunner of the movement, but that he also advocated and engaged in that distinctly Pentecostal phenomenon, speaking in tongues as the evidence of the Spirit's baptism.[23] More often than not, the point is found raised today in conversations among Pentecostal and non-Pentecostal Evangelicals, letters to the editor, and the popular press on the basis of hearsay evidence. The facts are, though, that there is no place in the great mass of published Moody sermons and comments where he either suggested that he had spoken in tongues or where he advocated speaking in tongues. In none of the many places where he discussed empowering for service did he make a connection between baptism by the Spirit and tongues speaking.

On the rare occasions when he referred to tongues in the New Testament, he hardly did so in the manner of a glossolalist. The "new tongues" of Mark 16:17 he interpreted as tongues that were not slanderous. On one occasion he applied Paul's prohibition of speaking in unknown tongues to choirs which sing such fine, operatic music in church that no one understands, so that all but the select few go to sleep! On still another occasion he saw a parallel between the tongues of Acts 2 and the new eloquence and power that ministers who had received power for service had.[24] Moody's exegesis can obviously be questioned, but that he did not take a Pentecostal interpretation of these passages cannot be questioned.

23. Stanley Howard Frodsham, *With Signs Following* (Springfield, Mo.: Gospel Pub., 1946), pp. 9-10. Recently, Donald W. Dayton, librarian of North Park Seminary, Chicago, and a graduate student at the University of Chicago, has been investigating the origins of Pentecostalism. Most students of Pentecostalism have sought for antecedents of its most unusual feature, glossolalia; and it has been generally recognized that Pentecostalism has its roots in the nineteenth-century holiness movement. However, Dayton is attempting to trace more specifically the rise of the complex of theological ideas that constitute Pentecostalism. He has concentrated on what he believes was a shift in emphasis from a Christocentric exposition of Christian perfection at mid-century to "baptism of the Holy Ghost language" by the 1870s. He sees Asa Mahan, first president of Oberlin College, as a key figure in this shift; Mahan's two books, *The Scripture Doctrine of Christian Perfection* (1839) and *The Baptism of the Holy Ghost* (1870) illustrate this shift. I am indebted to Mr. Dayton for copies of papers he has written on the subject. The first, "Asa Mahan and the Development of American Holiness Theology," was read at the Wesleyan Theological Society, Asbury Theological Seminary, on Nov. 2, 1973; a condensed version appeared in the *Wesleyan Theological Journal* 9 (Spring 1974): 60-69. The second, "From 'Christian Perfection' to 'Baptism of the Holy Ghost': A Study in the Origin of Pentecostalism," was read at The Society for Pentecostal Studies, Nov. 30, 1973, Lee College, Cleveland, Tenn.; it is to be published in *Aspects of Pentecostalism*, ed. H. Vinson Synan. At present, Dayton's conclusions are tentative, but his discussion of the subject sheds light on the evangelical milieu as it involved perfectionism and baptism of the Holy Ghost in the second half of the nineteenth century.

24. *New Sermons*, p. 587; *To All People*, p. 424; *Secret Power*, p. 110; Daniels, *Moody: His Words, Work, and Workers*, p. 399.

The closest link that can be established between Moody and the tongues phenomenon is a report that in the fall of 1873 in Sunderland, England, Moody addressed the local YMCA on a Sunday afternoon; that evening the reporter told of coming into a meeting where the young men were speaking in tongues and prophesying. However, Moody was not in that evening meeting and only a few weeks later Moody and Sankey were being warmly received in Scotland precisely because their brand of revivalism did not cater to such phenomena as had sometimes characterized earlier awakenings. He discouraged all displays of what he considered excess emotion. If someone would cry out uncontrollably or swoon, Moody would call for the singing of a song while the person was taken out, or he might even abruptly conclude the meeting. The report of an observer at Stockton-on-Tees in early November, 1873, is well worth quoting:

> Another important feature was the *absence of noise* in the meetings. The experience of the past few days in Stockton will, we think, have convinced them that the best and most successful prayer-meetings held in Stockton have been the quietest, reminding us of the old lady's description, "God Almighty was so near that nobody had to shout to Him."[25]

Equally in error is the temptation to put Moody simplistically in the perfectionist movement of the nineteenth century on the basis of shared terminology. William McLoughlin could hardly have made a more glaring mistake than when he said that Finney and Moody shared the "perfectionist belief that a truly converted Christian is free from sin and all its temptations." Even Findlay, whose discussion is more careful, wavers between saying Moody was a latent perfectionist or was led along the road to perfectionism and suspecting that Moody would have denied perfectionist beliefs.[26] Unjustifiably, Findlay felt Moody's public statements on the matter were ambiguous and that his emphasis on separation from worldliness bent Moody in a perfectionist direction.

25. Hall, *The American Evangelists, D. L. Moody and Ira D. Sankey, In Great Britain and Ireland*, p. 30. The account of the Sunderland incident and later reports of Moody and Sankey in Scotland is found in several sources with some obvious plagiarism involved: Robert Boyd, *The Wonderful Career of Moody and Sankey, In Great Britain and America* (New York: Henry S. Goodspeed, 1875), pp. 402, 425, 447, 459, 464; Daniels, *D L. Moody and His Work*, 1875, pp. 247-48, 313; Goodspeed, *Wonderful Career of Moody*, 1876, pp. 61-62, 85, 107, 119, 124. For express mention of the absence of excitement in Edinburgh, see "The Awakening in Edinburgh," *The Christian*, Jan. 29, 1874, p. 3.
26. McLoughlin, *Modern Revivalism*, p. 169; Findlay, *Dwight L. Moody*, pp. 245-46.

Findlay's conclusions from Moody's stance on worldliness point up a problem of definition that should be recognized before the discussion goes any further. What was perfectionism? What was the holiness movement? What was the Keswick movement? To say that separation from worldliness tends to perfectionism is to forget that such antiworldly attitudes have been a part of American religion since the days of the Puritans, quite apart from the nineteenth-century perfectionists. Furthermore, it is to forget that, historically, perfectionists have been subject to the charge of antinomianism and have sometimes actually moved in that direction.

The point is that the religious perfectionist tendencies of nineteenth-century America (and England) do not present a homogeneous face. They reflect in varying degrees the optimistic, romantic mind of the age and differing theological motifs such as postmillennialism, Oberlin perfectionism, Wesleyan perfectionism, and John Humphrey Noyes' antinomian perfectionism. And in Moody's early years there were the innovations of William E. Boardman, Walter and Phoebe Palmer, and Hannah and Robert Pearsall Smith. And one should not forget the rise and evolution of the Keswick movement.

It is beyond the scope of this study to trace these strands of and developments out of perfectionism in the nineteenth century with their interweaving and influence upon one another. Timothy Smith and Whitney Cross have given splendid treatments of different aspects of the phenomenon; and B. B. Warfield's massive work, though marked by his own theological biases, still is a standard in the field.[27] The point to be made here is that before one attributes perfectionism to Moody, he should define what is meant by the allegation and recognize the different streams. Such precision becomes much less critical, though, if it can be shown that there is no ground for ascribing any kind of perfectionism to Moody.

Findlay refers to a few statements made by Moody indicating that the new nature cannot sin.[28] Actually, Findlay could have cited Moody statements sounding much more perfectionistic. Such statements in-

27. Whitney R. Cross, *The Burned Over District: The Social and Intellectual History of Enthusiastic Religion in Western New York, 1800-1850* (New York: Harper & Row, 1950), pp. 238-51; Smith, *Revivalism and Social Reform*, pp. 103-47; Timothy L. Smith, *Called Unto Holiness: The Story of the Nazarenes: The Formative Years* (Kansas City, Mo., 1962), pp. 11-26; Benjamin Breckinridge Warfield, *Perfectionism*, vol. 2 (New York: Oxford U., 1931).
28. Findlay, *Dwight L. Moody*, p. 245.

clude allusions to being delivered from sin; Christ keeping from sin day by day; Christ delivering from all sin, all appetite, and all lust; and the new birth taking away sin and the desire for it and giving victory.[29] However, in nearly every instance which could be cited, Moody also makes some affirmation of the continuance of the old Adam nature within the immediate context. He would affirm that the old man was not dead and that Christ knows the believer by his defects. Such statements applied only to the new nature and the basis of victory over the old nature that it provided. However, the old nature remained and one could not necessarily expect perfect victory over it.

Here it is necessary to recall Moody's doctrine of regeneration. Regeneration gives birth to a new nature but does not alter the old nature. In one of his earliest extant statements on the subject (Edinburgh, Jan. 16, 1874), he affirmed that the flesh was not changed at conversion, so that a continual warfare goes on between the flesh and the spirit. The flesh is unchanged and unchangeable and is not dropped until the grave or until Christ returns.[30] Nearly every time Moody preached on the new birth he referred in the clearest of terms to the conflict that continually went on between the two natures, often affirming that he himself was a saved sinner who still sinned. He said he had more trouble with D. L. Moody than any other man. He found something to repent of every day. And Moody's statements between 1874 and at least 1897 do not change on this matter. He would often bring Romans 7 into the discussion, interpreting the conflict there portrayed as that which the believer experiences between the old and the new nature. At this point he was in obvious opposition to Finney's understanding of Romans 7.[31]

There is another theological subtlety that should be brought into focus at this point, and that is the matter of postmillennialism versus premillennialism. There is a compatibility between perfectionism in its

29. *New Sermons*, pp. 223-24, 263-64, 266, 273, 584-85; "Ninety-First Psalm. Address delivered by Mr. D. L. Moody, Young Women's Conference, Saturday Evening, July 15, 1899," p. 3 of a typed manuscript, Moodyana.

30. Hall, *The American Evangelists, D. L. Moody and Ira D. Sankey, In Great Britain and Ireland*, p. 433. Cf. pp. 123-24.

31. *Glad Tidings*, pp. 95, 236, 363, 365; Shanks, ed., *College Students at Northfield* (1888), pp. 85-86; *New Sermons*, pp. 123, 128, 259, 584-85; *To All People*, pp. 421-22; Shanks, ed., *A College of Colleges* (1887), pp. 243-44; D. L. Moody, "New Things in the Kingdom," *The Christian Herald*, Mar. 30, 1910 (preached Feb. 19, 1897), pp. 311-12. Cf. Charles G. Finney, *Lectures to Professing Christians* (Oberlin, Ohio: E. J. Goodrich, 1879), originally delivered in 1836-37, pp. 320-38.

various forms and postmillennialism with its optimistic aspirations of bringing to fruition God's Kingdom on earth before Christ's personal return; there is a basic incompatibility between perfectionism and pre-millennialism and its mediately pessimistic view that righteousness will not finally prevail, that is, God's Kingdom rule, until Christ Himself returns to set up His Kingdom on earth. More than one author has noted this correlation.[32] This probably explains in part why very few Methodists in either the nineteenth or twentieth centuries have been attracted by premillennial theology. One finds Finney linking his per-fectionism with his postmillennial hopes.[33] And by the same token, Moody denies that perfection is possible for the Christian, and relates that to his premillennialism![34]

Divorcing Moody from the perfectionist strands accords well with other available clues. For instance, the May 12, 1870, issue of *The Advance* (Chicago) complains of those who have been riding the hobby of the theory of perfection in the YMCA meetings. It is not clear that Moody is the one complaining, but his leadership in the local "Y" makes it likely that it truly reflected his views. In early 1874 R. Pearsall Smith and W. E. Boardman were in the British Isles preach-ing their views of entire sanctification. *The Christian*, which carried notices of their meetings throughout the year, also reported a statement by Moody which was critical of those who were always emphasizing the "higher Christian life."[35] John Farwell was later to recall Moody's annoyance with Smith's preaching of entire sanctification in the famous Brighton meetings.[36]

The influences of Boardman, the Smiths, and the Brighton conven-tion eventually issued in the Keswick movement with its distinctive emphasis on Christian holiness.[37] Moody's later sympathies with the Keswick movement and his invitations to Keswick-type speakers to the Northfield platform are well known.[38] However, it must be remembered that in the early days when the embryonic movement was still feeling

32. McLoughlin, *Modern Revivalism*, pp. 103-5; Smith, *Revivalism and Social Reform*, pp. 148-62; Sandeen, *Roots of Fundamentalism*, pp. 141, 163, 177.
33. Finney, *Lectures to Professing Christians*, pp. 339-44, 352.
34. *New Sermons*, p. 373; *To All People*, p. 511.
35. *The Christian*, May 7, 1874, p. 292; cf. Feb. 5, p. 12; July 16, p. 469; Aug. 13, p. 523.
36. Farwell, *Early Recollections of Dwight L. Moody*, pp. 110-11, 116.
37. For a helpful history of the early years of the movement and its distinctives, see J. C. Pollock, *The Keswick Story* (Chicago: Moody, 1964), pp. 11-79.
38. Ibid., pp. 116-19; Sandeen, *Roots of Fundamentalism*, pp. 176-81; Findlay, *Dwight L. Moody*, pp. 341-43, 407-8.

its way along, Moody remained aloof, if not critical, of its perfectionist tendencies and language. Much is often made of the fact that Moody sent a word of cordial greeting to the Brighton convention on its opening day.[39] But this must be balanced by Moody's earlier and later criticism of Smith's emphasis. It was only when the Keswick movement repudiated the concept of eradication of inward sin and substituted an emphasis on the Holy Spirit's power to lead away from sin that Moody began to really feel comfortable with Keswick teaching and people.[40] In the 1880s and 1890s, as the movement gradually achieved some theological maturity with a stress on holiness of life without straying in the direction of perfectionism, Moody's transatlantic connections with Keswick became closer, with Moody even preaching at the Keswick convention in 1892.[41] However, Moody never allowed it to become a hobby horse, and in the presence of Keswick leaders, Moody said, "I dare not make any professions of being holy."[42]

39. Steven Barabas, *So Great Salvation: The History and Message of the Keswick Convention* (Westwood: N. J.: Revell, n.d.), pp. 23-24.
40. Sandeen, *Roots of Fundamentalism*, p. 179; Pollock, *The Keswick Story*, pp. 66-67; Smith, *Called unto Holiness*, p. 25. It should be added that this shift made the Keswick teaching acceptable to American premillennialists.
41. This took place largely under the influence of Bishop Handley C. G. Moule. See Pollock, *The Keswick Story*, pp. 64-76.
42. Ibid., pp. 66-67.

8

THE BEST INSTITUTION UNDER HEAVEN

IT IS IRONIC that there has been a more adequate treatment of Moody's ecclesiology in books about Moody than of any other aspect of his theology. The fact that it is so ironic is because Moody said so little about the Church and attempted to avoid those matters of theological dispute that led to ecclesiastical division and denominational barriers, or as he put it, "this miserable sectarian spirit."[1] He was especially reticent to commit himself on such matters of obvious denominational difference as baptism and church polity.

But it is the very fact of Moody's relative silence on the Church and his practice of cooperative interdenominational evangelism which accounts for the recent interest in Moody's ecclesiology, such as it is. The Oxford dissertation of John Wesley White focuses on the effects of Moody's cooperative evangelism and on his contacts with men and movements which were the forerunners of twentieth-century ecumenism. James Findlay's biography deals more with the broad scope of Moody's relationships with churches, both in his personal experience and in his evangelistic campaigns, with only a brief discussion of his doctrine of the Church. Stan Nussbaum's recent thesis specifically treats Moody's doctrine of the Church with special reference to the possible influence this may have had on the ecclesiology of twentieth-century Evangelicals. Although his work is unduly colored by his own biases and marred by lapses of research in some areas, Nussbaum's specific exposition of Moody's ecclesiology is the most serious study to

1. *Great Joy*, p. 19.

date.[2] In the work of all three men the same themes are clearly heard: the primacy of evangelism in Moody's work, his avoidance of divisive questions, and his ecumenism in both spirit and practice.[3]

In the midst of these recent and helpful treatments of Moody's ecclesiology, I have not intended to plow the same ground again, at least not in the same direction. Instead I have related Moody's statements and practice with reference to the Church to what has already been described as his proclamation theology. This will serve as a corrective to some misplaced emphases in previous studies. Special attention is given to what Moody said in explanation of what he was doing, a point at which other studies are noticeably weak. Moody's statements of his own ecclesiology were intentionally vague and were so infrequent and occasional as not to be readily apparent. But a few statements are in the published materials as well as typed manuscripts.

Moody's ecclesiological statements defy systematic arrangement, for they are ad hoc statements which never occur in the context of an extended discussion of the Church. As a consequence of this and of his purposeful silence on divisive questions, a discussion of Moody's expressed doctrine of the Church will be characterized by many gaps. Thus, the arrangement of his statements in a study of this nature becomes quite arbitrary. However, whatever order and method are followed, Moody's statements about the Church must always be seen from the combined perspectives of his personal Congregationalism, his interdenominational evangelism, and the general framework of voluntaristic American denominationalism.[4]

THE CHURCH AND SALVATION

The thing that Moody's audiences heard him say most frequently about the Church was that no church, nor its ordinances, could save a person. "Mark me, all the churches in Christendom never saved a soul," Moody would declare. "Don't think joining a church is going to save you." He warned against what he understood to be the exclusivistic

---

2. See pp. 14-15.
3. Findlay, *Dwight L. Moody*, pp. 64, 75, 80, 109-10, 118-19, 125-27, 161-68, 206, 246-48, 262-74, 294, 304-5, 354-55, 371-72; White, "The Influence of North American Evangelism in Great Britain between 1830 and 1914 on the Origin and Development of the Ecumenical Movement," especially chaps. 2 and 3; Nussbaum, "D. L. Moody and the Church," pp. 63-102.
4. See pp. 28-31. Nussbaum fills in these gaps with conjecture, with no documentation or with secondary documentation of dubious value; his chap. 7, pp. 82-94, is typical.

claims of Roman Catholics, Baptists, Episcopalians, Presbyterians, and Methodists, suggesting that too many listened to the voice of the church rather than the voice of God. "It is the Son of God who is the Saviour of the world." Moody's sermons on the new birth or regeneration almost invariably warned that it was not to be confused with church membership or participation in the ordinances (sometimes he spoke of the sacraments).

Moody would often hasten to add that "forms and ordinances are all very good, but they do not make a new creature." "They are not Christ." "Ordinances and salvation are things apart and have nothing to do one with the other." Though Moody would affirm the value of the ordinances in that Christ had commanded their observance, he never specifically stated what their value or significance really was. It may even be questioned whether he had an accurate understanding of denominational distinctives on these points. For instance, he apparently believed Baptists taught that immersion was necessary to salvation when, in fact, Baptists did not and argued with "Campbellites" on this very point.

Be that as it may, as a matter of practicality, Moody was convinced that many of his hearers had misplaced their hope of salvation in the Church and its ordinances. This reveals the controlling idea in his statements about the Church and its ordinances. He would avoid preaching for or against denominational distinctives so as not to detract from the centrality of the Gospel as he understood it; but he would repudiate any suggestion that either the Church or its ordinances had any salvatory efficacy, even if it offended the denominational scruples of some. It is significant that in Baltimore he explicitly spoke against transubstantiation and the idea that "spiritual life" or "salvation" is in either baptism or the Lord's Supper. In Dublin he spoke against the confessional and priestly absolution.[5] Moody was not anti-Roman Catholic in sentiment and tried to avoid offending Catholics, but only so far as his understanding of the Gospel would allow.

Consistent with his warnings against trusting in the Church to obtain salvation for oneself, Moody also warned that the churches cannot help

---

5. *New Sermons*, pp. 121, 224, 268-69, 583; "Moody and Sankey," *Daily Courant* (Hartford, Conn.), Jan. 28, 1878; "Moody's Ministrations," *Daily Inter-Ocean* (Chicago), Nov. 9, 1876; "The Bread and the Wine" and "Mr. Moody's View of Churches and Ordinances," undated newspaper clippings from the *Baltimore Sun*, Moodyana; "Convention of Ministers of the Gospel," *Daily Express* (Dublin), Nov. 25, 1874.

keep one in the way of salvation. The preceding discussion makes the reasons for his saying this obvious. Salvation is wholly of God, and it is the Son of God who keeps the believer.[6] Why then did Moody not divorce his work from the work of the churches, and why did he urge new converts to affiliate with some church?

The Church and the Believer

Moody's statement that the Church does not keep a person is in his farewell sermon delivered in Boston in 1877. But in that very sermon, within just a few moments of this warning, Moody strongly and lengthily urged the new converts to affiliate with some church. And as usual he urged them to do so because the church was a place to work; in fact, it was from this very sermon that many of Moody's comments about work cited in chapter 7 were drawn.[7] As indicated there, the church's significance for the believer was that, first and foremost, it is the place for the believer to work. Moody did not speak so much of joining a church or of becoming a member of a church as of going into church work or finding some work in a church. Sometimes he would cite what he identified as "John Wesley's definition of a church—'All at it, and always at it.' Every Christian ought to be a worker."[8] In fact, one of the basic criteria to consider in searching for a church home was whether or not it gave one something to do, and if the first church did not have work to be done, try a second and a third. If this failed, one could generate his own work either within or without a church, as Moody himself had done.

Moody justified his revival meetings by arguing that sometimes God has to work outside the regular channels to get the work done. But he maintained that the revival work begun in his meetings should be carried back to the churches so that the work would not end when the meetings did.[9] Although Moody did not make frequent public statements on this matter, it followed quite naturally that he did not think the unregenerate should be admitted into church membership. Not

6. *New Sermons*, p. 637.
7. See pp. 144-53.
8. D. L. Moody, *The Overcoming Life and Other Sermons* (New York: Revell, 1896), p. 119.
9. *New Sermons*, pp. 91, 574-78, 638-39; *To the Work! To the Work!*, pp. 14-15; "Questions answered by Mr. Moody, at General Conference, Tuesday Afternoon, August 16, 1898" and "Questions and Answers, General Conference, Wednesday Morning, August 2, 1899," typed manuscripts, Moodyana.

only might the unbeliever put a false hope in the church, but the very nature of the church was that it was the place where believers worked, that is, witnessed.[10]

But this by no means exhausts Moody's understanding of the church's relationship to the believer. Just as it would be wrong to say that Moody's concept of the Christian life was exclusively activistic without reference to quality, so it would be wrong to conclude that the church was only a place to work. He spoke of the Church as the "nursing mother of all Christians." He warned the newly converted that they could not sustain themselves outside of a church. Indeed, he even warned that pastoral ministry should not be merely evangelistic; the flock must be fed, and this ministry was just as important, if not more important, than evangelism. By the same token the services of a church should be of three types: worship, edification of believers, and evangelism.[11]

Moody was apparently not too concerned what kind of a church his converts chose so long as it was an evangelical church that provided the opportunity to work. To have done anything else would have alienated his supporters. Once he suggested that Jesus is the way, "and if we follow His footsteps we will be in the right Church." As for himself, he said he would rather be of Paul's persuasion than a Baptist, Methodist, or Presbyterian. Besides, there was not a "snap of the fingers" difference among them; they nearly all believed the same thing.[12]

But he did warn against trying to find a perfect church, and in so doing he seemed to be warning against the separatism and exclusivism practiced by the Plymouth Brethren. Moody had been influenced by individual Brethren and had sympathy with some of their distinctive teachings. But he, like so many other American Evangelicals, adopted their dispensationalism without adopting their exclusivistic ecclesiology.

Instead, he advised to find a church and be loyal to it. "Most any one can tear down. What we want is to build up, and if the church is not

10. "Thursday Afternoon, August 18, 1898, Quesitons and Answers at General Conference," typed manuscript, Moodyana; "The Bread and Wine," *Baltimore Sun*, undated newspaper clipping, Moodyana.
11. *New Sermons*, p. 576; Shanks, ed., *College Students at Northfield* (1888), p. 182; "Questions answered by Mr. Moody, at General Conference, Tuesday Afternoon, August 16, 1898," typed manuscript, Moodyana; "Moody and Sankey," *Daily Courant* (Hartford, Conn.), Jan. 28, 1878; *New York Witness Extra*, Mar. 29, 1876; *Signs of Our Times*, Mar. 10, 1875, p. 149.
12. *New Sermons*, pp. 269, 637; "Questions and Answers, Wednesday Afternoon, August 17, 1898," typed manuscript, Moodyana.

what it ought to be let us try and purify it—do what we can to make it
better." Those truly born of God would want to be identified with the
Church of God. "It is not only a duty but a glorious privilege to be in
the bosom of some church."[13] Estimates vary as to the long-range benefits realized by the churches from Moody's campaigns, but there can be
no doubt that Moody's intention was that his work should contribute to
that of the churches.[14]

THE CHURCH AND ITS MINISTERS

Nussbaum briefly argues that Moody did not experience any special
call to Christian ministry and that in Moody's judgment no special call
was necessary, at least no special call to an evangelistic ministry of
Moody's sort.[15] Moody's failure to seek ordination and his insistence
that he simply be called Mister Moody lend some credence to Nussbaum's suggestion. Also, his emphasis on every believer's responsibility
to work might seem to suggest that Moody thought that every Christian
should give his life to evangelism as he had done. Even his concept of
"gap-men" or irregulars and bushwhackers, that is, unordained laymen
with only a basic training in the English Bible, suggests the possibility
that Moody depreciated the importance of the educated and ordained
clergy and minimized the importance of a special call to Christian
ministry.[16]

However, one should not read too much into the fact that Moody
never sought ordination. A very practical consideration was that he
probably realized that he could not have passed any sort of rigorous
ordination examination. Ordination would have given him an un-
wanted denominational identity. Furthermore, he was an evangelist
and never claimed to be more than that.

Even though he was the dominant personality and guiding light in
his Chicago Sunday school and church, he was not its pastor and made
no pretensions of being such. Nor should one conclude too much from
the gap-men concept. Moody felt that there were lay people who could

13. *Glad Tidings*, p. 453; *Great Redemption*, pp. 470-71; J. M. (Mrs. J. McKinnon), *Recollections of D. L. Moody* (printed for private circulation, 1905), p. 65; Sandeen, *Roots of
Fundamentalism*, p. 101; Hall, *The American Evangelists*, pp. 294-95.
14. Findlay, *Dwight L. Moody*, pp. 262-302; William Garden Blaikie, *The Religious Awakening in Edinburgh, in Connection with the Visit of Messrs. Moody and Sankey* (Manchester:
n.p., 1874), p. 7.
15. Nussbaum, "D. L. Moody and the Church," p. 49.
16. See pp. 147-49.

relate to the unchurched masses in the cities in a manner that the clergy could not. But these people had not been sufficiently trained for this work in the churches; the Bible institute in Chicago would train such people, both men and women. That some people at that time and later interpreted this as a repudiation of an educated and ordained ministry is understandable; but Moody specifically denied these suggestions and said that more ministers were needed with a full seminary education. The gap-men were gap-fillers between the clergy and the laity, which in itself affirmed the clerical office.[17]

The idea of lay preachers was not new either to the American or English scene, as Findlay rightly points out. But Moody adapted the concept to urban evangelism and wanted to provide them with some formal training. Likewise, there had been a historic rivalry between the settled, ordained ministry and evangelists, especially lay evangelists. However, Moody had no intention of fanning these fires or of undermining the position of the ordained minister.

Some very clear indications of Moody's positive attitude toward the ministry also exist. In his meetings he sought the cooperation of the local ministers and turned the new converts over to their care. He did not engage in the kind of diatribe against ministers for which George Whitefield became infamous. And in the presence of ordained ministers he took the attitude of the learner, at least on matters of Bible and theology. At the Northfield conferences, he did not monopolize the platform but rather called in well-known professors and clergymen to speak. On the matter of ordination to the ministry he was silent, perhaps because this would have involved him in denominational disputes. But on the necessity of a divine call to the ministry he could hardly have been more clear, in spite of what Nussbaum has said.

Moody made a distinction between those who are called to be disciples and those who are called to the ministry. All are called to be disciples, "but we are not all called to give up our occupation and devote our whole time to the ministry." Moody said he never advised a person to go into the ministry; "it is too high a calling, it seems to me, for men to be influencing one another to go into it." He warned the college students assembled at Northfield in 1888 that "no man ought to go into

17. Shanks, ed., *A College of Colleges* (1887), pp. 212-13; cf. Findlay, *Dwight L. Moody,* pp. 328-29.

the ministry unless he is forced into it by the Spirit of God." The year
before he had told a similar group:

> Some young men look down upon the ministry; but I tell you to be a
> herald of the cross—to be appointed by God to preach the Gospel—is
> the highest position offered to any mortal. I have not doubt that men
> have come to this convention that look down upon the ministry; but
> I tell you, if a man is called by God, and qualified by God, and sent
> into the Christian ministry, he will be heard of not only in this life, but
> in the life to come—he will shine not only in time, but in eternity.[18]

THE CHURCH AND SECTARIANISM

It has become common to speak of Moody's ecumenical spirit and of
the influence that he had on what came to be the ecumenical movement
in the twentieth century. John Pollock identifies the two chief springs
of the movement as the Northfield Conference of 1885 and the student
conference of 1886, held in the neighboring Mount Hermon School.
The streams from these two springs flowed together, says Pollock, under
John R. Mott's chairmanship of the Edinburgh Conference of 1910.
John R. Mott himself had been deeply influenced by Moody. But there
is more that qualifies Moody for Pollock's appellation, "grandfather of
ecumenism," for the Moody and Sankey campaigns themselves "were
the strongest force for Christian unity in the nineteenth century."[19]
Pollock's eulogistic description needs to be balanced with consideration
of other trends that parallel and antedate Moody and his influence, but
he is quite right in identifying Moody as a significant force for Christian
unity in the late nineteenth century.[20] We turn now to Moody's concern
for such unity with the hope that such a consideration will both illumine
Moody's spirit and the purpose and basis of Christian unity as conceived
by this man who was such a force in the embryonic stages of Christian
ecumenism.

Moody decried any and all forms of what he called a "party spirit."

18. *To All People*, p. 279; Shanks, ed., *College Students at Northfield* (1888), pp. 223-24;
Shanks, ed., *A College of Colleges* (1887), p. 217; cf. *Sermons and Addresses, Question
Drawer*, p. 1013.
19. J. C. Pollock, "Dwight L. Moody—Grandfather of Ecumenism," *Christianity Today*
7 (Nov. 23, 1962): 189-90.
20. Cf. Smith, *Revivalism and Social Reform*, pp. 95-102; White, "The Influence of North
American Evangelism in Great Britain between 1830 and 1914 on the Origin and Development of the Ecumenical Movement," the entire dissertation is relative to this point; Nussbaum, "D. L. Moody and the Church," pp. 74-81; Carter, *The Spiritual Crisis of the Gilded
Age*, pp. 181-85, 190-98.

Manifestations of this spirit were especially scandalous to Moody because he felt that it was nothing more than petty bickering over inconsequential matters. This consumed the energies of the churches and distracted them from the fundamental work of evangelism. In addition, such bickering and lack of love among Christians had become a matter of disrepute before the world so that again the Church was hindered in its witness to the Gospel. Unity was not conceived so much as an end in itself, but rather as essential to evangelism.

Moody did not suggest that sectarian divisions could be erased, but he was bold enough to suggest that they could be forgotten in carrying out the responsibility to evangelize, and no one prior to him had been so successful in bringing together Christians in a spirit of unity for this purpose.[21] One of the first emphases to come out early in his campaigns was that unity, which meant praying and working together, was essential to the success of the meetings; and if he felt matters had gone well, at the close of the series he would refer gratefully to the unity that had prevailed, as he did in his closing prayer in Boston in 1877: "We would thank Thee for the Spirit of harmony which has prevailed among the various denominations, and that the hearts of their members have been bound together in the carrying on of the great work of the revival." He might refer to "this miserable sectarian spirit that once held despotic hold on men," as he did when beginning meetings in Chicago; and then he would appeal that no such spirit mar this meeting:

> Talk not of this sect and that sect, of this party and that party, but solely and exclusively of the great comprehensive cause of Jesus Christ. . . . In this ideal brotherhood there should be one faith, one mind, one spirit, and in this city let us starve it out for a season, to actualize this glorious truth. . . . Oh, that God may so fill us with His love, and the love of souls, that no thought of minor sectarian parties can come in; that there may be no room for them in our atmosphere whatever; and that the Spirit of God may give us one mind and one spirit here to glorify His holy name.[22]

21. Though Finney sometimes seemed to provoke as much disunity as unity, he had earlier insisted on unity as the prerequisite for revival; cf. *Lectures on Revivals of Religion*, pp. 267-70, 290. For an example of Moody's influence on union movements in Scotland, see Rufus W. Clark, *The Work of God in Great Britain: Under Messrs. Moody and Sankey, 1873 to 1875* (New York: Harper & Bros., 1875), pp. 172-75.

22. *London Discourses*, p. 8; *New Sermons*, pp. 644-45, 13-15; cf. pp. 40, 618, 643-44 and *Great Joy*, p. 19.

From the beginning to the end of his career in evangelism, Moody expressed the hope that the sectarian walls would be broken down, so that all one would ask of another would be, "Are you washed in the blood?" He even censured the antisectarian sects that said, "Come out!" Moody said, "*Stay in,*" rather than create another sect. Some of the most eloquent passages in Moody's sermons are these appeals for Christian unity. On one occasion he raised this possibility:

> Suppose Paul and Cephas were to come down to us now, they would hear at once about our Churchmen and Dissenters. "A Dissenter!" says Paul, "what is that?" "We have a Church of England, and there are those who dissent from the Church." "Oh, indeed! Are there two classes of Christians here, then?" "I am sorry to say there are a good many more divisions. The Dissenters themselves are split up. There are Wesleyans, Baptists, Presbyterians, Independents, and so on; even these are all divided up." "Is it possible," says Paul, "that there are so many divisions?" "Yes; the Church of England is pretty well divided itself. There is the Broad Church, the High Church, the Low Church, and the High-Lows. Then there is the Lutheran Church; and away in Russia they have the Greek Church, and so on." I declare I do not know what Paul and Cephas would think if they came back to the world; they would find a strange state of things. It is one of the most humiliating things in the present day to see how God's family is divided up. If we love the Lord Jesus Christ the burden of our hearts will be that God may bring us closer together, so that we may love one another and rise above all party feeling.[23]

In the 1870s and 1880s Moody seems to have been optimistic that the sectarian walls were in fact coming down; but in the 1890s, perhaps as a result of the controversies over higher criticism, Moody sounded a more pessimistic tone. Shortly before his death he asked:

> Shall we have a great and mighty harvest, or shall we go on discussing our differences? As far as I am concerned, I am terribly tired of it, and I would like before I go hence to see the whole church of God quickened as it was in '57, and a wave from Maine to California that shall sweep thousands into the kingdom of God.[24]

If Moody's spirit and practice are to be described as ecumenical, it

---

23. *Wondrous Love*, p. 65; *Prevailing Prayer: What Hinders It?*, p. 75; cf. pp. 71-77; Hall, *The Amercian Evangelists*, pp. 294-95.
24. *Moody's Latest Sermons*, p. 125; cf. Shanks, *A College of Colleges* (1887), p. 241.

must be emphasized that it was an ecumenism of the Gospel as he understood it and as it was apparently understood by most Evangelicals in Great Britain and America at the time. W. G. Blaikie, Moody's host in Edinburgh in 1873-1874 and professor at New College, reported that it was "ministers of all evangelical denominations" who took part in the services, "forgetting their past controversies and estrangements." Similarly Beadenkopf and Stricklen reported that in Baltimore in 1878-1879, "The pastors of all evangelical denominations rejoiced to have a common platform on which to unite for Christian work." It is no wonder the Universalist, Ryder, had complained of the exclusion of non-Evangelicals from active participation in the earlier Chicago campaign.[25] Evangelism was the purpose that drew the Evangelicals together under Moody's leadership, and the more or less common understanding of the Gospel was the platform upon which they stood, an understanding expounded in chapters 3-5.

While Moody normally tried to avoid sectarian differences, as he would have called them, he did not trim his message if it involved what he thought to be a vital truth of the Gospel. Since he understood assurance to be a vital part of the Gospel, he did not de-emphasize it to please his Methodist supporters. He was in Salt Lake City twice and the second time even preached in the Mormon Tabernacle. But his message was the same as ever. In fact, on his first visit to the Mormon capital he openly repudiated the alleged revelations to Joseph Smith.[26]

Much has been made of the fact that Moody was on friendly terms with the Roman Catholics in Northfield and elsewhere and that he was greeted with friendly courtesy by the Catholics of Ireland. One Chicago newspaper in 1897 reported that the stage of the Auditorium was filled by ministers, "Roman, Anglican, Protestant," while Moody preached at the desk to a packed theater. Indeed, some of Moody's supporters were critical of Moody's failure to take a hard line against the Catholics.

Typical of his response to such critics is his statement to a Detroit reporter in April, 1899: "When I was here before, some people came to me and wanted me to pitch into the Catholics. I told 'em I would,

25. Blaikie, *The Religious Awakening in Edinburgh, in Connection with the Visit of Messrs. Moody and Sankey*, p. 2; Thomas M. Beadenkopf and W. Raymond Stricklen, *Moody in Baltimore* (Baltimore: The Sun Printing Office, 1879), p. 6; Ryder, *An Open Letter from W. H. Ryder, D. D., of Chicago, Ill., to D. L. Moody, Esq., The Evangelist*, pp. 2-3.
26. *Moody's Latest Sermons*, p. 120; Ira D. Sankey, *My Life and the Story of the Gospel Hymns* (New York: Harper & Bros., 1907), p. 79.

after I had all the Protestants converted." The summer before he had told the General Conference at Northfield, "Now the way I get a Catholic I say everything good I can about them. There is such a thing as tact, and if you can say a good word for the Catholic church, say it, and at the same time you want to put the truth in."[27] "Put the truth in," that was Moody's concern. Examination of sermons preached in Baltimore, 1878-1879, and in Dublin, 1874, 1883, and 1892 reveals that not only did his message not change before audiences likely to contain significant numbers of Catholics, he also took special pains to show how he understood his message to differ with Catholicism on the confessional, priestly absolution, works, and the sacraments![28]

Moody was probably even more severe on those in the Protestant tradition that he felt were either subverting or denying the Gospel. He typically warned a London audience in 1875, "If you are in a church, either Dissenting or Established, and the minister doesn't preach the blood, get out of it as Lot out of Sodom." The next spring in his closing meeting in the New York Hippodrome, he warned the new converts, "If the minister does not preach the gospel, go out of his church and get into some church where the gospel is preached."

Moody the ecumenist was a separatist if he thought the Gospel was at stake. This raises the question of his attitude toward higher criticism and theological liberalism when they became known in the late 1800s. Detailed discussion of this point is in chapter 10, but it should be noted here that in 1898 he said that he would get out of a church that made light of the Bible and discredited the supernatural, just as Lot got out of Sodom (the same simile as used above in 1875). The context of the statement clearly shows he was referring to liberal higher criticism.[29]

27. Findlay, *Dwight L. Moody*, pp. 165, 248, 371-72; "Wages War on Sin," unidentified 1897 newspaper clipping, Moodyana; "To Stir Up the Churches and Convert Christians," *Detroit Free Press*, newspaper clipping, simply dated Apr. 1899, Moodyana; "Questions answered by Mr. Moody, at General Conference, Tuesday Afternoon, August 16, 1898," typed manuscript, Moodyana.
28. "Convention of Ministers of the Gospel," *The Daily Express* (Dublin), Nov. 25, 1874; *Irish Times* (Dublin), "Messrs. Moody and Sankey in Dublin," Jan. 9, 1883; and "Messrs. Moody and Sankey," Jan. 11, 1883; D. L. Moody, "A Friendly Message to Irishmen from America," reprinted from the *Irish Daily Independent*, Nov. 3, 1892; "Illustrations from the Record of the Penitent Thief Upon the Cross—Faith and Repentance the Necessary Steps—Mr. Moody's View of Churches and Ordinances" and "The Bread and Wine," *Baltimore Sun*, undated newspaper clippings, Moodyana.
29. *London Discourses*, p. 182; *Glad Tidings*, p. 453; "Questions answered by Mr. Moody, at General Conference, Tuesday Afternoon, August 16, 1898." Cf. Nussbaum, "D. L. Moody and the Church," pp. 77, 82-89. Cf. pp. 112, 115 (this book).

For the sake of the total picture, it also needs to be pointed out that Moody did not intend to imply that denominational distinctives were either avoidable or inherently wrong. He bent over backward to avoid such controversial questions as baptism, yet he admitted that he had his own views on the subject. In fact, he said there was a time and a place for such matters, and that was the local church. "It is very proper that all these things should be taught, but it's the work of the ministers." "I can have my views on baptism," Moody said, "and if I had a church I would teach the people what I believe, but in these meetings it would be unfair to do it." This was also at the very heart of Moody's understanding of his calling as an evangelist. He was an evangelist, not a pastor. He said in response to a question on baptism, "Why don't I preach baptism? The Lord has sent me to preach the Gospel. I leave these doctrines to your pastors. I have not come to get up a quarrel in England."

It was not Moody's calling to debate such matters. His job was to preach the Gospel.[30] Though the Gospel did not erase sectarian differences, it did transcend them; and all true Christians should unite together in evangelism and fellowship because of devotion to a common Lord and a common Gospel. And this common purpose and loyalty was totally incompatible with "party-spirit."

It is true that Moody can be and was criticized by ecclesiastical purists for loose and undefined views of ecclesiology.[31] But it has been shown that he did not despise such points of ecclesiastical debate, nor did he consider them to have no legitimate place in discussion. Rather, they had no place in his ministry. But his ministry did emphasize the purpose and message that should bring all of Christ's Church together—preaching the Gospel. It is at this point that his high regard for the Church is really seen. Moody's working with and through the churches was not just a pragmatic expedient. It was Christ's Church, and that was why it was good to see the party spirit fading and the denominational walls coming down. To the college students assembled at Northfield in 1887, Moody said:

30. *To All People*, p. 173; "The Bread and Wine," *Baltimore Sun*, undated newspaper clipping, Moodyana; *Signs of Our Times*, Mar. 10, 1875, p. 149; Shanks, ed., *A College of Colleges* (1887), pp. 216-18; cf. Goodspeed, *Wonderful Career of Moody*, pp. 567-70 for a typical series of questions put to Moody and the manner in which Moody sidestepped "controverted points."

31. J. A. Singmaster, "Modern Evangelism," *Quarterly Review of the Lutheran Church and Lutheran Quarterly* 7 (July 1877): 407-8.

> If I know my own heart I love the Church more than anything else on this earth. I believe it is the dearest thing on this earth to the heart of my Master. And if there has been any criticism here it has been from its friends, and out of love. We are here as Christians, to see how we can improve the Church of God, and the way to make it stronger and better in our day. We are inside the Church, and trying to lift it up.

Whatever the Church's shortcomings, Moody believed, "It is the best institution under heaven. It is the only institution I want to belong to. 'He purchased it with his own blood.' "[32]

32. Shanks, ed., *A College of Colleges* (1887), pp. 242-43; *Great Redemption*, pp. 471-72; cf. Nussbaum, "D. L. Moody and the Church," pp. 89-90.

9

WATCH AND PRAY, FOR YE KNOW NOT WHEN THE TIME IS

> I look on this world as a wrecked vessel. God has given me a life-boat, and said to me, "Moody, save all you can." God will come in judgment and burn up this world, but the children of God don't belong to this world; they are in it but not of it, like a ship in the water. This world is getting darker, and its ruin is coming nearer and nearer. If you have any friends on this wreck unsaved, you had better lose no time in getting them off.[1]

DWIGHT L. MOODY'S PREACHING of Christ's second coming and the relation of that coming to the millennial Kingdom marked a new departure in evangelistic preaching in America. Prior to Moody the well-known preachers of revival and evangelism had preached a postmillennial message, and most Protestants who preached the doctrine of the second coming were postmillennial. The two most noteworthy examples were Jonathan Edwards and Charles Finney, but they were by no means isolated instances. Though other systems of eschatology were existent before and during their times, the postmillennial hope that the millennial Kingdom would be brought to actualization by Christian witness, work, and influence prior to the last judgment and Christ's return to earth had been the message generally preached from Protestant pulpits in America. It was a view of Christianity as an all-conquering faith destined to convert the world and to turn it into one vast realm under Christ's spiritual rule. As such, it also accorded well with the optimistic and hopeful outlook from colonial days through the early days of the republic.

1. *New Sermons*, p. 535.

In 1742, Jonathan Edwards wrote *Some Thoughts Concerning the Present Revival of Religion in New England* in which he expressed the hope that "what is now seen in America, and especially in New England, may prove the dawn of that glorious day," by which he meant the millennial Kingdom. Almost one hundred years later Charles Finney was lamenting the fact that if Christians in the United States had gone to work ten years earlier, "the millennium would have fully come in the United states before this day." But all was not lost. "If the church will do all her duty, the millennium may come in this country in three years."[2]

Lest we dismiss the significance of variant eschatological theories too lightly, it must be emphasized that much more was involved in these debates than the question of the timing of the second advent. Postmillennialism provided a rationale for the conversion of mankind and the amelioration and cure of the ills of the world. It was a philosophy of history, and a generally optimistic one at that. Through the sanctified efforts of Christians, the Kingdom would be brought to reality before Christ returned. Society itself would be reorganized in accordance with the laws of God. The postmillennial philosophy of history was the cornerstone in the foundation of most, if not all, of the social-reform movements promoted by American Evangelicals in the mid-nineteenth century, and the view continued after the Civil War, though it began to lose ground. The prayer revival of 1857-1858 served to quicken these hopes that had long lived in American Protestantism.[3]

However, even in the pre-Civil War years, premillennialism revealed signs of resurgence, not only in the United States but also in Great Britain. The most sensational and public evidence of this was the crusade of William Miller to convince the nation that Christ would return in 1843 to judge the world and cleanse it by fire, a prediction that had also

2. Jonathan Edwards, *Some Thoughts Concerning the Revival of Religion in New England* in John E. Smith, ed., *The Works of Jonathan Edwards*, vol. 4: *The Great Awakening*, C. C. Goen, ed. (New Haven: Yale U., 1972), p. 358; Finney, *Lectures on Revivals of Religion*, pp. 289-90. For a survey of early postmillennialism in America beginning with Massachusetts Bay, see Robert Kieran Whalen, "Millenarianism and Millennialism in America: 1790-1880" (Ph.D. thesis, State University of New York at Stony Brook, Oct. 1971), pp. 21-27, 45-47.
3. Timothy Smith gives a helpful description of this phenomenon with much documentation in *Revivalism and Social Reform*, pp. 225-36. Cf. McLoughlin, *Modern Revivalism*, pp. 105-6; Findlay, *Dwight L. Moody*, pp. 249-50; Handy, *A Christian America: Protestant Hopes and Historical Realities*, pp. 95-101. Whalen, "Millenarianism and Millennialism in America: 1790-1880," pp. 102-38, contains a very lucid description of the essential doctrinal features of pre-Civil War premillennialism and postmillennialism in America.

been made by premillennialists in Great Britain. Although the Millerite brand of premillennialism had its own peculiarities, such as rejection of the idea that Israel would be restored as a nation, it held much in common with premillennial eschatology as it generally had been stated up to that time. Specifically, Miller, like most contemporary premillenarians, belonged to the historicist school of interpretation.

Historicists tied themselves to a prophetic timetable, derived primarily from the books of Daniel and Revelation, which they understood to be in the process of being fulfilled in the present age. Although non-Millerite premillennialists of the historicist school seldom set dates as Miller had, the temptation was always there to do so. When that luxury was engaged in, disappointment was the result. But all historicists shared a common problem that derived from the fact that their eschatology was based on a past chronology. As history advanced without the return of Christ to set up His Kingdom, the schemes of reputed fulfillment of prophecy in the present age had to be repeatedly updated to accommodate more recent history. The validity of such interpretations could only be shown by matching history and prophecy, and history continued to advance with no return. As a result of such needs of constant adjustment, "after 1844 the historicists position began to lose the almost undisputed position that it had held during the first generation of the millenarian revival."[4]

In the 1840s the futurist premillennial position began to gain more and more attention in both the British Isles and United States. In general, the futurists looked upon the present age of the Church as a parenthesis in God's prophetic program. Consequently, futurists were not bound to finding correspondencies between historical events of the age of the Church and the prophetic Scriptures, and thus they escaped the embarrassment of the historicists who constantly had to be reshuffling to make presumed prophecy correspond to presumed fulfillment up to that time. Those prophecies of the Old Testament that they did not understand to have been fulfilled either prior to or by Christ's first advent, they placed in the future, after the parenthesis of the Church was over. By the same token, they understood the fulfillment of the

---

4. Sandeen, *Roots of Fundamentalism*, p. 60. In chaps. 1 and 2, pp. 3-58, Sandeen discusses the revival of British and American millenarianism (premillennialism), 1800-1845. Whalen, "Millenarianism and Millennialism in America: 1790-1880," pp. 27-101, surveys early American premillennial literature. He suggests that pre-Civil War premillennialism was more virile than has been previously recognized.

Olivet discourse (Mt 24-26) and of the greater part of the book of Revelation to be future to the age of the Church.

It seems to have been the Plymouth Brethren in the British Isles who initially popularized futurist premillennialism. This sect originated in Ireland in 1827-28 and took root in Plymouth, England, in 1830. As a separatist group, they believed that the Church could not be identified with state churches and denominational structures, and they did not possess an organized ministry. Although the Plymouth Brethren in the British Isles were torn by various disputes, especially disputes over details of eschatology, the position of John Nelson Darby won the day in the last half of the century. Darby's views of eschatology and ecclesiology became known as dispensationalism. They were spread by the Plymouth Brethren far beyond the bounds of their own movement in both the British Isles and America. Much to the chagrin of Darby, many within the denominations adopted his eschatology without accepting his separatist ecclesiology. Darbyite dispensationalism came to dominate late nineteenth-century American premillennialism and essentially became embodied in the famous *Scofield Reference Bible*.[5]

D. L. Moody was one of the many whose theological outlook was significantly influenced by the writings of and contacts with the Plymouth Brethren, thus making him the first noteworthy premillennial preacher of revival and evangelism in America. Certain aspects of this influence have already been alluded to in this study, such as his refusal to accept their exclusivistic ecclesiology while sharing their rejection of perfectionism. Some mention has also been made of his early contacts with the Plymouth Brethren and of his later invitations to premillennialists to speak from the Northfield platform.[6] Moody lacked a refined system of eschatology, which is hardly surprising; nevertheless, his preaching reflects a premillennial outlook, and sometimes even a dispensational outlook.

Other authors have very adequately described the nature of Moody's contacts with the Plymouth Brethren and other premillennialists, both in the earlier and later years.[7] What has not been done previously is to

5. Sandeen, *Roots of Fundamentalism*, pp. 59-62. Whalen challenges the view that the Plymouth Brethren were the main introducers of and popularizers of dispensationalism in America, but he does so by improperly defining dispensationalism and by ignoring the evidence of Plymouth Brethren influence; cf. "Millenarianism and Millennialism in America: 1790-1880," pp. 272-95.

6. See pp. 44-46, 54-55.

7. See Sandeen, *Roots of Fundamentalism*, pp. 70-102, 172-87; Findlay, *Dwight L. Moody*, pp. 125-27, 249-53, 351-52, 406-7.

examine Moody's sermons thoroughly for the purpose of ascertaining the nature and extent of premillennial and dispensational themes in his message.

DISPENSATIONALISM COMES TO AMERICA

Plymouth Brethren were apparently in North America before Darby arrived, but his visits gave the Brethren more visibility and spread their influence. Darby's journeys to and through the United States and Canada began in 1862 with a four-week stint in Canada, but between 1862 and 1877 he was to visit North America seven times. He spent nearly seven of those sixteen years in the United States and Canada. Many of the Brethren were immigrants from Europe, and Darby ministered to these assemblies of Brethren. By 1873 Darby had carved out a sphere of influence in the larger cities of the Midwest and East, preaching publicly and teaching laymen and clergymen privately. His preaching and teaching were paralleled by the missionary work of lesser lights of the movement and by the spreading influence of the writings of Plymouth Brethren authors such as F. W. Grant, William Kelley, William Trotter, and C. H. Mackintosh. The last named became famous simply as C. H. M., author of the widely read *Notes on the Pentateuch*.[8]

Just when young Moody came under the influence of the Plymouth Brethren is uncertain. Some lines of evidence suggest that Moody came in contact with this teaching as early as 1867 or 1868. On one occasion Moody is reported to have said that he had held to premillennialism since 1867, and this would accord with the fact that during his 1867 trip to the British Isles Moody had close contacts with the Brethren. Moody's son William claimed that Moody had entertained Brethren in his home in Chicago prior to that trip and that one purpose of his trip to Britain was to learn from them. It was the next year that Moorhouse followed Moody back to America and began to exert such an influence over him. Moorhouse was numbered among the Plymouth Brethren.[9]

On the other hand, A. P. Fitt, Moody's son-in-law, said that Moody

8. Sandeen, *Roots of Fundamentalism*, pp. 70-80; H. A. Ironside, *A Historical Sketch of the Brethren Movement* (Grand Rapids: Zondervan, 1942), pp. 70-82; C. Norman Kraus, *Dispensationalism in America: Its Rise and Development* (Richmond, Va.: John Knox, 1958), pp. 46-56, cited as *Dispensationalism in America*.
9. W. R. Moody, *Moody* (1930), pp. 101-4; D. L. Moody, *Ten Days with D. L. Moody, Comprising a Collection of His Sermons* (Chicago: J. S. Ogilvie, 1886), p. 151.

first heard of "dispensational truth" in 1872, a claim that is supported
by another of Moody's reported statements that he had been in the
church fifteen or sixteen years before he had heard a sermon on the "return of the Lord to this earth."[10] Though Darby had been in the Midwest
and in Chicago, there is uncertainty as to when the two first came into
contact.[11] The weight of evidence seems to favor an earlier date for
Moody's initial exposure to Plymouth Brethren teaching, but that is
hardly a crucial question. In view of Whalen's minimizing of the role
of the Brethren in introducing dispensationalism to America, it is significant that Moody had to go to the Brethren to learn "dispensational
truth." By the time Moody's star rose in the mid-1870s he was clearly
preaching premillennialism as opposed to postmillennialism, an assertion which is vindicated later.

It is also clear that Moody to the end of his life had a high respect
for the Plymouth Brethren teachers as well as for evangelists and ministers outside of the Brethren movement who had been influenced by
their futurist premillennialism and dispensationalism. Moody himself
was not at all reticent to admit to what he regarded as the benefits that
he had received from their teaching. An advertisement that appeared
very widely in the 1880s and 1890s contained a glowing testimonial by
Moody to the value he placed on the writings of C. H. Mackintosh, one
of the more significant Plymouth Brethren writers. The testimonial
read, grammatical infelicities and all:

> Some year's since I had my attention called to C. H. M.'s notes, and
> was so much pleased and at the same time profited by the way they
> open up the Scripture truths, that I secured at once all the writings of
> the same author, and, if they could not be replaced would rather part
> with my entire library, excepting my Bible, than with these writings.
> They have been to me a very key to the Scriptures.[12]

Moody's continuing sympathies with certain aspects of Plymouth
Brethren teaching are reflected in the names of those men with whom
he closely worked or who were invited to speak at the Northfield conferences. The following list includes those who were, if not Plymouth
Brethren, at least premillennial or Darbyite premillennial: D. W. Whit-

---

10. Arthur Percy Fitt, *Moody Still Lives: Word Pictures of D. L. Moody* (New York: Revell, 1936), p. 55, but cf. p. 50; *New Sermons*, p. 529.
11. See Findlay, *Dwight L. Moody*, p. 251.
12. D. L. Moody, *Heaven; Where It Is; Its Inhabitants; and How to Get There* (Chicago: Revell, 1880), on the first page of advertisements after the text of the book.

tle, George Pentecost, A. T. Pierson, George Needham, Nathaniel West, A. J. Gordon, William E. Blackstone, James Brookes, W. G. Moorehead, and C. I. Scofield.

But Moody's sympathies were much broader than those of the Plymouth Brethren. He is not to be identified with the movement, nor did he partake of the divisiveness that the movement tended to produce and in fact existed within the movement.[13] Even though he is properly identified with the resurgence of premillennialism in America following the Civil War, Moody did not make the question of eschatology either a test of fellowship or of cooperation in his crusades and conferences. When the split within the ranks of American premillennialists over the question of the secret rapture of the Church began to develop in the mid-1880s and widened in the 1890s, Moody seems to have attempted to stay aloof.

DISTINCTIVE EMPHASES OF DISPENSATIONALISM

One of the most common mistakes in analyzing dispensationalism is to take its name too seriously.[14] The essence of dispensationalism, contrary to what many have assumed, is not the division of history into dispensations. Findlay seems to have fallen into this trap when he concluded that Moody was not an "outright advocate of dispensationalism" because he used "only once or twice the term 'dispensation,' and he never developed, as did the dispensationalists, a structured series of ages."[15] Actually, Findlay is wrong on two counts. Moody does use the term "dispensation" with some frequency, but in any event, this use or lack of it would neither prove nor disprove that Moody was a dispensationalist. Sandeen correctly cites several examples of the word "dispensation" being used by nondispensationalists, and to his list may be added such nondispensationalists as Charles Finney, John Tomline Walsh, and Francis Wayland.[16] If the periodization of history were the genius

13. See p. 165.

14. Sandeen, *Roots of Fundamentalism*, pp. 60-70, 219-20 is one of the more fair and objective treatments by a nondispensationalist; for unsympathetic analyses, see Kraus, *Dispensationalism in America*, and Clarence B. Bass, *Backgrounds to Dispensationalism: Its Historical Genesis and Ecclesiastical Implications* (Grand Rapids: Eerdmans, 1960); for a sympathetic analysis, see Charles Caldwell Ryrie, *Dispensationalism Today* (Chicago: Moody, 1965).

15. Findlay, *Dwight L. Moody*, p. 408; Whalen, "Millenarianism and Millennialism in America, 1790-1880," pp. 271-77.

16. Sandeen, *Roots of Fundamentalism*, pp. 68-69, 86; Charles G. Finney, *Lectures to Professing Christians* (Oberlin, O.: E. J. Goodrich, 1879, originally delivered in New York City in 1836-37), pp. 271, 355; Walsh, *Moody versus Christ and His Apostles: A Vindication of the Truth of the Gospel*, p. 25; Francis Wayland, *The Elements of Moral Science*, cited in McLoughlin, *The American Evangelicals, 1800-1900: An Anthology*, p. 113.

of the movement, these men would seem to qualify as dispensationalists, although in fact they were not. Furthermore, if that were the essential point, it would seem that there should be fairly close agreement among dispensationalists as to the identity and number of the dispensations, a situation which does not exist and has not existed among them. What then is dispensationalism?

To its adherents dispensationalism is first of all a hermeneutic, that is, a consistent application of grammatico-historical principles of interpretation to the text of the Bible. Other premillennialists made the same claim. Obviously, since there are different interpretations that can be arrived at even on the basis of grammatico-historical principles, there is not absolute uniformity among dispensationalists. In their efforts to follow through this hermeneutical principle consistently, dispensationalists arrived at certain typical conclusions. First, they were led to premillennialism, refusing to take in any figurative or spiritual sense the Old Testament prophecies of the Messiah's reign on earth, and interpreting literally the reference to 1,000 years in Revelation 20. Second, they made a hard and fast distinction between Israel and the Church, with Israel having its proper place in God's economy and the Church its place. They read numerous prophecies made to the Nation Israel which they could not find fulfilled in history past and so concluded that they had to be fulfilled for the nation of Israel in future history, that is, the Messianic Kingdom, the Millennium.

Third, they could not escape references, such as Paul's, to the evil character of the last days. So, in contrast to postmillennialism, they took a pessimistic view of the effectiveness of human, even Christian, efforts to bring the Kingdom of God to actuality on earth. There was no theological reason to hope for the betterment or conversion of the world until Christ Himself returned to inaugurate His personal rule in the millennial Kingdom. It can be added that the crises of society at the end of the century seemed to confirm this pessimism. But they insisted that they were only mediately pessimistic; ultimately they were optimists, for Christ would return to establish His righteous rule.

Fourth, most and perhaps all of the early dispensationalists did periodize history into separate dispensations. But the exact periodization was not necessarily significant, except that Israel and the Church were to be kept dispensationally distinct at all costs. Dispensationalists attached significance to the idea that in each of these periods man is given a test by God which man fails and which results in divine judgment. This was tied in with the pessimistic view of present efforts to bring in the Kingdom and was a refinement of the pessimism common to premillennialists.

Fifth, the economy of one dispensation could not validly be imposed on succeeding dispensations, unless obviously transdispensational or specifically repeated for a future dispensation. For example, the Mosaic Law, including the Ten Commandments, was not the rule of life for the Christian. Moral and spiritual principles of unending value expressed in that Law were still binding on the Christian. But that was true because they were to be found in the New Testament, especially the epistles, not because they were in the Law. This is related to the previously stated principle that the distinction made and maintained between the Church and Israel demands that passages intended for Israel should not be transposed to the Church, and vice versa.

Sixth, with Darby and those who were influenced by him, the above considerations led to the view that the Church was something of a parenthesis in God's program in history, a parenthesis between phases of God's dealings with Israel and a parenthesis not foreseen in the Old Testament. This parenthesis also involved the futuristic interpretation of Revelation. Israel had rejected its Messianic King at His first coming; but since the promises of the King and Kingdom remained to be fulfilled, the actualization of the Kingdom was future (the Millennium). The Kingdom had been postponed and the Church age fills the interval. This distinction between the Church and Israel also meant that the Church would have to be removed from earth before God began dealing with Israel as a nation. Since God was understood to renew these dealings in the seven-year period of Tribulation before Christ's return to earth to establish His millennial rule, Christ's coming for the Church was conceived to be a return in the clouds (not to the earth) to which the Church would be caught up. This view has been designated the "secret, any moment rapture" or the "pretribulation rapture." Exegetical arguments were also advanced to support this position.

On this and related points, the Plymouth Brethren movement in England was seriously divided by the controversy between J. N. Darby and B. W. Newton. This cleavage that broke apart the British Plymouth Brethren in the 1840s developed and widened in American premillennialism in the mid-1880s and the 1890s when Robert Cameron and

Nathaniel West, two prominent American premillennialists, began to question the secret, any moment, pretribulational rapture and its related doctrines. Darbyite pretribulational premillennialism, which had apparently dominated the American premillennial movement since the Civil War, now found itself opposed by posttribulational premillennialism which used many of the arguments used earlier by B. W. Newton. A rift developed in American premillennialism that still divides the movement and is still the subject of hot controversy.[17]

Finally, since they held the pessimistic premillennial view of history prior to Christ's second coming, evangelization of the world was not thought of in terms of conversion of the world. Rather, evangelization was taking the Gospel message to the whole world. Nineteenth-century premillennialists tended to be Calvinistic and postmillennialists Arminian.

It should not be concluded from this resumé that all dispensationalists were in complete harmony on these points, nor should it be assumed that there are no other dispensational distinctives to be identified. However, this description is adequate for the purpose of determining the extent that Moody had been influenced by dispensationalism.[18]

DISPENSATIONALISM IN MOODY'S PREACHING

It is generally recognized that Moody was a premillennialist, although often this is not taken into acount by those who have analyzed related areas of Moody's theology. However, beyond this the efforts to discover possible dispensational motifs in Moody's sermons have been inadequate. As has been stated in other connections in this study, Moody simply did not enter into systematic and theoretic discussions of such subjects. The best one can hope for is a rambling sermon that reveals the basic outlines of his thinking; beyond that, one must rely on incidental references and allusions to be found throughout his sermons.

17. For example, cf. Leon Wood, *Is the Rapture Next?* (Grand Rapids: Zondervan, 1956); John F. Walvoord, *The Rapture Question* (Findlay, O.: Dunham, 1957); George Eldon Ladd, *The Blessed Hope* (Grand Rapids: Eerdmans, 1956); Robert H. Gundry, *The Church and the Tribulation* (Grand Rapids: Zondervan, 1973).

18. This resumé is largely based on my personal acquaintance with the movement and its literature. Those desiring to examine the source materials should read the writings of J. N. Darby, William Kelly, C. H. Mackintosh, and C. I. Scofield among the earlier dispensationalists, and such authors as John F. Walvoord, J. Dwight Pentecost, and Charles Ryrie among contemporary dispensationalists. Analyses similar to that above can be found in Sandeen, *Roots of Fundamentalism*, pp. 60-102, 208-32; Bass, *Backgrounds to Dispensationalism: Its Historical Genesis and Ecclesiastical Implications*, pp. 18-47; Kraus, *Dispensationalism in America*, pp. 57-68; Ryrie, *Dispensationalism Today*, passim.

In this case, such sermons are available, and the evidence gleaned from them will be supplemented by the incidental evidence. Normally, Moody would preach at least one sermon on Christ's return toward the end of an extended series of meetings.

A typical example from the mid-1870s was when Moody began a sermon by affirming the inspiration and profit of all Scripture (2 Ti 3:16).[19] It would be wrong, he argued, to ignore the prophecies of the Bible since they were so numerous and "taught in the New Testament as clearly as any other doctrine." He lamented that the churches had been so silent on the subject, but explained it as due to the fact that "the devil does not want us to see this truth, for nothing would wake up the church so much." With this statement emerges what is perhaps Moody's major emphasis in his preaching of premillennialism, and that is the practical effect of the preaching of the doctrine. In terms of this opening statement he said that the doctrine would wake up the Church in that the knowledge of Christ's return would cause the world to lose its hold on the Christian. "Gas-stocks and water-stocks, and stocks in banks and horse-railroads, are of very much less consequence to him then. His heart is free, and he looks for the blessed appearing of his Lord, who at His coming will take him into His Kingdom."

A little later in the sermon Moody said that the proper state of the believer is to be watching and waiting for Christ's return. He was convinced that appreciation of this doctrine would wake the Church up from its coldness and formality. Moody offered his own experience as testimony: "I have felt like working three times as hard ever since I came to understand that my Lord was coming back again," and with that comment Moody introduced the statement quoted at the beginning of this chapter—God had given Moody a lifeboat to rescue people off this world as off a wrecked vessel.

Thus the doctrine of Christ's return in judgment, followed by His Kingdom, was to impart a sense of urgency to the evangelistic task. But the doctrine also should impress upon the unbeliever a sense of urgency because of the imminent danger. "This world is getting darker and darker, and its ruin is coming nearer and nearer." On another occasion Moody warned, "Lose no time! If you want a part and lot in that com-

---

19. "Our Lord's Return," *New Sermons*, pp. 529-36. A similar sermon is found in *To All People*, pp. 499-512.

ing Kingdom of the Lord you had better press into it now while the door is open. By and by 'Too late! too late!' will be the cry."[20]

To suggest that Moody adopted premillennialism as a "sophisticated scare tactic" or simply because it would serve as a convenient and effective weapon of evangelism is not warranted by the evidence. As has been shown, postmillennialism in its own way could likewise be used as such an instrument, as indeed it was by Finney, that is, to evangelize to bring in the Kingdom. But it is true that Moody used the doctrine of Christ's premillennial return to incite believers to witness and to warn unbelievers to go in the door while it was still open, and it was a frequent theme.[21]

In the sermon being examined, Moody then moved to the interpretation of the image portrayed in Daniel 2. He took the classic premillennial interpretation of that image, declaring that the first four parts of the image had been fulfilled in the kingdoms of Babylon, Medo-Persia, Greece, and Rome. Only the stone, depicting the return of Christ to establish His Kingdom, had yet to come, to become a great mountain and to fill the whole earth.

In another sermon devoted entirely to the interpretation of Daniel 2, Moody stated his belief in the "literal fulfillment" of this prophecy, reflecting both a premillennial and dispensational orientation, with the emphasis on a literal hermeneutic. He also spoke of the coming Kingdom as the "Fifth Monarchy." With the introduction of the premillennial interpretation of Daniel 2, especially verse 45, the theme of the premillennial advent became a matter of recurring reference through the rest of the sermon. He spoke of the time when he did not accept the doctrine. He cited the premillennialism of Dean Henry Alford, the well-known English exegete, and of Charles H. Spurgeon, the famous Baptist preacher of London. He referred to postmillennialism and rejected it. Did not the Bible tell him to watch for the coming of the Lord, not the Millennium? Besides, "I don't find any place where God says the world is to grow better and better."

His other sermons often contained similar affirmations of premillen-

---

20. Ibid., pp. 529-30, 534-35, cf. 527-28; *Bible Characters*, p. 16; cf. Moody's letter to the International Prophetic Conference, 1886, in which he testifies to the inspiration this doctrine had been to him, George C. Needham, ed., *Prophetic Studies of the International Prophetic Conference* (Chicago: Revell, 1886), p. 41.

21. Cf. Findlay, *Dwight L. Moody*, p. 253. Whalen discusses the manner in which postmillennialists regarded their view to be the nerve of missionary activity, "Millenarianism and Millennialism in America: 1790-1880," pp. 95-96, 150-59.

nialism as opposed to postmillennialism, though at times he could speak somewhat inconsistently of Christ presently having the Kingdom. Occasionally he would even emphasize the Jewishness of that Kingdom, in true dispensational fashion. But usually his statements were rather simple affirmations of premillennial faith without any careful argumentation.[22]

In this sermon on the Lord's return, Moody next repudiated those who "have gone beyond prophecy, and tried to tell the very day He would come." The statement is directed quite obviously against the kind of date-setting represented by William Miller. But Moody also used rejection of date-setting as a lead-in to his view of the suddenness and unexpectedness of Christ's coming. Dates could not be set because Christ's coming might be at any moment and would be unexpected.

At this point the question must be faced to what extent Moody had accepted the Darbyite dispensational view of a secret, any-moment rapture of the Church. Dispensationalists said it would precede the seven-year Tribulation and that it would antedate by at least seven years Christ's return to establish His millennial rule. It should be recalled that dispensationalists argued for this exegetically and on the basis that the Church was a parenthesis between phases of God's dealings with Israel; since God was going to resume His dealings with the nation during the seven-year Tribulation, they argued that the Church would be raptured before the Tribulation began. Thus, Christ's coming for the Church would be secret and imminent, that is, it could be unexpected and happen at any moment.

It is very difficult to discover precisely what Moody believed on this point, and one is led to the conclusion that his belief was not very precise, at least not as precise as that of most dispensationalists. As has been seen already, he claimed to follow a literal interpretation of prophetic passages which led him to a literal belief in a 1,000-year rule of Christ. In dispensational fashion, he at least maintained enough of a distinction between Israel and the Church that he insisted upon the regathering of the Jewish people, the restoration of the nation of Israel, and the literal fulfillment of prophecies with reference to Israel. And in this sermon he clearly insisted that the believer should expect Christ to return suddenly, unexpectedly, and secretly. He even said he couldn't

22. *New Sermons*, pp. 530-36, 203-4, 527, 541, 565, 572; *Wondrous Love*, p. 64; *Bible Characters*, pp. 15-16.

find anything in the Bible that tells the believer to look for signs of the coming of the Millennium. Rather, the believer was simply to be ready, watching, and waiting for the Lord who would come as a thief in the night.

In one of his clearest statements on the matter, he said that Christ would take the bride (the Church) out of the world to the place He had prepared for her before He came in judgment. This all sounds very much like the dispensational concept of a secret, any moment, pretribulational rapture to remove the Church from the world before God resumes his dealings with Israel.

Problems remain, however. He did not identify himself as a futurist nor did he speak of the Church age as a parenthesis. Not once did Moody mention a seven-year interval between Christ's coming for His Church and His return to inaugurate the millennial Kingdom. In many references to Christ's return it sounds as if he made no distinction between a secret coming and a coming in power and glory. He never described a period known as the Tribulation, seven years in length. On many occasions it sounds as though Christ's return to earth as King is indeed the next event expected—a premillennial advent, and that alone. On the occasion of his speaking in Boston on the return of Christ, Moody spoke of Christ returning for the Church without making any distinction between that and the establishment of the millennial peace.

The most that can be said is that Moody adopted the concept of an any-moment return and some of its attendant vocabulary from the dispensationalists. But that he had a carefully thought-out and expressed dispensational distinction between a pretribulational rapture and a posttribulational coming cannot be demonstrated.[23]

Moody's statements on this matter become even more interesting after the rift among premillennialists on the question of the secret, any-moment rapture became evident and grew from the mid-1880s on.[24] Robert Cameron had broached his doubts about the doctrine of imminency to Nathaniel West, another prominent premillennialist, in 1884, and West promised to give the matter serious attention. He even promised to refute the view if he came to the conclusion that it was unscriptural.

23. *New Sermons*, pp. 531-35, 204, 554-57; *Glad Tidings*, pp. 434-35; *Bible Characters*, p. 26; *To All People*, pp. 504-6; *Pleasure and Profit in Bible Study*, p. 40.
24. See pp. 181, 183-84. See also the account as given in Sandeen, *Roots of Fundamentalism*, pp. 208-19.

Sandeen indicates that the results of that review by West began to appear in the 1890s when West attacked the secret-rapture theory publicly. But, as early as 1886, signs of impending rupture appeared. That summer at Northfield, Nathaniel West spoke on Daniel 12:1-3, a key passage for students of prophecy. Though his sermon contained some typical dispensational themes, it did not contain a clear statement of the secret rapture, and it contained the suggestion that West was moving away from that doctrine. At one point in the sermon he quoted S. P. Tregelles in support of his interpretation of the first resurrection. Significantly, Tregelles was not only a noted British Old Testament scholar, he also was one of the British Plymouth Brethren who had dissented from Darby's views of the secret rapture. A. T. Pierson later said that "the prominent idea of this convention was *Dispensational Truth.*" It seems significant that West was so vague on this characteristic dispensational note at such a convention.

Whether or not those who heard West speak knew what was going on in his mind cannot be definitely determined. However, it may be significant that Major Whittle, a lay evangelist and close friend of Moody, spoke at that same conference and clearly taught the pretribulation rapture. Was he referring to West when he said, "There is where some of us feel we have our hope of the rapture of the Church. Some people think we are going to be put through tribulations—going to be sifted and tested"?[25]

In November of the same year, West spoke at the International Prophetic Conference in Chicago. There the trend in West's thinking seems to be even clearer. It not only appears that he spoke of Christ's coming to establish the Kingdom as the hope of the Church, but he also spoke of Israel's conversion through the missionary activity of the Church. These are not things that a pretribulation rapturist would say, for the Church would have been removed from earth before these events.[26]

It was in 1893 that West publicly attacked the secret-rapture idea, and the more or less solid front that American premillennialism had presented began to become fragmented. Moody's response to this situation was to say that *"when* His coming will be, we don't know," a

25. Shanks, ed., *D. L. Moody at Home,* pp. 145-51, 162-65; Arthur T. Pierson, *Forward Movements of the Last Half Century* (New York: Funk & Wagnalls, 1900), p. 158.
26. Needham, ed., *Prophetic Studies of the International Prophetic Conference,* pp. 133, 135.

statement he made at the 1886 conference in Northfield. "The true attitude of every child of God is just to be waiting and watching." Since Moody had not set forth a chronological scheme of future events, but only insisted that Christ could return at any moment and that the time of His return was otherwise unknown, he did not become directly involved in the debate. His previous statements had been sufficiently vague that there was hardly any reason for him to become involved.

Moody continued to preach an any-moment return between 1886 and 1899, but by 1897 a note had crept into his preaching that reflects his concern over the controversy raging in the premillennial ranks with which he had been identified. He told a congregation in Tremont Temple, Boston, "Don't criticise if our watches don't agree about the time that we know he is coming." He even extended an olive branch to the postmillennialists and said, "We will not have division." Apparently Moody was becoming more convinced that matters concerning eschatology were areas of legitimate disagreement that should not produce division. Though he continued to preach his own brand of an any-moment coming in terms that were both vague and yet somewhat dispensational in tone, he warned his auditors:

> Now, I believe truth has suffered more from its so-called friends than from others. We have been making out a programme to tell us what is going to happen, and one who does that has a big job. If anyone had tried to tell what Jesus would do when he first came, he would have had a job indeed. We have been told that he would be born in Bethlehem and live in Jerusalem. But when you come to make out a programme, I differ. I don't know! I don't think any one knows what is going to happen.

The next day, with almost identical words, Moody repeated his personal agnosticism on the details of the second coming, simply preaching a premillennial return with no clear distinction between a pretribulational rapture and a posttribulational return.[27]

Although he was clearly a premillennialist and he had obviously been influenced by the dispensationalists, Moody's preaching of the Lord's return would not have been fully satisfactory to his dispensational

---

27. Dwight L. Moody, "When My Lord Jesus Comes," *The Christian Herald*, Feb. 23, 1910, pp. 168-69; Dwight L. Moody, "When Jesus Comes Again," *The Christian Herald*, Dec. 21, 1910, pp. 1208-9.

friends. This is even more characteristic of his preaching in his later years.

One more major theme from Moody's sermon on the Lord's return remains to be discussed—the world as a wrecked vessel. As a premillennialist, he had a philosophy of history that would normally be regarded as pessimistic. It is an emphasis that is frequently found in Moody's preaching. In this sermon he declared that the world was getting darker and darker and that its ruin was coming nearer and nearer. He set his understanding of history against that of the postmillennial optimism and said, "I don't find any place where God says the world is to grow better and better. . . . I find that the earth is to grow worse and worse, and that at length there is going to be a separation." In addition to the usual pessimistic outlook of premillennialism, he also held that historically man proved himself a failure in each dispensation, a special emphasis of the dispensationalists. Not only was the present age getting worse, but this had been the story of each age.

> But some one will say, "Do you, then, make the grace of God a failure?" No; grace is not a failure, but man is. The antediluvian world was a failure; the Jewish world was a failure; man has been a failure everywhere, when he has had his own way and been left to himself.[28]

Moody would quote biblical passages predicting perilous times and godlessness in the last days, and then would identify what he regarded as the symptoms of these conditions in contemporary society. "Let us get at facts," he challenged in 1897. "Isn't the nation declining?" Everything from disobedience to parents, to drunkenness, to love of money, to open theaters on Sundays was cited as evidence of this decline, and he predicted the possibility of riots and revolution. But Moody insisted that he was not a pessimist, and though predictions of doom seem to become even more frequent toward the end of the nineties, he insisted that he should be judged in terms of his ultimate outlook.

> It is darkest just before the dawn. I think it is getting very dark, but don't think for a moment that I am a pessimist. If I should live ten thousand years I couldn't be a pessimist. I haven't any more doubt about the final outcome of things than I have of my existence. I believe

28. *New Sermons*, pp. 534-35; cf. *Glad Tidings*, pp. 415-16, and D. L. Moody, *Twelve Select Sermons* (Chicago: Revell, 1880), pp. 22-23.

Jesus is going to sway His sceptre to the ends of the earth, that the time is coming when God's will is to be done on earth as it is done in heaven, and when man's voice will be only the echo of God's.

Though things might look dark now, "We are on the winning side."[29] Like most premillennialists and perhaps all dispensationalists, Moody was pessimistic about the immediate future, but thought of himself as ultimately optimistic. It was this that gave Moody courage to stay at the work, and he tried to communicate this same outlook.

Examination of Moody's sermon on the Lord's return as given in *New Sermons, Addresses and Prayers,* supplemented by other materials, has revealed a clearly premillennial outlook which frequently had dispensational overtones, but not a rigidly or consistently dispensational scheme. Other considerations bear out this conclusion. For instance, at times Moody made a distinction between Law and grace similar to that usually made by the dispensationalists, but at other times he would declare that the Ten Commandments are "as binding as ever they have been."[30] Similarly, his rather frequent references to dispensations suggest acceptance of distinctively dispensational language and concepts, but Moody did not bother to define these concepts nor did he set out a complete plan of the ages in the usual dispensational fashion. Indeed, many of his references to dispensations are so vague that they could have been made by a nondispensationalist.[31] The term itself, it must be remembered, was used commonly, though not as frequently, outside of dispensational circles.[32]

Although the notes of pessimism about the course of history prior to Christ's return and agnosticism about the sequence of events in connection with that return become more prominent in Moody's later years, his basic emphasis remained the same: Watch and pray, for ye know not

29. *To All People,* pp. 508-11; Dwight L. Moody, "A Sermon on Backsliders," *The Christian Herald,* Sept. 28, 1910, p. 860; Dwight L. Moody, "When Jesus Comes Again," *The Christian Herald,* Dec. 21, 1910, pp. 1208-9; *Moody's Latest Sermons,* p. 116; *To the Work! To the Work!,* pp. 54-55. See also the comments of Findlay, *Dwight L. Moody,* pp. 253-54; McLoughlin, *The American Evangelicals, 1800-1900: An Anthology,* pp. 24, 172; White, "The Influence of North American Evangelism in Great Britain between 1830 and 1914 on the Origin and Development of the Ecumenical Movement," 8:3-7, 40-41; Arthur Percy Fitt, *Moody Still Lives: Word Pictures of D. L. Moody,* p. 146.
30. *New Sermons,* pp. 106-8, 420-28; *Glad Tidings,* pp. 161-62, 410-15; *Weighed and Wanting, passim.* Cf. C. H. Mackintosh, *Notes on the Book of Exodus* (New York: Revell, n.d.), pp. 247-64.
31. *New Sermons,* pp. 159, 566, 611; *Glad Tidings,* p. 161; *Bible Characters,* pp. 61, 71-72; *Wondrous Love,* pp. 47, 48, 69; *Moody's Latest Sermons,* p. 76.
32. See pp. 181-82.

when the time is.[33] It was clearly premillennial, vaguely dispensational, and held with such tolerance as to not create a barrier between himself and those who might differ, even postmillennialists.

---

33. For good examples of Moody's later sermons on Christ's return, see the two sermons cited in note 27 above.

10

A MATTER OF REVELATION,
NOT INVESTIGATION

AS THE MOST VISIBLE American religious leader of the last quarter of the nineteenth century, there was no way that D. L. Moody could remain unaware of, untouched by, and irresponsive to the current intellectual challenges to Christianity's system of thought. Untutored though he was in theology, science, and philosophy, he *was* aware of the Huxleys, the Tyndalls, the Ingersolls, the German critics, the men of science, and the preachers of moral essays.

Though such a statement hardly needs confirmation, the pages of two different newspapers provide striking examples of the intellectual currents flowing around Moody. The first is the front page of the *Chicago Daily Tribune* for June 2, 1893. In one column are the headlines, "Dr. Briggs Must Go. General Assembly Suspends Him from the Ministry. He Refuses to Recant." The reference to the famous trial of Dr. Charles Briggs of Union Theological Seminary for his higher critical views of the Old Testament is obvious. Several columns to the right and equally prominent on the front page was this headline, "Offer Moody Advice. Evangelist Importuned to Preach and not to Preach." The reference of the latter headline is not so obvious, but it involved the question of whether or not Moody should preach on the Sunday opening of the World's Fair in Chicago. Letters and telegrams from all over the city and country were coming in to him, giving advice on this Sabbath question. And within a few weeks, the question was to be even more acute: Should he preach at the Parliament of Religions being held in connection with the fair? The other striking example of the currents flowing around Moody is a full-page spread in the *New York*

Journal on Sunday, November 29, 1896. The editor had accomplished on paper what had not occurred in the flesh—Dwight L. Moody and Colonel Robert G. Ingersoll were brought together on the same platform. The two men are caricatured by a cartoonist as facing opposite directions with each expounding his own viewpoint. On the Moody side are these headlines, "The Bible is Truth and Life. The Famous Revivalist's Strongest Argument for Christianity." On the side of Ingersoll is this declaration, "The Bible is a Delusion. The Best Argument Ever Advanced Against Christianity."

INTELLECTUAL CHALLENGES TO CONSERVATIVE CHRISTIANITY

Ingersoll, who was dubbed "the Dwight L. Moody of Free Religion," devoted his mature years to preaching agnosticism. His eloquent attacks on Christianity were representative of the thinking of the Free Religious Association formed in 1867. Its confident humanistic message was in the free-thought tradition of Thomas Paine and eighteenth-century rationalism. Though the association did not attract a large number of adherents, the effect of Ingersoll's message reached beyond the borders of organized movements, contributing its share to a growing naturalistic mentality at the popular level.

Not all of the challenges to traditional Christianity were as radical as those of the free thinkers. Slightly to the right were the earliest religious liberals in the American tradition, the Unitarians. They came from the stream of New England Calvinism as modified by Jonathan Mayhew and Charles Chauncy. Philosophically and ethically, Unitarianism also stemmed from the Enlightenment. William Ellery Channing in 1819 gave the classic expression of the basic doctrines of rational Christianity, and from this movement came the new American denomination known as Unitarianism. From within the Unitarian tradition emerged another movement known as transcendentalism. Ralph Waldo Emerson and Theodore Parker were key figures. Its optimistic, romantic, and pantheistic view of nature, man, and God became the prevailing form of Unitarian theology, mellowing some of the "commonsense" theology represented by Channing. The acceptance in Unitarianism of Parker's humanitarian view of Jesus marked the final break with traditional Christology. But so-called romantic liberalism was not confined to the Unitarians; it cast its spell far beyond those bounds.

Not all of the liberals were sympathetic with a thoroughly humanitarian view of Jesus, though, so another stream of liberalism can be identified, beginning at least with Horace Bushnell. Although it is simplistic to suppose that the streams flowed in neatly defined channels, these liberals have been called "evangelical" or "Christocentric liberals." In the early twentieth century they were generally known simply as "liberals." Their attempt was to construct theology in terms of the person and work of Christ, although their Christology was clearly a "modernized" version. Just as significant was their general acceptance of the evolutionary world view, the acceptance of higher criticism as a tool of biblical scholarship, and the appropriation of philosophical idealism. The result was rejection of the traditional Protestant view of inspiration, an emphasis on the immanence of God that bordered on pantheism, an insistence on the inherent worth of man, acceptance of the moral theory of the atonement involving rejection of the idea that Christ came to "satisfy" God's wrath, preaching of the Fatherhood of God and the brotherhood of man, and a social interpretation of the Gospel in terms of the actualization of the Kingdom of God as revealed in the life and teaching of Jesus.[1]

These intermingling streams of theology represent both reactionary and creative responses to the intellectual and scientific trends of the times, such as Enlightenment rationalism, European romanticism imported to New England, philosophical idealism, uniformitarian geology, the theory of evolution, the empirical sciences, and historico-critical studies.

The issues raised and the struggles occasioned by the advent into America of higher criticism of the Bible are more readily delineated. Perhaps they are also more obviously typical of the points at issue between liberals and conservatives, since the former usually adopted or adapted themselves to the method with its premises and conclusions, whereas the latter usually rejected the same. Higher criticism had its beginnings in the seventeenth and eighteenth centuries and may be

1. Ahlstrom, *A Religious History of the American People*, pp. 597-614, 763-66; Carter, *The Spiritual Crisis of the Gilded Age, passim;* H. Shelton Smith, Robert T. Handy, and Lefferts A. Loetscher, *American Christianity: An Historical Interpretation with Representative Documents* (New York: Charles Scribner's Sons, 1963), 1:493-502; 2:223-28, 255-65; Arthur Meier Schlesinger, "A Critical Period in American Religion, 1875-1900," pp. 523-48; Bert James Loewenberg, "Darwinism Comes to America," *Mississippi Valley Historical Review* 28 (Dec. 1941): 339-60; Charles Howard Hopkins, *The Rise of the Social Gospel in American Protestantism: 1865-1915* (New Haven: Yale U., 1940), pp. 55-63, 123-34; Boller, *American Thought in Transition: The Impact of Evolutionary Naturalism*, pp. 22-46.

traced through the work of Thomas Hobbes, Baruch Spinoza, Jean Astruc, and J. S. Semler.

This new biblical scholarship flourished in nineteenth-century Germany in the universities. During the first half of the century, the critical learning from Germany was imported into New England. On the liberal side, Harvard provided support for Edward Everett and George Bancroft for their studies abroad under German biblical scholars, and Andrews Norton and George Noyes attempted to create a critical Unitarian biblical scholarship at Harvard. On the conservative side, Moses Stuart taught his students the art of biblical criticism at Andover Seminary. At mid-century the movement was in decline, and by the end of the Civil War it was practically gone. The activist concerns of the American clergy, the disruptions of war, and the death of most of the early leaders had marked this practical demise.

When higher criticism again became an important force in the United States, it was not by recollection of the pre-Civil War American heritage, but by means of a fresh importation from abroad. W. Robertson Smith, professor at Aberdeen in Scotland, had studied in Germany and presented Wellhausen's view of the Pentateuch and Old Testament history in the ninth edition of the *Encyclopaedia Britannica* (1875 ff.). These articles and the publicity in the American press of his trial for heresy by the Free Church of Scotland served to mediate these views to America. After his removal from the professorship in 1881, he wrote two more works that had a wide circulation on this side of the Atlantic. Ten years later Oxford professor S. R. Driver wrote an Old Testament introduction that became the standard for American theological students.

The great debate over higher criticism in this country began in the 1880s, with Charles A. Briggs of Union Theological Seminary and William Rainy Harper, editor, Yale professor, and future president of the University of Chicago, being the most vocal scholarly advocates of the discipline. But other scholars were involved in the crusade, including George Foot Moore of Andover, Paul Haupt of Johns Hopkins, John Peters of Yale, Benjamin Bacon of Yale, and Henry Preserved Smith of Lane Seminary. Outside of academia, the Boston Unitarian minister, Minot J. Savage, and three Congregational ministers, Henry Ward Beecher, Washington Gladden, and Lyman Abbott, were very effective in their preaching and writing in popularizing higher criticism.

One of the more spectacular outbreaks of the controversy in Moody's lifetime was the previously mentioned trial of Briggs. In 1890 he was appointed to the professorship of biblical theology at Union Theological Seminary. He had already gained a reputation as a higher critic, but his inaugural address resulted in the veto of his appointment by the General Assembly of the Presbyterian Church (U.S.A.) and his trial for heresy. In 1893 he was finally condemned and suspended from the ministry. His address, which had occasioned these drastic actions, had advocated reason and the Church as well as the Bible as sources of religious authority, had denied the inerrancy of the Bible, had seriously questioned the validity of Messianic prophecies and their alleged fulfillments, had denied Mosaic authorship of the Pentateuch, and had endorsed dual authorship of Isaiah.

Liberal higher critics treated the Bible as a human book, not as a verbally inspired divine oracle. Since many of the critical theories were constructed on evolutionary presuppositions, such as Wellhausen's exposition of Israel's history and the authorship and composition of the Pentateuch, it became obvious to the conservatives that higher criticism as it was being taught was not consistent with their views of inspiration and inerrancy. The conservatives challenged these views with men like Charles Hodge, B. B. Warfield, and William Henry Green leading the way.[2]

Where Did Moody Stand?

That such a question should even be asked, let alone require an answer, might seem strange in view of what has been discovered about the theology implicit in Moody's preaching. However, the question has often been asked, and not without some justification. While no one with any knowledge of Moody would suggest that his theology was anything but of a conservative, evangelical stripe, the suggestions persist that Moody had a liberal spirit with reference to the theological trends under discussion. For instance, C. Howard Hopkins, historiographer of the Social Gospel and of the YMCA, claimed that while the "Fundamentalists took over the Moody Bible Institute, the Y.M.C.A. was the more legitimate heir of Moody's warmly evangelical but open-minded

2. Jerry Wayne Brown, *The Rise of Biblical Criticism in America, 1800-1870: The New England Scholars* (Middletown, Conn.: Wesleyan U., 1969), pp. 6-9, 94-95, 128, 140-49, 164-70, 180-81; Ira V. Brown, "The Higher Criticism Comes to America, 1880-1900," *Journal of The Presbyterian Historical Society*, 38, Dec. 1960, 193-211.

and essentially liberal spirit." Hopkins made the statement within the context of a description of the association's almost imperceptible gravitation toward liberalism.[3]

Of Moody's two sons, William was a conservative Evangelical and Paul was more in sympathy with the liberalism of the early twentieth century. Paul even argued that his father was for his days a liberal and that if he "were living today [1923], . . . he would be . . . more in sympathy with the men who, like Fosdick, are preaching what he loved to spread—the love of God and the power of Christ—than with those who are attempting to persecute them because they will not subscribe to certain shibboleths." Within a few days of Moody's death, George Adam Smith, the renowned Old Testament critic and professor at the Free Church College in Glasgow, wrote, "To me it is very clear that we have lost not only one of the strongest personalities of our time, but a man who was more able than any other to act as a reconciler of our present divisions." Lyman Abbott's "snap-shot" of Moody lauded him for his "catholicity of spirit" which did not estimate men by "the accidents of their creed" and which made him "indifferent to theological theories."[4]

The evidence commonly cited to support these claims usually is either information Moody allegedly communicated in personal conversations or an appeal to the fact that Moody had a close personal relationship with Henry Drummond in spite of Drummond's later theistic evolution and "evangelical liberalism." It is also pointed out that Moody used Drummond as a speaker at Northfield in 1887, and it is claimed that Moody wanted to use him again in his 1893 World's Fair campaign in Chicago. Likewise, it is pointed out that at Northfield Moody used William Rainy Harper, George Adam Smith, and other men who were clearly aligned with higher criticism. Although rumblings could be heard earlier, it was an editorial in the July 12, 1923, *Christian Century* that seems to have sparked the great debate with charges and counter charges flowing freely. Was Moody Bible Institute in the true tradition of Moody, or were the Northfield Schools? Would Moody have been with the modernists or the Fundamentalists?

3. Hopkins, *History of the Y.M.C.A. in North America*, p. 511.
4. Paul D. Moody, "Moody Becoming 'a Veiled Figure,'" *The Christian Century*, Aug. 2, 1923, p. 979; George Adam Smith, "Dwight L. Moody: A Personal Tribute," *The Outlook*, Jan. 20, 1900, p. 163; Lyman Abbott, "Snap-Shots of My Contemporaries: Dwight Lyman Moody—Evangelist," *The Outlook*, June 22, 1921, p. 326.

"Where Would Mr. Moody Stand?" *The Christian Century* asked. Its answer was obvious: Not with the fundamentalist stance of Moody Bible Institute. The literature evoked by this controversy is fascinating, but more for what it reveals about the modernist-fundamentalist battles of the 1920s than for the light shed on D. L. Moody. Looking at that debate from a distance, it seems just to conclude that the Fundamentalists appealed to Moody's undeniably conservative theology, while playing down the significance of his catholic spirit on the personal level toward those of differing theological positions. The liberals appealed to Moody's catholic spirit and his tendency to subordinate theological and critical questions in the interests of evangelism, while minimizing the significance of his admittedly conservative theology. Beyond that, the debate centered around what Moody allegedly did or did not do or say with reference to such controversial figures as George Adam Smith and Henry Drummond. At times it is the recollection of a George Adam Smith or Paul Moody against the recollection of an R. A. Torrey (Bible Institute of Los Angeles and former associate of Moody) or Charles Blanchard (Wheaton College president).[5] For every assertion that Moody welcomed higher critics to the Northfield platform because he saw in these men genuine Christianity, one can find counterassertions that Moody invited these men in ignorance and regretted his invitations after he knew better. The debate proved little more than both sides of the debate claimed to be the true heirs of Moody's mantle.

The polarization between the two forces in the 1920s was much more pronounced than it was in Moody's time. Although the forces pulling

5. For those who would like to examine this sidelight to the modernist-fundamentalist debate, the following articles, listed in chronological order, should be consulted: "Where Would Mr. Moody Stand?" *The Christian Century*, July 12, 1923, pp. 870-72; L. W. Munhall, "An Attack upon the Moody Bible Institute," *Eastern Methodist*, July 19, 1923, p. 5; Paul D. Moody, "Moody Becoming 'a Veiled Figure,' " *The Christian Century*, Aug. 2, 1923, p. 979; R. A. Torrey, "Mr. Paul D. Moody's Gross Calumny of His Honored Father, D. L. Moody," *The Moody Bible Institute Monthly*, Oct. 1923, pp. 51-52; R. A. Torrey, "Where Would D. L. Moody Stand?" *The Moody Bible Institute Monthly*, Dec. 1923, pp. 171-73; "Echoes of Dr. Torrey's Defence of D. L. Moody," *The Moody Bible Institute Monthly*, Dec. 1923, pp. 173-74; W. H. Griffith-Thomas, "Are Liberals Liberal?" *The Presbyterian*, Feb. 14, 1924, pp. 9, 26; Elmer William Powell, "D. L. Moody and the Origin of Fundamentalism," *The Christian Work*, Apr. 19, 1924, pp. 496-97, 500-502; Charles Blanchard, "Mr. Moody's Modernism," *The Presbyterian*, May 22, 1924, pp. 8, 29; "D. L. Moody and the Origin of Fundamentalism," letters to the editor from Henry P. Crowell and Paul D. Moody, *The Christian Work*, July 12, 1924, p. 60; R. A. Torrey, "Did Dwight L. Moody Favor Modernism?" *The Presbyterian and Herald and Presbyter*, Nov. 12, 1925; Charles T. Page, "D. L. Moody and George Adam Smith—R. A. Torrey Corroborated," *The Moody Bible Institute Monthly*, Feb. 1926, p. 263; "D. L. Moody and Henry Drummond," *The Moody Bible Institute Monthly*, Mar. 1926, p. 307. Cf. Paul D. Moody, *My Father: An Intimate Portrait of Dwight Moody*, pp. 182-99.

at Moody are evident in the 1890s, it is difficult, perhaps impossible, to determine precisely where he would have stood in the 1920s. That his theology would have been essentially unchanged seems to be a reasonable conclusion. But what his relationships with and attitudes toward the two poles would have been is a moot question. Those who asked the question, "Where Would Moody Stand?" did not distinguish between their own time and Moody's time. The question is legitimate only if phrased, "Where did Moody stand?"

MOODY'S THEOLOGICAL POSITION

Before turning to Moody's responses to the intellectual challenges to Christianity in the last of the nineteenth century, it will be helpful to briefly review the outlines of Moody's evangelical theology. Contrary to what some interpreters have suggested, including the early liberals, theology was not a matter of indifference to Moody. While he disdained the party spirit that separated the denominations into hostile camps, he recognized the validity of their theological concerns and in terms of his own work of evangelization insisted upon an evangelical understanding of the Gospel.

His own theological concerns centered on the nature of the Gospel. Under the rubrics—ruin by the fall, redemption by the blood, and regeneration by the Spirit—we have seen that his understanding of man's need and God's provision was quite consistent with the views of individual salvation traditionally held by conservative Evangelicals and quite out of step with the concepts of both the older and newer liberalism. To be specific, sin is man's ruination, the atonement is to be understood in terms of penal substitution and satisfaction, and man cannot reform himself since he as sinner stands in need of regeneration by the Spirit. This message is the Good News, not the preaching of moral essays of reform.

Examination of Moody's view of the Christian life and of eschatology revealed a dim view of the possibility of perfection in this life or age, whether individual or societal. Although his appeal to the human will in the matter of personal faith in Christ sounded very Arminian, it was also shown that other emphases have a distinctly Calvinistic ring to them. Moody was personally imprecise on many points of theological debate and his cooperative evangelism emphasized the goal toward which Christians could work together; but he also insisted on agreement as to the nature of the Gospel, and even counselled believers to leave churches that were not true to the Gospel. While it must be remembered that Moody was big enough to be able to recognize genuine Christian faith in those whose theology he rejected, it also must be kept in mind that by his own choice Moody's closest associates were among the most conservative Evangelicals at the close of the century, namely, the premillennialists and dispensationalists, of whom R. A. Torrey would be the most noteworthy example.

The conservative orientation of Moody's theology also is to be seen in other areas. Implicit in his view of the atonement was a Christology that viewed Jesus as the God-man. Characteristically, Moody did not discuss Christ's deity or trinitarianism in theoretical or abstract terms, but his affirmations of the deity of Christ and of trinitarianism are not only implicit in his view of the atonement; they are also frequently explicit. He had an entire sermon devoted to "Jesus Christ the God-Man" in which he posed two alternatives. Either Jesus Christ was only a man and hence "the vilest imposter that ever trod this earth," or He was the "God-man," "the Son of God from heaven." And whichever He is, "the quicker we know it the better," for salvation hinges on that question. Moody occasionally discussed his conversion from Unitarianism to trinitarianism, using explicitly trinitarian terminology. He even spoke of the deity and personality of the Holy Spirit and His being "equal with the Father and Son."[6]

In view of the contemporary discussions of the nature and character of the Bible and its authority, Moody's bibliology has more than passing interest. His view of the Bible is no surprise, though. His sermons reveal an awareness that the Bible was the focal point of many critical and theological debates. In his judgment he simply took the Bible as it stood, without alteration. His preparation of new sermons basically consisted of Bible study, and one of the most formative influences upon his developing theological views in the sixties and early seventies was his eager reading of the Bible. One element of faith was simply taking God at His word, by which he meant accepting what the Bible said without reservations. Moody's acceptance of premillennialism involved allegiance to the principle of literal interpretation, and Moody himself

6. *New Sermons*, pp. 274-75, 387-94, 558, 572, 667, 696; *Glad Tidings*, pp. 274-75, 360, 483; *Great Redemption*, pp. 288-89; "Sermon of D. L. Moody on the Atonement, Tremont Temple, Thursday A.M., Feb. 11, 1897," typed manuscript, Moodyana.

claimed to accept this principle. Wherever one turns in Moody's sermons, one finds his conviction that the Bible is the sufficient and sole authority and that it may be understood properly without critical helps. Moody's frequent advice to new converts on Bible study was that they needed three books: a large-print Bible, a *Cruden's Concordance,* and a topical textbook of the Bible.

Moody's view of the Bible became most explicit in the various versions of his sermon, "How to Study the Bible," and in his book, *Pleasure and Profit in Bible Study.* Since we are "not to believe the best man living if it is contrary to the Word of God," it is not surprising to find that Moody's view of the Bible ranked with the most conservative of the Evangelicals of his time. General affirmations that the Bible is true were sharpened with statements that all the Bible is inspired, "yes, every word of it." Although not all actions or incidents recorded in the Bible are inspired, "Someone was inspired to write it, and so all was given by inspiration and is profitable. Inspiration must have been verbal in many, if not in all cases."

Moody rejected attempts to set aside literal interpretation of the crossing of the Red Sea, the story of Jonah and the whale, and the feats of Samson as being essentially objections to the supernatural character of the Bible, and not worthy of the Christian's serious consideration. "I notice," said Moody, 'if a man goes to cut up the Bible and comes to you with one truth and says, 'I don't believe this and I don't believe that'—I notice when he begins to doubt portions of the Word of God he soon doubts it all."[7] Verbal, plenary inspiration involved "verbal infallibility of the scriptures as originally given in Hebrew, Aramaic, and Greek, and the King James Version and the Revised Version are substantially accurate translations of the original."[8]

Ernest Sandeen in his analysis of the roots of Fundamentalism has argued that nineteenth-century premillennialists developed sharply defined views of inspiration and inerrancy as an apologetic necessity to maintain premillennial hermeneutics. To be literally interpreted, a Bible had to be literally inspired. Something of this has already been

---

7. *New Sermons,* pp. 342-43, 347, also pp. 269, 275, 667; *Wondrous Love,* pp. 266-67; *Thou Fool,* pp. 163-64; *Pleasure and Profit in Bible Study,* pp. 25-26; "Mr. Moody's Meeting," *Montreal Daily Star,* Nov. 29, 1894.

8. "Inspiration of Bible," *Evening Post* (Chicago), Apr. 5, 1897. This article is of interest for what it reveals about the views of a cross section of prominent Chicago pastors on inspiration; it consists of their responses to a questionnaire distributed by the *Evening Post.*

seen in Moody.[9] But that was not the key point for Moody. Moody's defenses of the inspiration of Scripture characteristically grew out of his concern to protect the one source from which one could learn of Christ. "If you want to know about God, read His blessed Word." "How are you going to get faith? Read your Bibles." Young converts should be in love with the Bible, because that is how they may grow in love and knowledge of Christ. In one address on "How to Study the Bible," he advised the new converts:

> Dig deep, read it again and again, and even if you have to read it twenty-eight times do so, and you will see the man Christ Jesus, for He is in every page of the Word; and if you take Christ out of the Old Testament, you will take the key out of the Word.

Moody immediately moved into an attack on those who cut and slash away at the Bible and don't believe in the first five books (a clear reference to Pentateuchal higher criticism in the context).[10]

After his return to America in 1875, Moody composed a letter addressed to converts of his meetings, many of whom had written him for advice. In this letter published in the columns of *The Christian*, Moody wrote, "Do not above all, forsake your Bibles. You can never separate Jesus the Word made flesh from the written Word. He who proclaimed Himself *the Way*, declared also that He was *the Truth*."[11] Moody's insistence on verbal inspiration and infallibility grew from concerns much deeper and more spiritually dynamic than an apologetic necessity dictated by premillennial hermeneutics; and on this very score, one must question whether or not Sandeen has done justice to nineteenth-century premillennialists.

Moody's claim of "taking God at His Word" raises the question of Moody's critical approach to the Bible. Anyone who takes the Bible seriously approaches it with some critical method, whether he realizes it or not. Moody's claim was to take the Bible literally, which meant to him that he would accept the Bible according to its originally intended meaning. But that is a hermeneutical goal to which both liberal and conservative biblical scholars could subscribe. The heart of the critical question is, by what methods is that goal achieved? Liberal

9. Sandeen, *Roots of Fundamentalism*, pp. 103-31, 168-70; *New Sermons*, p. 533; "The Bible to be Taken Literally—Nothing Figurative About It—How the Prophecies Have Been Fulfilled," *Baltimore Sun*, undated newspaper clipping, Moodyana.
10. *New Sermons*, pp. 140-41, 143, 345-47, 552, 561, 661.
11. *The Christian*, Dec. 2, 1875, p. 7.

critical scholars would not have been happy with Moody's hermeneutics, as indeed George Adam Smith was not.[12] But even by the standards of conservative critical scholarship, Moody's interpretation of specific passages of Scripture would often be judged as very inadequate. He was not equipped with the tools of scholarship, and it is with justification that no one claims that he was a careful exegete. Fortunately, he himself recognized this and often deferred to others who were more qualified than he. In their presence, his position was that of the learner, not the teacher.

This weakness is so evident in Moody's preaching that there is no point in even demonstrating it. But what is of historical interest is to trace the evidence of Moody's developing awareness of the contemporary intellectual challenges to Christian thought and to analyze his own apologetic stance in the face of these challenges.

MOODY'S DEVELOPING AWARENESS OF INFIDELITY

Through the nineteenth century, "infidelity" was a catch-all term used to designate rationalistic tendencies in religion. It often meant what the user needed it to mean in defining his own contrasting position.[13] In its frequent occurrences in the sermons of D. L. Moody, the term functioned similarly; but more specifically, it designated doubt or disbelief in the inspiration of the Bible. "An infidel is one who doesn't believe in the inspiration of Scripture. . . . If he tries to say that the Bible is not inspired from back to back he is an infidel." "These men want us to give up the Bible." He classed them with skeptics, pantheists, and deists who said they couldn't believe the Bible. The evidence shows that the term carried connotations specifically involving the inspiration of Scripture throughout his mature ministry.[14] By the term Moody designated all those tendencies both inside and outside the churches that were casting doubt on the doctrine of inspiration. He used the term without making a distinction between a Huxley and a higher critic in the pulpit. They were all of the same fabric. Unitarians and German critics were both infidels.

12. George Adam Smith, "D. L. Moody: A Personal Tribute," *The Outlook*, Jan. 20, 1900, p. 166.
13. For a helpful history of the image of the infidel in American religion, see Marty, *The Infidel: Freethought and American Religion.*
14. *New Sermons*, pp. 190, 269, 343, 448; *Thou Fool*, p. 163; "Moody's Ministrations," *Daily Inter-Ocean* (Chicago), Nov. 9, 1876; D. L. Moody, "Sabbath School Teachers and the Bible," *The Superintendent and Teacher*, Nov. 1895, p. 1.

If historians of the following century have had difficulty in sorting and separating the tangled threads of what made up liberalism in the last half of the nineteenth century, perhaps Moody can be forgiven for not carefully sorting out and critically distinguishing the various strands. In view of the fact that some have argued that Moody was indifferent to the issues raised by higher criticism and liberalism and that he was "liberal" in spirit, whatever that may mean, a careful chronological description of Moody's developing awareness of and responses to these trends should clarify his position.[15] In this survey, it must be kept in mind that he indiscriminately lumped all "infidelity" into one mass.

The earliest volumes of sermons from the English campaigns, particularly the London campaign of 1875, contain very general allusions to disquieting trends that Moody discerned. He referred to those who believe that it does not make any difference what one believes just so long as he is sincere. He cited "deceivers going out into the world" and "error coming in on all sides" that would do "away with Christ, with hell, and even with heaven." He had a special word of warning against those ministers "who preach a bloodless religion" and who "speak not of the death of Christ, but His life, because it is more pleasing to the natural ear."[16]

The accounts of sermons preached in the first two or three years after his return to America contain such clear and frequent references to the various foes of the faith that it is almost overwhelming. One quickly gets the impression that whatever may have been Moody's shortcomings in terms of critical and philosophical sophistication, he was quite sure there were some rotten apples in the basket. This impression is best communicated by scanning in order of occurrence the numerous allusions to be found in the 1877 volume, *New Sermons, Addresses and Prayers.*[17]

In preaching on "Power of Faith" he spoke of those who "reason out all the miracles of Christ" and "tell us that there is nothing of the supernatural that can not be explained. Everything is in accordance with scientific laws." They were later identified as infidels and skeptics who do not believe in prayer, Christianity, or their mother's Bible (pp. 34-36).

15. His apologetic response is considered in the next section.
16. *Wondrous Love*, pp. 47, 50, 71, 264-67.
17. For convenience, page numbers are included in the text.

He warned the new converts of the pantheistic denials of transcendence (p. 79).

In another sermon on faith, he spoke of infidels and scoffers who won't believe the Bible and who say that any creed is good so long as a man is sincere (pp. 139-40).

He warned that there were preachers and denominations that did not preach the blood (p. 161).

In his sermon on excuses, he cited the "infidels, skeptics, pantheists, deists" who said they couldn't believe the Bible because they couldn't understand everything in it (p. 190).

Moody became a little more specific with his reference to those preaching the goodness and greatness of man in the churches; he continued with a reference to those who "preach in eloquent words" and who "preach sermons on science" (p. 220). This is the first of many references to science in the volume.

"Behold men of science—scientific men they call themselves—going down into the bowels of the earth, digging away at some carcass, and trying to make it talk against the voice of God" (p. 292).

In Moody's sermon "How to Study the Bible" he again referred to the "scientific men" who say the Bible is "only a bundle of fables," and again he spoke of them as "men who dig down for stones with shovels in order to take away the Word of God." He also referred to those who would take away the Old Testament and who were attacking the books of Moses. What was of even greater concern to Moody was the fact that there were many in the churches espousing these views. To these he said, "You are deluded by Satan." There should be less talk about "metaphysics and science" and more exposition of the Word of God in the pulpit. Significantly, this discussion took place in connection with the question of inspiration (pp. 343-49).

Again Moody is found speaking of the scientific men, but this time as men who claim to be wiser than the Bible and who fight against the Bible. The presence of this infidelity in the Church of God is cited with the assertion that such men are not Christians and that there should be a separation from such men (pp. 398-400).

The next sermon in the volume was directed toward young men, warning them of those who would say the Bible is a myth (pp. 405-6).

The theme of infidelity in the pulpits is found again in a sermon on the "isms," though Moody suggested that ministers would feel insulted to be called infidels (pp. 446-48).

In Boston he declared, "I think there is no city in this country where the Bible has been attacked as much as it has been here" (p. 561). In the follow-up sermon he spoke of those who say Christ was an ordinary man (p. 562). And in a still later Boston sermon he warned of those who accuse John the Baptist and Jesus of collusion and who "see nothing supernatural about Christ" (pp. 616-17).

In a sermon on prayer Moody took note of the "infidels, and scoffers, and scientists" who "tell us that the world must move along in a certain way, and a divine answer to a prayer is absurd—the affairs of the world are, and always have been going along in a regular way" (p. 658). This was apparently Moody's pedestrian way of describing uniformitarianism.

Preaching on "Noah's Carpenters," he poked fun at the "Tyndalls and their scientific men" who denied that there was anything supernatural about the animals going two by two into the ark (p. 687). Tyndall and Huxley had spoken to the British Association for the Advancement of Science in Belfast in the fall of 1874, shortly before the meetings of Moody and Sankey. It had created quite a stir, for they had spoken of the conflict between science and revelation.[18]

Finally, in one of the last reports in this volume, Moody warned against "liberal Christianity" and "a great curse abroad in the land, called 'German infidelity' " (p. 698).[19]

In addition to revealing Moody's early awareness of what were to him disturbing indications of infidelity, this series of statements confirms that he made little if any distinction between those inside or outside the churches who were questioning the traditional views. Nor did he regard them as people wrestling with honest intellectual doubts, but as people who were at best deluded by Satan and at worst purposefully out to undermine the faith. It is also surprising to discover that Moody with his educational deficiencies had even a vague awareness of higher criticism, uniformitarianism, and geology at this early date. It is probably an indication of a general public awareness through the press more

18. White, "The Influence of North American Evangelism in Great Britain between 1830 and 1914 on the Origin and Development of the Ecumenical Movement," 2:3, 44.

19. For a similar series of statements in another volume of early sermons, see *Glad Tidings,* pp. 26, 112, 140, 316, 387, 453, 484.

than an indication of Moody's wide reading. In terms of Moody's attitude toward these matters, it is significant that even then he insisted that such manifestations of infidelity should not be tolerated in the churches.

Examination of sermons preached in the late 1870s and the 1880s reveals no measurable shift in Moody's assessment. References to infidelity, critics of the Old Testament, antisupernaturalism, and professed friends of Christianity who stab it in the dark continue as in the earlier sermons.[20] It comes to this, then: Did Moody's attitudes change in the 1890s?

A reporter for the *Chicago Tribune* asked Moody in 1899 "if it were true, as had been reported, that he had weakened somewhat in his belief in the literal truth of the Bible." One wonders, if in fact there were rumors circulating, what might have given rise to them. They may have grown out of George Adam Smith's participation at Northfield that summer. Moody replied, "I never knew any more about that than what I read in the papers. I always read the Chicago papers to find out things about myself." Asked then if he denied the report, Moody said, "Pooh! When a man has become 60 years of age he does not change his belief. He leaves that for younger men." In a way, that seems to be a rather insipid reply, but as the interview continued Moody typically insisted on literal interpretation of the Bible and decried the preaching of negations. "People are tired of negation. They will listen to a man who can get up with something definite to tell them."[21]

Moody had begun criticizing the preaching of negations at least as early as 1894.[22] In the 1890s, it was actually much more common for Moody to be criticized for having a theology that had not changed through the years of his ministry. In such cases Moody would try to turn the criticism into an asset by saying that if his theology were not 6,000 years old he would have pitched it into the Mississippi. On one

20. For representative examples from this period see: "Mr. Moody Treats of the Sundry Forms of Unbelief" and "The Bible to be Taken Literally—Nothing Figurative About It—How the Prophecies Have Been Fulfilled," *Baltimore Sun*, undated newspaper clippings but from the 1878-79 Baltimore meetings, Moodyana; *Great Redemption* (contains sermons preached in Cleveland, 1879), pp. 136, 145-46, 226-27; *Ten Days with D. L. Moody, Comprising a Collection of His Sermons* (preached in Northfield in the 1880s), pp. 19-22; "Moody and Sankey," *Burlington Hawk-Eye* (Iowa), Feb. 17, 1888.
21. "Moody Comes to Exhort," *Chicago Tribune*, Sept. 30, 1899.
22. "The Moody Meetings," *News* (Providence, R. I.), Jan. 22, 1894; cf. *Moody's Latest Sermons*, p. 42.

such occasion in Detroit in 1899, he expressed the view that there was no need for a restatement of theology.[23]

References to throwing his theology into the Mississippi appear to be jocular alongside other statements from the 1890s indicative of Moody's continuing deep feelings on the subject. He still spoke of the necessity of believing the whole Bible and of rejecting the claims of those who said the Old Testament did not have the authority of the New Testament. Those who insisted that one should reject the supernatural elements and those elements that cannot be understood, still received sharp criticism from Moody. "If you are going to throw out that part, you might as well burn it up and throw it away." On the same subject, he warned Sabbath school teachers, "I think the time has come to sound a warning in no uncertain tone in regard to the Bible," and then he proceeded to criticize the teacher or minister who "uses his penknife on the Bible, clipping out this and that part because it contains the supernatural or something he cannot understand."

In response to the *Evening Post*'s questionnaire on inspiration, he spoke disparagingly of "superficial preachers" who "have thought it was a mark of scholarship to accept the so-called conclusions of destructive criticism." If they would just study the Bible and get filled with the Spirit, "they will not need to run off after some new theology." Available statements from the last three years of Moody's life indicate that his repudiations of higher criticism and new theology were as frequent and strong as ever.[24] Indeed, Moody was advocating separation in terms that seem stronger than ever. In 1898 he told those at the Northfield General Conference:

> I tell you the time has come for the laity to speak out, and if a minister begins to pick the Bible to pieces, get up and go out. I have said it the length and breadth of this country, and I am going to say it. I believe that a minister that gets a white cravat on and goes into the pulpit and picks the Bible to pieces is doing the devil's business better than he could do it himself; and I think the time has come for the laity

23. "To Stir up the Churches and Convert Christians," *Detroit Journal*, newspaper clipping dated Apr. 1899, Moodyana; "Mr. Moody's Meetings," *Montreal Daily Star*, Nov. 29, 1894; D. L. Moody, "A Sermon on Backsliders," *The Christian Herald*, Sept. 28, 1910 (preached Jan. 20, 1897), p. 860.

24. "The Necessity of Faith," *News* (Providence, R. I.), Jan. 23, 1894; D. L. Moody, "Sabbath-School Teachers and the Bible," *The Superintendent and Teacher*, Nov. 1895, pp. 1-2; "Inspiration of Bible," *Evening Post* (Chicago), Apr. 5, 1897; D. L. Moody, "The Good Samaritan," *The Christian Herald*, Nov. 16, 1910 (preached Jan. 15, 1897), pp. 1048-49; *Thou Fool*, pp. 43, 87, 124, 150, 155, 159; *Moody's Latest Sermons*, pp. 30, 34, 42.

to speak right out and give no uncertain sound. Not be whining and moaning because your pastor does so and so, but stand on your feet and fight it out, in a Christian spirit, of course. . . . I propose if I am going to have my Bible cut up, to do my own cutting. I don't propose to let some German infidel cut my Bible for me; and if I have a right to say this isn't authentic, you have a right to say that isn't, and there wouldn't be two of us with a Bible alike. We would be cutting it all the time.[25]

However, it must be also said that in these last years, and especially in the last months of his life, Moody began to express the concern that the debates over higher criticism were having negative effects on the cause of evangelism. While there are no indications that Moody's assessment of liberal theology or even of higher criticism had changed, there were growing indications that he was especially concerned about the preoccupation of the general public and of the ministry with these matters. Evidence also indicates that he was coming to deplore the divisions that the debates were creating in the churches. While his own rejection of these views was as strong as ever, and while his exhortations to the laity to take a stand against infidelity were quite clear, it is significant that he warned that it should be done "in a Christian spirit, of course."

Something of this concern can be found as early as February 19, 1897. Moody was drawing a comparison between an Israelite fleeing to one of the cities of refuge for safety and one fleeing to God for salvation. Emphasizing the urgency of the situation, Moody said:

I spring into the highway. I don't stop to discuss higher criticism or theology, I don't stop to discuss who wrote the Bible. My business is to get into that City. I don't think about the whale or Jonah now. I don't stop to hear rhetoric; I don't care about the elegance of flowers by the way. I may be stricken down, and I go leaping on the highway.[26]

But from the last month's of Moody's life come his most moving statements in this vein. Upon his arrival in Detroit in April, 1899, a reporter had asked Moody his views on higher criticism. Giving evidence of the shrewdness and humor that George Adam Smith was later to speak of, Moody replied:

25. "Questions answered by Mr. Moody, at General Conference, Tuesday Afternoon, August 16, 1898," typed manuscript, Moodyana.
26. *Thou Fool*, p. 150.

> You want to know what I think of the effect of higher criticism upon
> the Bible and upon Christians. Frankly, I don't know anything about
> the higher critics of late. I haven't seen 'em. I've been six months in
> the wilderness of Judea calling upon people to repent. But I'll tell you
> one thing—if people will busy themselves repenting of their sins they
> won't have much time to talk about higher criticism.[27]

Still further indications of Moody's concerns come from a letter he
wrote to the Glasgow Evangelistic Committee on May 23, 1899. Moody
had been invited to the city for an evangelistic campaign, but he was
declining. He wrote of his reasons:

> The work in this country has never been so promising as it is now.
> Destructive theology on the one side, and the no less evil spirit of ex-
> treme intolerance on the other side, have wrought wide dissension in
> many communities in America. Instead of fighting error by emphasis
> of truth, there has been too much "splitting of hairs," and only too
> often an unchristian spirit of bitterness. This has frequently resulted in
> depleted churches, and has opened the way for the entrance of still
> greater errors. Under these conditions, the question of the authorship
> of the individual books of the Bible has become of less importance than
> a knowledge of the teaching of the Bible itself; the question of the two
> Isaiahs less urgent than a familiarity with the prophecy itself.
>
> The facts are being recognized by many of our leading churches, and
> some of our ablest ministers are turning to the preaching of the Gospel
> as never before.[28]

That summer George Adam Smith was at Northfield. Smith, Torrey,
and Moody discussed critical questions among themselves. The discussions were later to be reported differently by Torrey and Smith, and
from this vantage point it is difficult to know precisely what was said in
each instance. However, Smith insisted that Moody several times said
"that the guilt lay not only with the critics' opinions, but equally with
the temper in which they were received by the opposite side." This
much is clearly evident from Smith's reports, and it is consistent with
the concerns Moody was expressing at that time. Moody was "weary
of this strife in the churches. It is ruining revival work and emptying the
churches. Couldn't we agree to drop the critical controversy and go on

---

27. "To Stir up the Churches and Convert Christians," *Detroit Journal*, newspaper clipping
dated Apr. 1899, Moodyana; cf. George Adam Smith, "Dwight L. Moody: A Personal
Tribute," *The Outlook*, Jan. 20, 1900, p. 166.
28. The Moodyana Collection has a clipping taken from *The Christian*, June 22, 1899,
which printed this letter.

in the Lord's work together?" "Couldn't they agree to a truce and for ten years bring out no fresh views, just to let us get on with the practical work of the Kingdom?"[29] It was a naive suggestion, but perhaps no more naive than Smith's suggestion that had Moody lived, he could have acted "as a reconciler of our present divisions."

Moody's position in the controversy was that of one who held to the conservative views on the theological and critical questions of the times. Yet he had the largeness of view to be able to recognize what he regarded as genuine Christian faith in those of his personal acquaintance who held differing views. If he had the further assurance that such men would not preach their views, he would even use them at Northfield. This explains the presence of such men as William Rainy Harper, Henry Drummond, and George Adam Smith at Northfield. Drummond seems to have been a special case, though, because of the close personal relationship that had developed between the two men in the first British Isles campaign and had continued through the years. When he was at the student conference in Northfield in 1887, Drummond quite freely expounded his own brand of evangelical liberalism. Although Moody's conservative friends expressed their dismay with Moody's relationship with Drummond, Moody remained loyal to Drummond and at the same time deplored his theology. Moody saw in Drummond true Christianity.[30] Moody was also concerned for the unity of the Church and the cause of evangelism that was dependent upon that unity. Had Moody lived through the polarization of the following decades, it undoubtedly would have been very painful for him.

MOODY'S DEFENSE OF THE GOSPEL

Moody's personal sympathies for some individuals with liberal tendencies reflects his regard for them as individuals, not his approval of

29. George Adam Smith, "Dwight L. Moody: A Personal Tribute," *The Outlook*, Jan. 20, 1900, p. 166; George Adam Smith's introduction to Henry Drummond, *Dwight L. Moody: Impressions and Facts* (New York: McClure, Phillips, 1900), pp. 25-30.

30. Cf. Drummond's addresses at Northfield in 1887, contained in Shanks, ed., *A College of Colleges* (1887). The Drummond controversy is reflected in the literature in note 5 above and in Smith's introduction to Drummond's biography of Moody. Moody's relationship with Drummond is a fascinating subject, but outside the scope of this study. At this writing, James R. Moore has a Ph.D. dissertation in progress at the University of Manchester (England) tentatively entitled "Coming to Terms with Darwin: The Protestant Struggle for an Evolutionary Faith in Great Britain and America, 1870-1900." Moore has indicated that in his Part Three, "Peacemaker Between Science and Faith: The Spiritual World of Henry Drummond, F.R.S.E., F.G.S.," something of the relationship between Drummond and Moody will be explored. The dissertation was scheduled for completion in 1975.

their theology or critical views. He saw all such trends as subversive to
the Gospel. Moody was neither a trained critic, theologian, nor apol-
ogist, and he was not prepared to respond to the intellectual challenges
to the faith on a scholarly level. But he did have an apologetic response
to these trends, and it was one that was quite consistent through the
years. It is of interest, not only for what it reveals of Moody's understanding of the Christian faith, but also for the fact that it must have
reflected the thinking of many other Evangelicals during those crisis
years.

Scattered throughout Moody's sermons one finds a wide variety of
apologetic responses. Occasionally he would argue for the Bible's inspiration on the basis of its harmony, or he might appeal to the miracles
of the Bible as its vindication. To those who questioned the deity of
Christ he would pose the alternative: either Christ was truly God or He
was the world's greatest impostor. To those who accepted His deity but
questioned the history and traditional authorship of the Old Testament,
Moody would argue that Christ was on every page of the Old Testament
and that He had given His authentication of the Old Testament. And
those who still had lingering doubts would be counseled to pray and
have faith. However, these do not represent the mainline of Moody's
defense. His defense against unbelief and all its subvarieties—infidelity,
atheism, deism, pantheism, skepticism, new theology, German critics,
and preachers of moral essays—fell into three basic categories.

One of these categories of defense was his arguments from history.
He would cite historical arguments for the resurrection of Christ, and
then argue that this established the truth of the Bible and of Christianity.
More frequently he would cite the survival of the Bible through the
fires of persecution, and argue that only a supernaturally inspired book
could thus survive to the present day. Similarly, he appealed to the
survival and growth of Christianity through 1,800 years as evidence
that "the religion of Christ" was not "built on a sham." But his most
frequent historical argument was appeal to history as containing evidence of fulfilled Bible prophecies. "Now look at these prophecies in
regard to Nineveh, in regard to Babylon, to Egypt, to the Jewish nation,
and see how literally they have been fulfilled to the letter," Moody
would declare. Or he might cite the destruction of Sodom and Gomor-
rah, the story of Jonah, or Jesus' fulfillment of Old Testament Messianic
prophecies. Fulfillment of prophecy with reference to the Jews was an

especially favorite argument and reflects the premillennial interests of Moody who also saw the day coming when the Jew would be back in the land—in fulfillment of prophecy. Moody was apparently oblivious of the fact that with the "infidels" the matter of fulfilled prophecy was the question, not the evidence. His appeals to fulfilled prophecy were used to establish the inspiration of Scripture, the deity of Christ, and the general truth of Christianity.[31]

The second basic category of defense was the argument from experience. This argument was more frequently used than the historical argument, and it is found through all of Moody's sermons. It took many forms. He might typically ask, "Did you ever hear of a Christian in his dying hour recanting?" Or he would declare, "You can not find a man who has changed masters and gone over to Christ who has regretted it. This is one of the strongest proofs to Christianity."[32] He appealed to the peace and joy that the Gospel had brought to suffering souls of all nationalities, and asked, "What more proof do you want than this?"[33] As verification of the Christian concept of regeneration he would appeal to the personal experience of the believer. Such statements frequently appear in his sermons on the new birth. "He knows that his eyes have been opened; that he has been born of the Spirit, that he has got another nature, a heart that goes up to God, after he has been born of the Spirit. It seems to me this is perfectly reasonable." A year before his death, Moody testified:

> I got God's nature, a new nature, distinct and separate from the old nature, and all the infidels that I have had come to me during these 40 years and try to take it out of me, they might as well try to take Gibralter. Don't I know that there came a marvelous change that night that transformed my life? I would doubt my existence as quick as I would doubt that fact.[34]

Similarly, to those who wanted some evidence that the Bible is true, Moody would say, "What greater evidence do you want? Look around

---

31. *New Sermons*, pp. 406, 448-49, 552, 667-69; *Ten Days with D. L. Moody, Comprising a Collection of His Sermons*, p. 23; "In Temples of God," *Atlanta Journal*, Nov. 16, 1895; "Mr. Moody Treats of the Sundry Forms of Unbelief," *Baltimore Sun*, undated newspaper clipping, Moodyana; "Moody and Sankey," *Burlington Hawk-Eye* (Iowa), Feb. 17, 1888.
32. *New Sermons*, pp. 411, 449.
33. *Glad Tidings*, p. 484.
34. *New Sermons*, pp. 123-25; *Glad Tidings*, pp. 92-93, 104; "Regeneration. Address delivered by Mr. D. L. Moody, General Conference, Thursday Evening, August 18, 1898," p. 11 of typed manuscript, Moodyana.

you and see what Christ is doing. See how He is saving the oppressed."
This also served as evidence to the scientific men who claimed, "It's
only a bundle of fables." "A bad book couldn't make a bad man
good."[35]

Still another form of the argument from experience was that unbelievers and doubters had no knowledge of the Bible nor experiential
knowledge of Christian truth. How could they refute something they
had neither carefully read nor personally experienced? "I contend that
those infidels who assail us, have no weight with us, and have no right
to speak about our faith, because they are talking about something they
know nothing about. They have no knowledge upon the subject."[36] In
fact, Moody argued that the unregenerate could not be expected to
understand the truths of the Bible. Many mysteries become understandable when a person is saved, and further mysteries are opened up to
the believer by the Holy Spirit. Indeed, empowering by the Spirit would
sweep away doubts, Moody said. In the words of Moody, "No uncir-
cumcised eye can read God's writing. That is the reason so many infidels and scoffers to-day can not understand the Bible; they try to make
it out, but fail."[37]

Moody's third basic apologetic category was the appeal to mystery.
This line of apologetics filled in any remaining gaps in the wall of defense. But the concept of mystery played more than an apologetic role
in Moody's thought. Theological questions that involved insoluble
problems were readily put in the realm of mystery. This included the
origin of sin, the origin of salvation and why God loves fallen mankind,
the nature of regeneration, the Trinity, and God Himself. "My God is
above reason," Moody said. "And if you never believe God until you
can reason who God is and all about Him, I am afraid you will never
be saved."[38] In other words, there are sufficient reasons to believe, but
God cannot be completely comprehended by reason.

This view of God and the nature of God's truth in tandem with the
idea that human reason has been perverted by the Fall was Moody's

35. *New Sermons*, pp. 125, 343, 568; *Glad Tidings*, pp. 112, 276, 484; "Moody and Sankey.
Opening of the Fifth Week," *Daily Courant* (Hartford, Conn.), Feb. 4, 1878.
36. *New Sermons*, pp. 140-41, 143, 190, 448, 509; *Thou Fool*, pp. 161-62; "Inspiration of
Bible," *Evening Post* (Chicago), Apr. 5, 1897.
37. *New Sermons*, pp. 123, 289, 546; *London Discourses*, pp. 98-99; "Moody and Sankey.
The Last Week at the Rink," *Daily Courant* (Hartford, Conn.), Jan. 28, 1878; "Last Regular
Day. Northfield Conference is Nearing End," unidentified newspaper clipping, Moodyana.
38. *New Sermons*, pp. 123, 165, 190, 701; *Glad Tidings*, pp. 92-93, 99, 103, 275; *London
Discourses*, pp. 51-52, 56, 98-99; *Sovereign Grace*, p. 88.

way out of inexplicable difficulties all the way from those cited above to the creation of the earth. The appeal, then, was, don't try to understand these mysteries. Indeed, these mysteries should not even be regarded as an albatross around the neck of the believer. In 1876 he said, "If everybody could understand everything the Bible said, it wouldn't be God's book." And in 1894 the message was unchanged:

> I thank God that in this old Book there are some heights that are too high for me, and some depths which are too deep for me. If I had been able to understand everything in it, I should have finished with it forty years ago, but because I cannot, I take that as one of the greatest proofs that it comes from God.[39]

This type of argument is characteristic of Moody's entire ministry. While he did speak critically of infidels, he normally put the accent on the positive, not the negative. Although Moody made some use of argumentation, as indicated above, he normally refused to argue with skeptics. It was not the way to get the best of them; knowledge of the Bible and prayer were more effective. Don't defend the Bible; let it be your defense. "It does not need defence so much as it needs studying. It can defend itself." Error should be fought by emphasis on the truth, not by hairsplitting. It was at this point that D. L. Moody most clearly is set apart from later Fundamentalists, and one can see this even within Moody's lifetime. Moody's son William was editor of the *Record of Christian Work,* a Northfield publication. For the November, 1899, issue he solicited responses from Christian leaders to this question, "What was the teaching of Christ regarding His disciples' attitude towards error, and towards those who held erroneous doctrines?" The responses make interesting reading, coming from such men as Lyman Abbott, G. Campbell Morgan, George Williams, and A. T. Pierson. But the responses of D. L. Moody and R. A. Torrey hold the place of first interest. Torrey, a close associate in charge of the Bible institute in Chicago and later to be a leader of the Fundamentalists, wrote:

> Christ and His immediate disciples immediately attacked, exposed and denounced error. We are constantly told in our day that we ought not to attack error but simply teach the truth. This is the method of the coward and trimmer; it was not the method of Christ.

39. *New Sermons,* pp. 190, 343; "Mr. Moody's Meetings," *The Montreal Daily Star,* Nov. 29, 1894; cf. "The Necessity of Faith," *The News* (Providence, R. I.), Jan. 23, 1894; *Pleasure and Profit in Bible Study,* pp. 17-18; *Secret Power,* p. 11.

Moody's reply to his son's question was:

> Christ's teaching was always constructive. He gave little attention to tearing down, because he knew that as light dispels darkness, so truth scatters error. His method of dealing with error was largely to ignore it, letting it melt away in the warm glow of the full intensity of truth expressed in love. . . . Let us hold truth, but by all means let us hold it in love, and not with a theological club.[40]

Moody continued to expose error and defend truth as he understood them. However, doubts would not be dispelled by argumentation alone. Christ would not be found by reason. Error would not be overcome by attacking the men who held the error. Moody said, "I find a great many people say their reason stands between them and God. Now, let me say here, the religion of Jesus is a matter of revelation, not of investigation." He said that in the mid-seventies; he was still saying it in essentially the same way at the end of his ministry.[41] That was the theology implicit in Moody's message from beginning to end—the Gospel is a matter of revelation, not of investigation.

40. "Progress of the Christian Work in This City," *Baltimore Sun*, undated newspaper clipping, Moodyana; *Pleasure and Profit in Bible Study*, p. 16; *Heaven: Where It Is; Its Inhabitants, and How to Get There*, p. 7; *New Sermons*, p. 79; *To All People*, p. 51; letter of D. L. Moody to the Glasgow Evangelistic Committee, *The Christian*, June 22, 1899; "Moody Comes to Exhort," *Chicago Tribune*, Sept. 30, 1899; *Ten Days with D. L. Moody, Comprising a Collection of His Sermons*, pp. 23-24; "What Was Christ's Attitude Towards Error? A Symposium," *Record of Christian Work*, Nov. 1899, pp. 600, 602.

41. *New Sermons*, pp. 290, 506-7; *Thou Fool*, p. 143; Shanks ed., *College of Colleges* (1887), p. 213. One is tempted to say that Moody's apologetic emphasis on experience and mystery may have come to him through Drummond and W. G. Blaikie, both of whom he knew well and whom he highly respected. But these themes were common property of Evangelicals in the pietistic heritage. It is of interest, though, to compare Moody's statements with those of Drummond and Blaikie. Cf. Shanks, ed., *College of Colleges* (1887), pp. 40-44; Henry Drummond, *The New Evangelism and Other Addresses* (New York: Dodd, Mead, 1899), pp. 257-58; William Garden Blaikie, *An Autobiography: Recollections of a Busy Life*, pp. 203-4.

CONCLUDING REMARKS

CURRENT BIBLIOGRAPHY testifies to the renewed interest of historians in the "Gilded Age of America," the period from the Civil War to the end of the century. Accompanying this has been a new examination of American Evangelicalism during the period, with studies of perfectionism, higher-life movements, the roots of Pentecostalism, revivalism, the premillennial movement, the roots of Fundamentalism, evangelical social concern in the period, and the responses of Evangelicals to the intellectual currents of the last quarter of the century.

Dwight L. Moody, evangelist, cannot be ignored long when studying Evangelicalism in the "Gilded Age." He was probably the most visible American religious leader of the period and can be profitably studied from all of the above perspectives. Although he was without formal theological training, this popular religious figure had acquaintances that were amazingly wide-ranging. James F. Findlay, Jr., recognized Moody's significance and produced a biography which critically yet sympathetically views the evangelist within his times.[1] Findlay's work was a step in the right direction, but even his treatment of Moody's message and theology was inadequate and somewhat inaccurate. While biographical data have been carefully handled, no one prior to this study has carefully worked through the entire compass of Moody's sermons for the purpose of recovering his theology. As a result, inaccurate caricatures and generalizations of the man and his message still prevail.[2]

Contrary to much that has been written about him:

1. James F. Findlay, Jr., *Dwight L. Moody: American Evangelist, 1837-1899* (Chicago: U. Chicago, 1969).
2. A recent example is Sydney E. Ahlstrom's *A Religious History of the American People* (New Haven: Yale U., 1972). Ahlstrom dismisses Moody's message as "a simple and relatively innocuous blend of American optimism and evangelical Arminianism." He is said to have "furthered the mounting tendency to convert the traditional message of Protestant Christianity into something dulcet and sentimental. . . . Thus a new pattern was set for revivalism, and in the process, a prophetic faith was transformed into a sentimental moralism" (p. 745).

219

1. Moody's message was not simply the product of Arminianized American Evangelicalism; one must also consider the influence upon him of British Evangelicals, many of whom were Calvinistic in orientation. Nor can one ignore the dynamics of his own understanding of the Bible and of his own Christian experience.

2. Moody did have a theology, albeit implicit; and in that theology, message ruled over method. That Moody was an innovator in evangelistic methodology is indisputable. But that Moody continued in the reputed tradition of Finney and thought that revivals and conversions could be produced by human effort is myth.

3. The heart of Moody's theology is summarized by ruin, redemption, and regeneration. Man, ruined by the Fall, stands in total dependence on God's grace in redemption and regeneration. He understood redemption as something God did for man on the cross, the atonement being understood in objective, penal terms. Regeneration is what God, and God alone, does in man in giving him a new nature.

4. Not being an academic theologian, Moody tried to avoid the vexing problems of human responsibility and divine sovereignty in the appropriation of salvation. As an evangelist, he quite naturally emphasized the former, but not to the exclusion of the latter. The two co-exist in unresolved tension in Moody's sermons.

5. Moody was neither a perfectionist nor a Pentecostal.

6. Although he resisted denominational identification and ignored many matters of dispute between the churches, Moody was not hostile to the churches nor to their concerns. He tried to build up the churches by putting believers to work in them, by sending new converts to them, and by bringing various theological traditions together in cooperative effort. His was an ecumenism of spirit and practice based on a shared evangelical understanding of the Gospel.

7. Although Moody did not spell out the details of a premillennial eschatology and rejected the infighting which developed among premillennialists, he was clearly premillennial in his basic outlook. In the past this has been generally recognized, but there has been a failure to take into account the ways in which Moody's premillennialism profoundly affected his view of history and theology. The primary cases in point are his views on success and methodology in evangelism, the nature of man and the direction of human history, and perfectionism.

8. As the guns were being primed for the opening volleys of the modernist-fundamentalist debate, Moody took a very traditional and conservative doctrinal stance. He tended to lump together the various intellectual challenges to traditional doctrine and dismiss them all as "infidelity." Although Moody repudiated liberal theology in no uncertain terms, there was a liberality of spirit about him which could accept and even use those whom he felt to be genuine Christians in spite of their accommodations to modern thought. He said the best way to overcome error was by a positive presentation of truth. While Moody was vaguely aware of the challenges to the faith very early in his public career, he did not develop an intellectual apologetic which seriously wrestled with the issues or which could be intellectually satisfying to many on either side. The apologetics that can be found in his preaching grew out of his own experience of Christianity. Although other themes were present, it was fundamentally an appeal to Christian experience and the mystery of God.

Certain unresolved questions remain which warrant further research and discussion:

1. To what extent did Moody's work ethic, individualistic approach to the solution of social problems, and warnings against preaching reform contribute to the mind-set of twentieth-century Fundamentalists or conservative Evangelicals on social issues? Through at least the first half of the century their fear was that social concern was at least the first step toward a liberal Social Gospel. It has only been in the last twenty-five years that there has been an increasingly sensitive social conscience among Evangelicals. Was Moody's approach cause, or symptom, or both?

2. Similarly, it needs to be asked to what extent Moody's experiential apologetic and failure to wrestle seriously with the intellectual challenges to the faith are causes and/or symptoms of anti-intellectual, obscurantist mentality characteristic of many in the American fundamentalist-evangelical tradition, especially at the popular level.

3. With the shattering of one of the key links in the evolution of American revivalism as portrayed by Bernard Weisberger and William McLoughlin, there needs to be a fresh appraisal of their portrayal of both Moody's predecessors and successors. If it can stand as essentially accurate, someone needs to tell the full story of the prostitution of

Moody's methods and message by his would-be successors in the first quarter of the century.

Dwight L. Moody will never be regarded as a great theologian, and rightly so. He failed to deal adequately with the great social and intellectual issues of his era and he did not systematically present his own understanding of theology. It has not been my intention to vindicate him in these areas; he would have admitted his own limitations. But I hope that this study is a first essential step toward recovering what Moody's message *really* was and what his true significance is in the history of American Christianity.

SOURCES CONSULTED

Introductory Essay

THE THEOLOGY of Dwight L. Moody is most clearly revealed in the sermons that he preached, and research in his sermons is best conducted in the library of the Moody Bible Institute, Chicago, Illinois. The Moodyana Collection at the institute has long contained an extensive list of the published versions of Moody's sermons, and in recent years it has begun more actively to seek materials that would round out its holdings. Very few sermon books of significance are missing from that collection, and its resources of sermonic material were more than adequate for the purposes of this study. Hundreds of hours were spent combing the entire Moodyana Collection for materials relevant to Moody's theology. To list everything examined would be equivalent to cataloging the Moodyana Collection, which is a job the library itself has yet to complete! It is neither practical nor necessary to do that here. The list of sources below include only those published materials actually cited or otherwise of enough significance to justify inclusion. However, I do want to indicate the kinds of materials examined in the Moodyana Collection which I have not individually listed.

Hundreds of newspaper clippings are to be found in the file drawers, many of them reporting Moody's meetings and giving verbatim reports of his sermons. Unfortunately, many of these were clipped out without the date or name of the newspaper or with partial information. Only rarely were such clippings cited. The material in many of the other clippings was duplicated in the more readily accessible sermon volumes; consequently, newspaper materials were normally cited only when they contained material of special significance or when they provided a time and place datum that was not otherwise available. Those articles having this value are included in the Source List below.

Other printed materials exist which are not included here because of their limited value. There are the various editions of Moody's anecdotes, quotations, and notes from his Bible and library which have been compiled and edited by people other than Moody. There are also many pamphlets and booklets containing one or two sermons of Moody that have been issued through the years, but these same sermons are readily available in the standard volumes of sermons.

The unpublished materials not listed below are of several types. The notes Moody used in preaching many of his sermons are in the Moodyana Collection in either the original or photocopy form. But these notes are so sketchy and ill-organized that one can barely catch the drift of the sermons preached from them. Of more value are the envelopes in which Moody stored these notes, for they have written on them the dates and places at which the sermon was preached. Although there is no assurance that these records are complete, this information was helpful in several instances. Also, some of Moody's personal correspondence is preserved in the Moodyana Collection. But it is hardly worth the effort to decipher Moody's poor penmanship and spelling. The letters relate to personal matters and activities and the business of the Bible institute; they contain next to nothing related to biblical or theological questions. The typed manuscripts of sermons Moody delivered at the Northfield summer conferences in his later years proved to be very valuable. A number of these are found in Moodyana, and I have frequently cited them. They are a very valuable source indicating Moody's thinking in his later years. In them he seems to open up more and to reveal his innermost thoughts more than he did when he was holding a large meeting away from his home base.

The materials which have been included in the Source List have been divided into three major categories: I. Primary Sources for Reports of Moody's Work, Sermons, and Comments; II. Biographies, Critiques, and Other Treatments of Moody's Message and Work; III. Helpful Background Studies Consulted. Researchers will find Parts I and II especially helpful as an updating and, in some cases, correction of Smith's annotated bibliography. Some judgments in classifying material were of necessity arbitrary. For instance, some of the early biographies of Moody contained significant sections devoted to reproducing Moody's sermons. In such cases, materials were classified according to their major significance for this study; either the title of the volume or the annotation will indicate significant subject matter that does not fit into the category of classification. Many books of Moody's sermons were published without his editorship or approval. However, books published in his name are listed under his name. Editors, compilers, and authors of introductory sketches, when known, are given either in the bibliographic entry or the annotation, as seemed appropriate. Normally, clippings of articles from newspapers or periodicals with incomplete bibliographic information were not used or included in the Source List, but those few of enough significance to be used in spite of this difficulty are included here with all the relevant information available.

There are two main sources where one can find Moody's sermons and public comments. In the nineteenth century it was common practice for the newspapers to give extensive reports of notable religious awakenings. Moody's meetings were no exception, and they usually made the front-page news in the local papers. There would be detailed reports often including either summaries of Moody's sermons or even verbatim reports of the sermons. This in itself was no easy task, for Moody's pronunciation of difficult words was often unique, his grammar poor, and his rate of speaking was said to have been very fast, especially in his earlier years. The *New York Daily Tribune* sent four stenographers to the New York Hippodrome in 1876 to capture his words that came forth at 230 words per minute.

Books of sermons are the other main source where Moody's sermons may be located. Many of them are simply reprints of the stenographic reports that appeared in the local papers. A few are the work of stenographers who worked independently. The volumes issued with Moody's approval were edited by his associates. And a few of the volumes give no indication of how the publisher obtained the sermon transcripts. Although there are some obvious mistakes discernible in the reports, there is a remarkable consistency in the substance of what Moody said as reported in the newspapers and various types of collections of sermons. The sermons as reported in newspapers, books based on newspaper reporting, and in most cases books by independent stenographers are the most valuable to the researcher. They usually tell when and where the sermon was preached, and there is less of a tendency to correct Moody's mispronunciations and grammatical infelicities. In fact, volumes edited by Moody's associates impose a homiletic style on the sermons that was foreign to Moody, so that some of the authentic color is lost which is often found in other sources. These same associates edited sermons that appeared in periodicals such as the *Ladies Home Journal, Northfield Echoes,* and the *Record of Christian Work,* so that their value is also limited. Moody repeated what he thought were his better sermons scores of times, and it is usually possible to locate different versions of the sermon in print in several places. There is no lack of evidence for what Moody preached. But careful research must consider the problem of how the resources are to be used, especially when the substantial content is found in several places.

I followed six basic principles in using these sources:

1. Where there was a choice, preference was given to those sources that seemed to have the least amount of editorial tampering. In effect this means that preference was given to the typed manuscripts of Moody's sermons preached in the late 1890s in Northfield, the newspaper accounts, volumes based on newspaper reporting or other independent stenographers, and the various published reports of Moody's discussions in question-and-answer periods, commonly called "The Question Drawer." This is not to suggest that sermons edited by Moody's associates are without value and were not used. Footnotes will indicate their frequent citation. It should be remembered that in spite of editorial modifications, their publication was still under Moody's control, and Moody's choice of sermons to be published itself indicates where his concerns were.

2. Preference was given to sources which give at least an approximate indication of when the sermon was preached. In most cases it has been possible to give a good representation of Moody's preaching on significant matters through the entire span of his public ministry.

3. In order to minimize the danger of being led astray by bad reporting, no major arguments have been based on an isolated and unusual account.

4. In cases where nearly identical material was available from more than one source, the more readily available source was used. This usually meant books were preferred over newspapers and sometimes meant that I cited the books that were most readily available to me.

5. Where there was a choice among equally valuable reports of similar material, preference was given to those volumes that contained the larger and more representative selections of Moody's sermons. For the years 1875-1878 this meant a strong dependence on *New Sermons,*

Addresses and Prayers with *Glad Tidings* and *To All People* close behind.

6. In many cases, alternate sources have been cited in footnotes in addition to the quotations or allusions actually in the text.

Source List

I. PRIMARY SOURCES FOR REPORTS OF MOODY'S WORK, SERMONS, AND COMMENTS

A. Books

Clark, Rufus W. *The Work of God in Great Britain: Under Messrs. Moody and Sankey, 1873 to 1875.* New York: Harper & Bros., 1875.

Also contains biographical sketches and an appendix of four sermons revised by Moody. The author was chiefly indebted to *The Christian, The British Evangelist, The Witness, Signs of Our Times,* and *Times of Blessing* for his narrative material. The primary value of this book for this study is that its summaries of Moody's sermons verify that in the tour of Great Britain Moody preached the same messages and implicit theology that were to be published soon in verbatim reports in the London and American campaigns.

Cook, Richard B. *Life, Work and Sermons of Dwight L. Moody the Great Evangelist.* Baltimore: R. H. Woodward, 1900.

Daniels, W. H., ed. *Moody: His Words, Work, and Workers.* New York: Nelson & Phillips, 1877.

"Comprising his Bible portraits; his outlines of doctrine, as given in his most popular and effective sermons, Bible readings, and addresses, and sketches of his co-workers." The editor has simply arranged excerpts from Moody sermons under a simple outline of basic theology without editorial comment. There is an 1879 edition expanded to include accounts of Moody's recent campaigns and his addresses to Christian workers. The latter are of special interest.

Goss, Charles F. *Echoes From the Pulpit and Platform.* Hartford, Conn.: A. D. Worthington, 1900.

Includes a biographical sketch and many of Moody's well-known sermons as preached in the late 1890s. Paul Moody felt this volume best preserved the flavor of his father's sermons. However, Goss admits to heavy editing (p. 4).

Hall, John and Stuart, George H. *The American Evangelists, D. L. Moody and Ira D. Sankey, In Great Britain and Ireland.* New York: Dodd & Mead, 1875.

Contains six sermons delivered by Moody in December, 1873, and January, 1874. These are the earliest sermons reported in full that I had access to.

Moody, D. L. *Addresses and Lectures of D. L. Moody, with a Narrative of the Awakening in Liverpool and London.* New York: Anson D. F. Randolph, 1875.

From verbatim reports originally appearing in *The Christian.* Also reprints R. W. Dale's review and analysis of the character and labors of Moody and Sankey which originally appeared in the *Congregational Quarterly.* The eleven sermons in this volume are also to be found in *London Discourses.*

————. *Arrows and Anecdotes.* New York: Henry Gurley, 1877.

Also contains a sketch of Moody's life and work. Of little value, except that pp. 104-60 consist of "Illustrations of Scriptural Theology." Compiled by John Lobb.

————. *Bible Characters.* Chicago: Revell, 1888.

First edition appeared in 1885. Different editions have somewhat different contents. Moody liked biographical preaching and excelled in relating the stories with modern trimmings in such a way that they really came alive.

————. *Bible Readings Delivered in San Francisco and Oakland, and Selections From His Sermons.* San Francisco: Bacon, 1881.

This is a very rare book. Recently, Wilbur M. Smith donated his copy, the only known one in existence, to the institute's Moodyana Collection.

————. *Evenings With Moody and Sankey: Comprising Sermons and Addresses at their Great Revival Meetings.* Philadelphia: Porter & Coates, 1877.

These sermons are to be found in other volumes as well. Compiled by M. Laird Simons.

————. *The Faithful Saying.* London: Morgan & Scott, 1877.

————. *50 Evenings at the Great Revival Meetings, Conducted by Moody & Sankey.* Philadelphia: W. Henry Rice, 1876.

Identical with *Holding the Fort.*

————. *Fifty Sermons and Evangelistic talks.* Cleveland: F. M. Barton, 1899.

A collection of Moody sermons published posthumously with no dates.

————. *The Full Assurance of Faith.* New York: Revell, 1885.

A clear expression of Moody's doctrine of assurance and its basis.

————. *The Fulness of the Gospel.* London: Robert Scott, 1907.

A reprint of articles prepared by Moody for the *Ladies Home Journal,* stating in popular form the fundamental doctrines of Christianity. Prepared in 1896, the articles appeared in 1899. They are obviously sermons of Moody, thoroughly edited by someone else.

—————. *Glad Tidings: Comprising Sermons and Prayer-MeetingTalks Delivered at the N.Y. Hippodrome.* New York: E. B. Treat, 1876.

"From Stenographic reports, taken *verbatim,* expressly for *The New York Daily Tribune.* Carefully revised and corrected, with a full index to anecdotes and illustrations. Arranged by Rev. H. H. Birkins." Delivered in February, March, and April, 1876. One of the most significant volumes of Moody's sermons. See note under *Holding the Fort.*

—————. *The Gospel Awakening, Comprising the Sermons and Addresses, Prayer-Meeting Talks and Bible Readings of the Great Revival Meetings Conducted by Moody and Sankey.* Ed. L. T. Remlap. Chicago: Fairbanks, Palmer, 1883.

Sermons delivered in Philadelphia, New York, Chicago, Boston, and Great Britain from newspaper reports. Also reports of the Christian conventions. A valuable early resource, although most of this material is also to be found scattered through other volumes. There was also an 1877 edition with biographical sketches by M. Laird Simons, published by J. S. Goodman, Chicago.

—————. *Grace, Prayer, and Work.* London: Morgan & Scott, n.d.

Consists of the separately published *Sovereign Grace, Prevailing Prayer,* and *To the Work! To the Work!*

—————. *Great Joy: Comprising Sermons and Prayer-Meeting Talks.* New York: E. B. Treat, 1877.

Delivered at the Chicago Tabernacle in 1876. From stenographic reports taken verbatim for the *Chicago Inter-Ocean.* One of the most significant volumes of Moody's early sermons.

—————. *The Great Redemption; or Gospel Light Under the Labors of Moody and Sankey.* Chicago: Century Book & Paper, 1889.

Contains sermons, addresses, prayer meeting talks, Bible readings, and prayers given in the Cleveland Tabernacle during October and November, 1879. From verbatim stenographic notes taken for the *Cleveland Leader.* Largely repetitious of material in other volumes, but a good sampling of the course of sermons delivered by Moody in a revival meeting. As an interesting sidelight, there is a two-volume work, *Moody's Gospel Sermons: Delivered in Europe and America* (Chicago: Rhodes & McClure, 1889). I have seen Vol. 2, and it is identical in every respect, including pagination, to *Great Redemption* from p. 255 on. Another volume, edited by Richard S. Rhodes and published by the same company in 1898, is almost identical to *Great Redemption*. Biographical and historical sketches have been slightly altered; all sermons except one are repeated in the same order. Only the proceedings of the Christian Convention are completely dropped.

————. *Heaven; Where It Is; Its Inhabitants, and How to Get There.* Chicago: Revell, 1880.

One of Moody's more famous series of sermons. On p. 3 Moody makes this interesting comment: "Many books have been published in this country in my name, but none of them with authority." That would imply that this is the first authorized volume of sermons published in America.

————. *Holding the Fort: Comprising Sermons and Addresses at the Great Revival Meeting conducted by Moody and Sankey.* Philadelphia: Quaker City, 1877.

Also includes the proceedings of the Christian convention of ministers and laymen and the lives and labors of Moody, Sankey, and Bliss. This volume is identical in content with *Fifty Evenings at the Great Revival Meetings Conducted by Moody and Sankey,* and nearly all the material in these two titles is also found verbatim in *Glad Tidings.* Delivered in the New York Hippodrome in February, March, and April, 1876.

————. *How to Study the Bible.* Rev. ed. New York: Revell, 1876.

————. *The London Discourses of Mr. D. L. Moody.* London: James Clarke, 1875.

Delivered in the Agricultural Hall and Her Majesty's Opera House and printed from the notes of special shorthand writers. Though sermons for some evenings are omitted, this volume does give a good idea of the general course of Moody's preaching in London. A very valuable resource. Eleven of the sermons in this volume are also to be found in *Addresses and Lectures of D. L. Moody.*

————. *Men of the Bible.* Chicago: Moody, 1898.

Another volume of biographical sermons.

————. *Moody's Great Sermons.* Chicago: Laird & Lee, 1900.

Contains many of Moody's better-known sermons, but they are undated.

————. *Moody's Latest Sermons.* Chicago: BICA, 1900.

"Authorized Edition printed from verbatim reports." Consists of seven sermons, three of which were preached in Northfield during the summer of 1899.

————. *Naaman, The Syrian.* London: Morgan & Scott, c. 1875.

A penny booklet. A handwritten note on the cover says, "Preached at the Agricultural Hall Islington on Sunday afternoon, 9 May 1875." Same sermon to be found in many sources.

————. *New Sermons, Addresses and Prayers.* St. Louis: N. D. Thompson, 1877.

Contains 73 sermons and 29 addresses of Moody, probably the largest collection in one volume. It is a very significant collection, containing most sermons he had and was to frequently preach. Internal references indicate that most, if not all, of these sermons were delivered in Chicago and Boston from mid-1876 to early 1877. This volume and *Glad Tidings* and *Great Joy* taken together are more than adequate to reveal Moody's early revival preaching. An almost identical edition was published the same year in Chicago by J. W. Goodspeed.

————. *The Overcoming Life and Other Sermons.* New York: Revell, 1896.

————. *The Peril of Unbelief and The Danger of Doubt.* Chicago: BICA, n.d.

Two messages delivered in Tremont Temple, Boston, in 1897. Editing appears to be minimal.

————. *Pleasure and Profit in Bible Study.* Chicago: BICA, 1895.

————. *Prevailing Prayer: What Hinders It?* Chicago: Revell, 1884.

————. *The Second Coming of Christ.* Rev. ed. New York: Revell, 1877.

This sermon is typical of Moody's preaching on the second coming and is to be found in substance in numerous other places.

————. *Secret Power; or, The Secret of Success in Christian Life and Christian Work.* Chicago: Revell, 1881.

————. *Sermons and Addresses, Question Drawer, and Other proceedings of the Christian Convention Held in Chicago, September 18th to 20th, 1883. Under the direction of D. L. Moody.* Chicago: Fairbanks, Palmer, 1884.

A very important volume in that it contains sermons and remarks made by Moody in September, 1883. Since Moody was in Great Britain most of the time between 1881 and 1885, very little is available in the American press from this period. Also contains addresses and remarks of other participants in the Christian Convention. The pagination begins with 865, suggesting that there was a first volume.

————. *Sovereign Grace: Its Source, Its Nature and Its Effects.* Chicago: Moody, 1891.

————. *Sowing and Reaping.* Chicago: Moody, 1886.

————. *Ten Days with D. L. Moody, Comprising a Collection of His Sermons.* Chicago: J. S. Ogilvie, 1886.

Also contains sermons and addresses given at the Christian Convention, Northfield, Mass. Reported for *The New York Weekly Witness.*

————. *Thou Fool: And Eleven Other Sermons Never Before Published.* New York: Christian Herald, 1911.

These sermons were preached in Tremont Temple, Boston, in 1897 and 1898 and are taken from the verbatim shorthand reports of a Reverend Wm. Bridge.

————. *To All People.* New York: E. B. Treat, 1877.

Consists of sermons, Bible readings, temperance addresses, and prayer meeting talks delivered in the Boston Tabernacle as reported in the *Boston Daily Globe.*

————. *"To the Work! To the Work!"* Chicago: Revell, 1884.

————. *Twelve Select Sermons.* Chicago: Revell, 1880.

Reproduces content of *Select Sermons* with two additional sermons.

————. *The Way and the Word.* Chicago: Revell, 1877.

————. *The Way to God and How to Find It.* Chicago: Revell, 1884.

————. *Weighed and Wanting: Addresses on the Ten Commandments.* Chicago: BICA, 1898.

————. *Wondrous Love: Fifteen Addresses.* London: J. E. Hawkins, c. 1875.

"Carefully revised from short hand notes." A helpful source of early sermons.

Morrow, Abbie Clemens. *Best Thoughts and Discourses of D. L. Moody, As Delivered in England, New York, Brooklyn, Chicago and Boston.* New York: N. Tibbals & Sons, 1877.

Norton, Fred L., ed. *A College of Colleges, Led by D. L. Moody.* New York: Revell, 1889.

Reports of the Northfield summer conference for college students, 1889.

Shanks, T. J., ed. *A College of Colleges: Led By D. L. Moody.* Chicago: Revell, 1887.

A report of the "Summer School for College Students," June 30 to July 12, 1887.

————. *College Students at Northfield; or, A College of Colleges, No. 2.* New York: Revell, 1888.

Reports of the Northfield summer conference for college students, 1888.

————. *D. L. Moody at Home: His Home and Home Work.* Chicago: Revell, 1886.

A description of the Northfield enterprises and a sampling of addresses given by Moody and others at the Northfield summer conference, 1886.

————. *Gems from Northfield: A Record of Some of the Best Thoughts*

Exchanged at the Thirty Days' Conference for Bible Study Convened by Mr. Moody at Northfield, Mass. Chicago: Revell, 1881.

Rhodes, Richard S., ed. *Dwight Lyman Moody's Life Work and Gospel Sermons.* Chicago: Rhodes & McClure, 1902.

————. *Dwight Lyman Moody's Life Work and Latest Sermons.* Chicago: Rhodes & McClure, 1900.

> This volume contains the same biographical sketch as the above entry, but the sermons are different. The pagination of this volume begins where the above volume ended. The two volumes together contain a good cross section of Moody's sermons, but they are undated.

Smith, Wilbur M., ed. *The Best of D. L. Moody.* Chicago: Moody, 1971.

B. Periodicals

The Advance (Chicago), Dec. 5, 1867—July 7, 1870.

> Reports of the Chicago Noon Prayer Meeting in which Moody took a leading role are found in this religious periodical. It is the best source for his early views before he came into prominence in England in 1873.

The Christian: A Weekly Record of Christian Life, Christian Testimony, and Christian Work, January 1, 1874—December 31, 1875; June 22, 1899.

> Reports of Moody's first famous evangelistic tour of Britain regularly appeared in this weekly periodical published in London by Morgan and Scott.

The Christian Cynosure, Sept. 24, 1885—Sept. 6, 1894.

The Christian Herald, Feb. 23, Mar. 30, Sept. 28, Nov. 16, Dec. 21, 1910; Oct. 25, 1911.

> Reprints of a series of sermons delivered by Moody in Boston's Tremont Temple in the late 1890s.

The Illustrated Christian Weekly, Mar. 11, Apr. 8, 1876.

Moody, D. L. "How to Pray Effectually," *The Temple Magazine,* Jan. 16, 1896.

————. "Sabbath-School Teachers and the Bible," *The Superintendent and Teacher: A Journal of Methods,* 1 (Nov. 1895): 1-2.

Northfield Echoes, 1 (1894)—10 (1903).

The Record of Christian Work, Jan. 1894—Dec. 1896; Jan. 1898—Dec. 1900.

Supplement to the Record of Christian Work: Daily Scripture Readings, 1889-1893.

C. Newspapers

Atlanta Journal. "In Temples of God: Evangelist Moody Preaches a Sermon of Extraordinary Strength at the Tabernacle," Nov. 16, 1895.

Baltimore Sun. The Moodyana Collection has a series of articles reporting Moody's meetings in Baltimore from this newspaper. The date written on the clippings is only 1879-80, but even this is wrong, for those meetings were held in 1878-79. Some of these reports are very significant.

Boston Daily Advertiser. "Moody and Sankey," Feb. 3, 1877.

Boston Journal. "Moody and Sankey: The Work of Evangelization Begun," Jan. 29, 1877. Several undated clippings from 1877 issues of the *Boston Journal* were also examined.

Burlington Hawk-Eye (Iowa). "Moody and Sankey," Feb. 17, 1888.

Chicago Daily News. Jan. 23, 25, 1886.

Chicago Record. "On Mary and Martha: Helpful Sermon by Mr. Moody," Oct. 4, 1899.

Chicago Times. "Glory of the Bible," Apr. 3, 1897.

This article also reports that Moody had filled the Auditorium eight times for a total of 48,000 people. His appeal to the masses was still strong late in his life.

Chicago Times-Herald. "Moody Talks of Grace," Apr. 1, 1897.

Chicago Tribune. Oct. 7, 1876; Jan. 21, 23, 1886; May 8, June 2, 5, 12, 1893; Apr. 1, 1897; Sept. 30, 1899.

Daily Courant (Hartford, Conn.). Jan. 28, Feb. 4, 6, 1878.

Daily Evening Review (Peterborough, Canada). "Dwight L. Moody and His Utterances," Oct. 21, 1897.

Daily Express (Dublin, Ireland). Nov. 23, 25, 1874.

Daily Inter-Ocean (Chicago). Oct. 2, 1876—Jan. 17, 1877; Jan. 23, 25, 1886; Sept. 11-30, 1893; Nov. 11, 1896.

Detroit Free Press. "Thousands Gathered to Hear Moody," Apr. 10, 1899.

Detroit Journal. "To Stir up the Churches and Convert Christians," Apr., 1899.

This was apparently a bi-monthly paper.

Evening Post (Chicago). "Inspiration of Bible," Apr. 5, 1897.

Irish Daily Independent. "A Friendly Message to Irishmen from America," Nov. 3, 1892.

Irish Times (Dublin). Jan. 9, 11, 1883.

Montreal Daily Star. "Mr. Moody's Meeting," Nov. 29, 1894.

New Haven Daily Palladium. Mar. 20—May 13, 1878.

Photostats of these issues in the Moodyana Collection provide a good idea of the course of a typical series of Moody's meetings with the sermons preached.

New York Journal. Nov. 22, 29, 1896; Oct. 7, 1899.

News (Providence, R. I.). Jan. 22, 23, 1894.

Norwich Bulletin. "Moody's Tolerant Spirit," Aug. 10, 1899.

Ottawa Daily Free Press. "Mr. Moody in Ottawa," Oct. 15, 1897.

St. Louis Daily Globe-Democrat. "Two Grand Gatherings," Apr. 8, 1897.

San Francisco Examiner. "Moody Weeps Like a Child When Over Two Thousand Men Stand Before Him as the Result of His Pleading, And Promise to Lead a Better Life," Mar. 27, 1899.

The Times—Philadelphia. "The Marriage Feast; Grant and Hartranft at Prayer; A Noticeable Beginning for Moody and Sankey's Fifth Week," Dec. 20, 1875.

World (New York). "We're All a Bad, Bad Lot," Nov. 11, 1896.

II. BIOGRAPHIES, CRITIQUES, AND OTHER TREATMENTS OF MOODY'S
    MESSAGE AND WORK

A. Books

Batt, John Herridge. *Dwight L. Moody: The Lifework of a Modern Evangelist.* London: S. W. Partridge, 1902.

Beadenkopf, Thomas M. and Stricklen, W. Raymond. *Moody in Baltimore.* Baltimore: Sun Printing Office, 1879.

Blaikie, William Garden. *The Religious Awakening in Edinburgh, in Connection with the Visit of Messrs. Moody and Sankey.* Manchester: n. p., 1874.

   Blaikie was a professor at New College, and Moody stayed in his home during the Edinburgh meetings.

Boyd, Robert. *The Lives and Labors of Moody and Sankey.* Toronto: A. H. Hovey, 1877.

   Basically a revision and updating of Boyd's earlier volume, *The Wonderful Career of Moody and Sankey.*

————. *The Wonderful Career of Moody and Sankey, In Great Britain and America.* New York: Henry S. Goodspeed, 1875.

   Part I consists of Moody's biographical sermons, but their literary polish seems to indicate considerable editorial reworking. Parts II, III, and IV treat the lives and careers of Moody and Sankey, and parts of these sections are identical with the Goodspeed volume listed below.

Bradford, Gamaliel. *D. L. Moody: A Worker in Souls.* New York: George H. Doran, 1927.

Chapman, J. Wilbur. *The Life and Work of Dwight L. Moody.* Philadelphia: International, 1900.

Chartier, Myron Raymond. *The Social Views of Dwight L. Moody and Their Relation to the Workingman of 1860-1900.* Hays, Kans.: Fort Hays Kansas State College, 1969.

Collins, Almer M. *The Contradictions of Orthodoxy; or "What Shall I Do to be Saved?" as Answered by Several Representative Orthodox Clergymen of Chicago.* Chicago: Central Book Concern, 1880.

Cuckson, John. *Religious Excitement, A Sermon on the Moody & Sankey Revival, Preached in the Unitarian Church, Newhall Hill.* Birmingham: A. J. Buncher, c. 1875.

Cumming, I. A. M. [pseud.]. *Tabernacle Sketches.* Boston: Times Pub., 1877.

A satire on the work of Moody and Sankey in Boston. Written under a pseudonym which was itself a satirical takeoff from the hymn, "Hold the Fort, for I am Coming." The author obviously regarded himself a clever, urbane, and intellectual critic of religious superstition, bigotry, and intolerance.

Curtis, Richard K. *They Called Him Mister Moody.* New York: Doubleday, 1962.

Daniels, W. H. *D. L. Moody and His Work.* Hartford, Conn.: American, 1875.

A good source of information about the British campaigns, 1873-75, and of Moody's work before that trip.

Davis, George T. B. *Dwight L. Moody: The Man and His Mission.* Chicago: Monarch, 1900.

Contains Moody's last sermon preached in Kansas City on Nov. 16, 1899, and tributes from 26 well-known friends and associates.

Day, Richard Ellsworth. *Bush Aglow: The Life Story of Dwight Lyman Moody, Commoner of Northfield.* Philadelphia: Judson, 1936.

Drummond, Henry. *Dwight L. Moody: Impressions and Facts.* New York: McClure, Phillips, 1900.

By the controversial theistic evolutionist who was one of Moody's dearest friends.

Erdman, Charles R. *D. L. Moody: His Message for Today.* New York: Revell, 1928.

Farwell, John V. *Early Recollections of Dwight L. Moody.* Chicago: Winona Pub., 1907.

By a close associate of Moody. Contains many recollections and letters of special value to biographers, but also giving some theological insights.

Findlay, James F., Jr. *Dwight L. Moody: American Evangelist, 1837-1899.* Chicago: U. Chicago, 1969.

The definitive scholarly biography on Moody. The chapter on Moody's theology is the weakest in the book.

Fish, William H., Jr. *Mr. Moody's Theories and the Gospel of Christ.* Colorado Springs: n.p., c. 1899.

Critique of Moody's view of the atonement by the pastor of All Souls Unitarian Church, Colorado Springs. Appears to have been privately published.

Fitt, Arthur Percy. *Moody Still Lives: Word Pictures of D. L. Moody.* New York: Revell, 1936.

Getz, Gene A. *MBI: The Story of Moody Bible Institute.* Chicago: Moody, 1969.

Goodspeed, E. J. *A Full History of the Wonderful Career of Moody and Sankey, In Great Britain and America.* Cleveland: C. C. Wick, 1876.

A detailed, eulogistic account of the work of Moody and Sankey from the 1873 beginnings in England through the early 1876 meetings in the New York Hippodrome. Uncritical, but many valuable details are to be found here. As noted above, Goodspeed has copied some lengthy sections out of Boyd verbatim. Even the titles are similar.

Gray, James M. *D. L. Moody's Theology: A Finger Post for Christian Workers.* Chicago: BICA, n.d.

Hanson, J. W. *The Life and Works of the World's Greatest Evangelist: Dwight L. Moody.* Chicago: W. B. Conkey, 1900.

Hartzler, H. B. *Moody in Chicago, or The World's Fair Gospel Campaign.* Chicago: BICA, 1894.

Houghton, Will H., and Cook, Chas. T. *Tell Me About Moody.* London: Marshall, Morgan & Scott, 1936.

John, J. *The Hippodrome Revival: An Essay Read at the Methodist Preacher's Meeting, New York, on Monday, September 18th, 1876.* New York: N. Tibbals, 1876.

M., J. (Mrs. J. McKinnon). *Recollections of D. L. Moody.* Printed for private circulation, 1905.

MacPherson, John. *Revival and Revival Work: A Record of the Labours of D. L. Moody & Ira D. Sankey.* London: Morgan & Scott, c. 1875 or 1876.

McDowell, John, et al. *What D. L. Moody Means to Me: An Anthology of Appreciations and Appraisals of the Beloved Founder of the Northfield Schools.* East Northfield, Massachusetts: The Northfield Schools, 1937.

Of special interest are the tributes by Washington Gladden and George Adam Smith.

Miller, Walter J. *Messrs. Moody & Sankey Weighed Again: Being a Reply to Mr. Leigh's "Messrs. Moody & Sankey Weighed in the Balances and Found Wanting."* London: Elliot Stock, 1875.

Moody, Paul D. *My Father: An Intimate Portrait of Dwight Moody.* Boston:
Little, Brown, 1938.

By Moody's younger son.

Moody, Paul Dwight, and Fitt, Arthur Percy. *The Shorter Life of D. L.
Moody.* 2 vols. Chicago: BICA, 1900.

Moody, William R. *D. L. Moody.* New York: Macmillan, 1930.

A reworking of the following volume.

————. *The Life of D. L. Moody.* New York: Revell, 1900.

By Moody's older son who had been commissioned by his father to
write this. It is indispensable, though eulogistic.

*Narrative of Messrs. Moody and Sankey's Labors in Scotland and Ireland.
Also in Manchester, Sheffield, and Birmingham, England.* New York:
Anson D. F. Randolph, 1875.

Compiled from the *British Evangelist* and *The Christian,* two weekly
journals published in London.

Nason, Elias. *The Lives of the Eminent American Evangelists Dwight
Lyman Moody and Ira David Sankey, Together With an Account of their
Labors in Great Britain and America.* Boston: B. B. Russell, 1877.

Northrop, Henry Davenport. *Life and Labors of Dwight L. Moody.* Cincinnati: W. H. Ferguson, 1899.

Pell, Edward Leigh. *Dwight L. Moody: His Life, His Work, His Words.*
Richmond, Va.: B. F. Johnson, 1900.

Pollock, J. C. *Moody: A Biographical Portrait of the Pacesetter in Modern
Mass Evangelism.* New York: Macmillan, 1963.

Popham, J. K. *Moody and Sankey's Errors versus The Scriptures of Truth.*
Liverpool: J. K. Popham, 1875.

By a Particular (Calvinistic) Baptist preacher.

By a Protestant Dissenter (*sic*). *Recent Ridiculous Religious (?) Revivals
Rationally Reprobated: The Moody & Sankey Humbug.* London: *The
West End News,* 1875.

Rilance, W. *D. L. Moody vs. Henry Varley at World's Fair on Nature of
Christ's Atonement.* Toronto: William Briggs, 1894.

Ryder, W. H. *An Open Letter from W. H. Ryder, D.D., of Chicago, Ill., to
D. L. Moody, Esq., The Evangelist.* Boston: Universalist, 1877.

A critique of Moody's theology by the pastor of St. Paul's Universalist
Church, Chicago.

Smith, Wilbur M., comp. *An Annotated Bibliography of D. L. Moody.*
Chicago: Moody, 1948.

An indispensable tool for those doing any kind of Moody research.
The fact that Smith is an avid admirer of Moody in no way detracts from
the value of this work. Researchers should note, however, that the work

is dated and sometimes gives inaccurate, misleading, or incomplete bibliographic information. It is unfair to fault Smith for this, though, for the problems surrounding Moody's bibliography can be very baffling. Hopefully, on matters germane to this study, some of these problems are cleared up in this bibliography.

Torrey, R. A. *Why God Used D. L. Moody*. Chicago: BICA, 1923.

Walsh, John Tomline. *Moody versus Christ and His Apostles: A Vindication of the Truth of the Gospel*. St. Louis: John Burns, 1880.
    A polemic against Moody by a member of the Disciples of Christ (Church of Christ, "Campbellites").

Wharton, H. M. *A Month with Moody in Chicago: His Work and Workers*. Baltimore: Wharton & Barron, 1894.

Williams, A. *Weak Points in Mr. Moody's Teaching*. London: William MacIntosh, c. 1875.

Williams, A. W. *Life and Work of Dwight L. Moody, The Great Evangelist of the XIXth Century*. Chicago: P. W. Ziegler, 1900.

Williamson, David. *The Life Story of D. L. Moody*. London: Sunday School Union, n.d.

B. Periodical Articles

Abbott, Lyman. "Snapshots of my Contemporaries: Dwight Lyman Moody—Evangelist." *The Outlook,* June 22, 1921, pp. 324-27.

Atwood, I. M. "Revivals and the Unchurched." *Universalist Quarterly* 33 (Jan. 1876): 87-97.

Barber, H. H. "Mr. Moody at the Tabernacle." *The Unitarian Review* 4 (Aug. 1875): 186-91.

Blanchard, Charles. "Mr. Moody's Modernism." *The Presbyterian,* May 22, 1924, pp. 8, 29.

Crespi, J. H. "Moody and Sankey." *Southern Review,* n.s. 19 (Jan. 1876): 181-205.

"D. L. Moody and the Origin of Fundamentalism." Letters to the editor by Henry P. Crowell and Paul D. Moody. *The Christian Work,* July 12, 1924, p. 60.

Drummond, Henry. "Mr. Moody: Some Impressions and Facts." *McClure's Magazine* 4 (1894-95): 55-69, 188-92.

Duffus, Robert L. "The Hound of Heaven," *The Amercian Mercury* 4 (Apr. 1925): 424-32.

Gotwald, L. A. "The Human Conditions of a Good Prayer Meeting," *Quarterly Review of the Lutheran Church and Lutheran Quarterly* 9 (Jan. 1879): 47-66.

Grant, G. M. "Christianity and Modern Thought." *The Canadian Monthly* 8 (1875-76): 437-41.

———. "Laon on 'Messrs. Moody and Sankey and Revivalism.'" *The Canadian Monthly* 8 (1875-76): 251-55.

L., M. P. "Things at Home (Freedom with Fellowship)." *Unitarian Review* 7 (May 1877): 559-64.

Laon [pseud.]. "Messrs. Moody and Sankey and Revivalism." *Canadian Monthly* 7 (June 1875): 510-13.

Moody, Paul D. "Moody Becoming 'A Veiled Figure.'" *The Christian Century,* Aug. 2, 1923, p. 979.

Moody Monthly 1 (Sept. 1900)—73 (July-Aug. 1974).
　　Vols. 1-10, *The Institute Tie*
　　Vol. 11, *The Institute Tie; The Christian Worker's Magazine*
　　Vols. 12-20, *The Christian Workers Magazine*
　　Vols. 21-37, *Moody Bible Institute Monthly*
　　Vols. 38-73, *Moody Monthly*

Munhall, L. W. "An Attack upon the Moody Bible Institute." *Eastern Methodist,* July 19, 1923, p. 5.

New York Witness Extra. Feb. 14, 20, 28; Mar. 6, 13, 20, 29, 30; (Apr.) 9th, 10th, 11th Weeks, 1876.

New York Witness Extra (Chicago Series), Nov. 1876 (No. 2, 3); Dec. 1876 (No. 4, 5, 6).

P., B. "Moody and Sankey." *Appleton's Journal* 15 (Mar. 25, 1876): 397-99.

The Peace Committee of the Middle District Conference of the General Conference of Mennonites of North America. "Dwight L. Moody and War." *The Mennonite* (North Newton, Kans.), Sept. 28, 1943.

Pollock, J. C. "Dwight L. Moody—Grandfather of Ecumenism?" *Christianity Today* 7 (Nov. 23, 1962): 29-30.

Powell, Elmer William. "D. L. Moody and the Origin of Fundamentalism." *The Christian Work,* Apr. 19, 1924, pp. 496-502.

Sedgwick, A. G. "Moody and Sankey." *The Nation* 22 (Mar. 9, 1876): 156-57.

"Shall the Church Rely on Revivalism or on Christian Nurture?" *New Englander* 38 (Nov. 1879): 800-806.

Signs of Our Times 8 (Dec. 17, 1874)—9 (Dec. 31, 1875).
　　A weekly religious journal advocating premillennialism. The weekly issues examined contained regular reports of Moody's activities and sermons.

Singmaster, J. A. "Modern Evangelism." *Quarterly Review of the Lutheran Church and Lutheran Quarterly* 7 (July 1877): 398-409.

Smith, George Adam. "Dwight L. Moody: A Personal Tribute." *The Outlook*, Jan. 20, 1900, pp. 163-67.

Thomas, W. H. Griffith. "Are Liberals Liberal?" *The Presbyterian*, Feb. 14, 1924, pp. 9, 26.

Torrey, R. A. "Did Dwight L. Moody Favor Modernism?" *The Presbyterian and Herald and Presbyter*, Nov. 12, 1925.

Weiss, John. "The Orthodox Basis of Revivalism." *The Radical Review*, 1 (1877): 308-23.

"Where Would Mr. Moody Stand?" *The Christian Century*, July 12, 1923, pp. 870-72.

C. Dissertations and Theses

Beers, V. Gilbert. "The Work and Influence of D. L. Moody in the Field of Christian Education." M.R.E. thesis, Northern Baptist Theological Seminary, May, 1953.

Campbell, Wilbur Fred. "Dwight L. Moody and Religious Education." An essay presented to the faculty of the Divinity School of Yale for the Degree of Master of Sacred Theology, 1949.

Curtis, Richard Kenneth. "The Pulpit Speaking of Dwight L. Moody." Ph.D. dissertation, Purdue U., 1954.

Findlay, James Franklin, Jr. "Dwight L. Moody, Evangelist of the Gilded Age: 1837-1899." Ph.D. dissertation, Northwestern U., 1961.
    Forms the basis of Findlay's published biography.

Fry, August J., Jr. "D. L. Moody: The Formative Years, 1856-1873." B. D. thesis, U. Chicago, 1955.

Graf, Dennis Erwin. "Dwight L. Moody and the 1893 Chicago World's Fair Campaign." M.A. thesis, Wheaton College, Ill., 1959.

Huber, Robert Bruce. "Dwight L. Moody: Salesman of Salvation—A Case Study in Audience Psychology." Ph.D. dissertation, U. Wisconsin, 1942.

Ladd, James M. "Dwight L. Moody's Use of the Aristotelian Modes of Persuasion. Ed.D. dissertation, Oklahoma State U., 1960.

Lunsford, Rowan. "The Evangelistic Campaigns of Dwight L. Moody." M.A. thesis, U. Redlands, 1945.

Nelson, James Melvin. "The Theological Significance of City Evangelism: Being chiefly a critical study of the theologies of Dwight L. Moody and his successors in urban evangelism." Th.M. thesis, Princeton Theological Seminary, 1945.

Nussbaum, Stan. "D. L. Moody and the Church: A Study of the Ecclesiological Implications of Extraecclesiastical Evangelism." M.A. thesis, Trinity Evangelical Divinity School, 1973.

Olenik, Dennis L. "The Social Philosophy of Dwight L. Moody." M.A. thesis, Northern Illinois U., 1964.

Penick, Frank W. "Dwight L. Moody and His Imagination: Being a Study of Moody's Sermons with Particular Interest in His Imaginative Portrayal of Biblical Characters and Events." Th.M. thesis, Princeton Theological Seminary, 1950.

Quimby, Rollin W. "Dwight L. Moody: An Examination of the Historical Conditions Which Contributed to His Effectiveness as a Speaker." Ph.D. dissertation, U. Michigan, 1951.

Schwalm, Vernon Franklin. "Moody and the Revival of the Seventies." M.A. thesis, Divinity School, U. Chicago, 1916.

Wells, Donald Austin. "D. L. Moody and His Schools: An Historical Analysis of an Educational Ministry." Ph.D. dissertation, Boston U., 1972.

D. Privately Printed Paper

Rockwood, Sandra S. "Consent to Jesus: The Revivalism of Dwight L. Moody." Read at the American Society of Church History on December 29, 1973, San Francisco, Calif.

III. HELPFUL BACKGROUND STUDIES CONSULTED

A. Books

Ahlstrom, Sydney E. *A Religious History of the American People.* New Haven: Yale U., 1972.

Althaus, Paul. *The Theology of Martin Luther.* Trans. Robert C. Schultz. Philadelphia: Fortress, 1966.

Aulén, Gustaf. *Christus Victor: An Historical Study of the Three Main Types of the Idea of the Atonement.* Trans. A. G. Hebert. London: SPCK, 1965.

Bangs, Carl. *Arminius: A Study in the Dutch Reformation.* Nashville: Abingdon, 1971.

Barabas, Steven. *So Great Salvation: The History and Message of the Keswick Convention.* Westwood, N.J.: Revell, n.d.

Bass, Clarence B. *Backgrounds to Dispensationalism: Its Historical Genesis and Ecclesiastical Implications.* Grand Rapids: Eerdmans, 1960.

Berkouwer, G. C. *The Work of Christ.* Grand Rapids: Eerdmans, 1965.

Blaikie, William Garden. *An Autobiography: "Recollections of a Busy Life."* Ed. Norman L. Walker. London: Hodder & Stoughton, 1901.

Boller, Paul F., Jr. *American Thought in Transition: The Impact of Evolutionary Naturalism, 1865-1900.* The Rand McNally Series on the History of American Thought and Culture. Chicago: Rand McNally, 1969.

Bonar, Marjory, ed. *Andrew A. Bonar: Diary and Life*. Great Britain: Banner of Truth Trust, 1960.

Bowden, Henry Warner. *Church History in the Age of Science: Historiographal Patterns in the United States 1879-1918*. Chapel Hill: U. North Carolina, 1971.

Bratt, John H., ed. *The Heritage of John Calvin*. Grand Rapids: Eerdmans, 1973.

Brauer, Jerald C., ed. *Reinterpretation in American Church History*. Chicago: U. Chicago, 1968.

Brown, Jerry Wayne. *The Rise of Biblical Criticism in America, 1800-1870: The New England Scholars*. Middletown, Conn.: Wesleyan U., 1969.

Bushnell, Horace. *Christian Nurture*. New Haven: Yale U., 1888.

Carter, Paul A. *The Spiritual Crisis of the Gilded Age*. DeKalb, Ill.: Northern Illinois U., 1971.

Cherry, Conrad. *The Theology of Jonathan Edwards: A Reappraisal*. Garden City, N.Y.: Doubleday, 1966.

Colleran, Joseph M., trans. *Why God Became Man and The Virgin Conception and Original Sin by Anselm of Canterbury*. Albany, N.Y.: Magi Books, 1969.

Cross, Whitney R. *The Burned-over District: The Social and Intellectual History of Enthusiastic Religion in Western New York, 1800-1850*. New York: Harper Torchbooks, 1950.

Dale, A. W. W. *The Life of R. W. Dale of Birmingham*. London: Hodder & Stoughton, 1898.

Drummond, Henry. *Addresses*. Philadelphia: Henry Altemus, 1893.

————. *The Ascent of Man*. New York: James Pott, 1894.

————. *Love—the Supreme Gift; The Greatest Thing in the World*. New York: Revell, 1887.

————. *Natural Law in the Spiritual World*. New York: James Pott, 1886.

————. *The New Evangelism and Other Addresses*. New York: Dodd, Mead, 1899.

Duffield, G. E. *John Calvin*. Grand Rapids: Eerdmans, 1966.

Edwards, Jonathan. *The History of Redemption*. Marshallton, Del.: National Foundation for Christian Ed., n.d.

Farwell, A. F. *Reminiscences of John V. Farwell by His Elder Daughter*. 2 vols. Chicago: Ralph Fletcher Seymour, 1928.

Ferm, Robert L., ed. *Issues in American Protestantism: A Documentary History from the Puritans to the Present*. Garden City, N.Y.: Doubleday, 1969.

Finney, Charles G. *Lectures on Revivals of Religion.* New York: Revell, reprint from 1868.

———. *Lectures on Systematic Theology.* New York: George H. Doran, 1878.

———. *Lectures to Professing Christians.* Oberlin, O.: E. J. Goodrich, 1879. Originally delivered in New York City in 1836-37.

———. *Memoirs of Charles G. Finney.* New York: Revell, 1876.

———. *Sermons on Gospel Themes.* New York: Revell, 1876.

Frodsham, Stanley Howard. *With Signs Following.* Springfield, Mo.: Gospel Pub., 1946.

Gaustad, Edwin Scott. *A Religious History of America.* New York: Harper & Row, 1966.

Gaustad, Edwin S., ed. *The Rise of Adventism: Religion and Society in Mid-Nineteenth-Century America.* New York: Harper & Row, 1975.

Geikie, C., et al. *Gateways to the Bible.* Philadelphia: Rice & Hirst, 1897.

Gerstner, John H. *Steps to Salvation.* Philadelphia: Westminster, 1960.

Glover, Willis B. *Evangelical Nonconformists and Higher Criticism in the Nineteenth Century.* London: Independent, 1954.

Goen, C. C., ed. *Jonathan Edwards: The Great Awakening.* New Haven: Yale U., 1972.

Gundry, Robert H. *The Church and the Tribulation.* Grand Rapids: Zondervan, 1973.

Handy, Robert T. *A Christian America: Protestant Hopes and Historical Realities.* New York: Oxford U., 1971.

Hopkins, C. Howard. *History of the Y.M.C.A. in North America.* New York: Association, 1951.

———. *The Rise of the Social Gospel in American Protestantism, 1865-1915.* New Haven: Yale U., 1940.

Hudson, Winthrop S. *The Great Tradition of the American Churches.* New York: Harper & Pubs., 1953.

Ironside, H. A. *A Historical Sketch of the Brethren Movement.* Grand Rapids: Zondervan, 1942.

Kirk, Edward Norris. *Lectures on Revivals,* ed. David O. Mears. Boston. Congregational Pub. Soc., 1875.
    By the pastor of Mount Vernon Congregational Church which Moody attended and joined as a young man in Boston.

Kraus, C. Norman. *Dispensationalism in America: Its Rise and Development.* Richmond, Va.: John Knox, 1958.

Ladd, George Eldon. *The Blessed Hope.* Grand Rapids: Eerdmans, 1956.

Mackintosh, C. H. *Notes on the Book of Exodus.* New York: Revell, n.d.

Mackintosh, H. R. *Types of Modern Theology.* London: Collins, 1964.

McIntyre, John. *St. Anselm and His Critics: A Reinterpretation of the Cur Deus Homo.* Edinburgh: Oliver & Boyd, 1954.

McLoughlin, William G., Jr., ed. *The American Evangelicals, 1800-1900: An Anthology.* Harper Torchbooks. New York: Harper & Row, 1968.

McLoughlin, William G., Jr. *Billy Sunday Was His Real Name.* Chicago: U. Chicago, 1955.

————. *Modern Revivalism: Charles Grandison Finney to Billy Graham.* New York: Ronald, 1959.

McNeill, John T. *The History and Character of Calvinism.* New York: Oxford U., 1954.

Marty, Martin E. *The Infidel: Freethought and American Religion.* Meridian Books. Cleveland: World, 1961.

May, Henry F. *Protestant Churches and Industrial America.* New York: Harper & Bros., 1949.

Mead, Sidney E. *The Lively Experiment: The Shaping of Christianity in America.* New York: Harper & Row, 1963.

————. *Nathaniel William Taylor, 1786-1858: A Connecticut Liberal.* Chicago: U. Chicago, 1942.

Mears, David O. *Life of Edward Norris Kirk, D.D.* Boston: Lockwood, Brooks, 1877.

The Message of Keswick and Its Meaning. London: Marshall, Morgan & Scott, n.d.

Moody Bible Institute Lectures: Delivered by Noted Speakers During the World's Fair Season at the Bible Institute of the Chicago Evangelization Society. Chicago: Tupper & Robertson, 1896.

Morgan, G. Campbell. *Exactly What Is Meant by "Northfield" and "Keswick Teaching."* Chicago: Revell, n.d.

Morris, Leon. *The Cross in the New Testament.* Grand Rapids: Eerdmans, 1965.

Morse, Richard C. *History of the North American Young Men's Christian Associations.* New York: Association, 1922.

Murray, A. Victor. *Abelard and St. Bernard: A Study in Twelfth Century "Modernism."* Manchester: Manchester U., 1967.

Needham, George C., ed. *Prophetic Studies of the International Prophetic Conference* (Chicago, Nov. 1886). Chicago: Revell, n.d.

Needham, George C. *Recollections of Henry Moorhouse, Evangelist.* Chicago: Revell, 1881.

Nevins, Allan. *The Emergence of Modern America, 1865-1878.* Vol. 8 of A History of American Life, eds. Arthur M. Schlesinger and Dixon Ryan Fox. New York: Macmillan, 1927.

Olmstead, Clifton E. *History of Religion in the United States.* Englewood Cliffs, N.J.: Prentice-Hall, 1960.

Orr, J. Edwin. *The Flaming Tongue: The Impact of Twentieth Century Revivals.* Chicago: Moody, 1973.

Pannenberg, Wolfhart. *Jesus—God and Man.* Trans. Lewis L. Wilkins and Duane A. Priebe. Philadelphia: Westminster, 1968.

Parrington, Vernon Louis. *Main Currents in American Thought: An Interpretation of American Literature from the Beginnings to 1920.* New York: Harcourt, Brace, 1927.

Pierson, Arthur T. *Forward Movements of the Last-Half Century.* New York: Funk & Wagnalls, 1900.

Pollock, J. C. *The Keswick Story: The Authorized History of the Keswick Convention.* Chicago: Moody, 1964.

Runyan, William M., ed. *Dr. Gray at Moody Bible Institute.* New York: Oxford U., 1935.

Ryrie, Charles Caldwell. *Dispensationalism Today.* Chicago: Moody, 1965.

Sandeen, Ernest R. *The Roots of Fundamentalism: British and American Millenarianism 1800-1930.* Chicago: U. Chicago, 1970.

Sankey, Ira D. *My Life and the Story of the Gospel Hymns.* New York: Harper & Bros., 1907.

Schlesinger, Arthur Meier. *The Rise of the City.* Vol. 10 of A History of American Life, eds. Arthur M. Schlesinger and Dixon Ryan Fox. New York: Macmillan, 1933.

Seeberg, Reinhold. *Text-book of the History of Doctrines.* Trans. Charles E. Hay. 2 vols. Grand Rapids: Baker, 1966.

Shindler, R. *From the Usher's Desk to the Tabernacle Pulpit: The Life and Labours of Pastor C. H. Spurgeon.* London: Passmore & Alabaster, 1892.

Sikes, J. G. *Peter Abailard.* Cambridge: U. Press, 1932.

Smith, George Adam. *The Life of Henry Drummond.* New York: Hodder & Stoughton, 1898.

Smith, H. Shelton; Handy, Robert T.; Loetscher, Lefferts A. *American Christianity: An Historical Interpretation with Representative Documents.* 2 vols. New York: Charles Scribner's Sons, 1960.

Smith, Timothy L. *Called Unto Holiness: The Story of the Nazarenes, The Formative Years.* Kansas City: Nazarene Pub. House, 1962.

————. *Revivalism and Social Reform in Mid-Nineteenth Century America.* New York: Abingdon, 1957.

Spurgeon, Charles H. *The Autobiography of Charles H. Spurgeon.* Compiled by his wife and private secretary. Philadelphia: American Baptist Pub. Soc., n.d.

Tarbell, Ida M. *The Nationalizing of Business, 1878-1898.* Vol. 9 of A History of American Life, eds. Arthur M. Schlesinger and Dixon Ryan Fox. New York: Macmillan, 1936.

Walvoord, John F. *The Rapture Question.* Findlay, O.: Dunham, 1957.

Warfield, Benjamin Breckinridge. *Perfectionism.* 2 vols. New York: Oxford U., 1931.

————. *Studies in Theology.* New York: Oxford U., 1932.

Weisberger, Bernard A. *They Gathered at the River.* Boston: Little, Brown, 1958.

Williams, George Huntston. *Anselm: Communion and Atonement.* St. Louis: Concordia, 1960.

Wood, Leon J. *Is the Rapture Next?* Grand Rapids: Zondervan, 1956.

B. Encyclopedia and Dictionary Articles

Brown, W. Adams. "Expiation and Atonement (Christian)." *Encyclopedia of Religion and Ethics.* James Hastings, ed. Vol. 5. New York: Charles Scribner's Sons (1914-27).

Grounds, Vernon C. "Atonement." *Baker's Dictionary of Theology.* Everett F. Harrison, ed. Grand Rapids: Baker, 1960.

C. Periodicals

Abbott, Lyman. "On Preaching Christianity as a Gospel." *Andover Review* 15 (Apr. 1891): 430-35.

Bear, James E. "Historic Premillennialism." *Union Seminary Review* 55 (May 1944): 193-222.

Brown, Ira V. "The Higher Criticism Comes to America, 1880-1900." *Journal of the Presbyterian Historical Society* 38 (Dec. 1960): 193-212.

Carey, Ralph A. "The Horatio Alger Myth." *Fides et Historia* 5 (Spring 1973): 1-9.

"Estimating Evangelistic Efforts." *The Congregationalist,* Apr. 29, 1897, pp. 598-99.

Loetscher, Lefferts A. "Presbyterianism and Revivals in Philadelphia Since 1875." *Pennsylvania Magazine of History & Biography* 68 (Jan. 1944): 54-92.

Loewenberg, Bert James. "Darwinism Comes to America, 1859-1900." *Mississippi Valley Historical Review* 28 (Dec. 1941): 339-68.

Marsden, George. "The Gospel of Wealth, the Social Gospel, and the Salvation of Souls in Nineteenth-Century America." *Fides et Historia* 5 (Spring 1973): 10-21.

Mears, David O. "Revivals and the Ordinary Working Condition of the Churches." *Congregationalist Quarterly* 23 (Jan. 1876): 20-26.

Powell, Elmer William. "Plymouth Brethrenism." *The Crozier Quarterly* 16 (Jan. 1939): 32-40.

Quint, A. H. "Are Revivals of Religion Natural?" *Congregationalist Quarterly* 11 (Jan. 1869): 34-41.

Schlesinger, Arthur Meier. "A Critical Period in American Religion, 1875-1900." *Massachusetts Historical Society Proceedings* 64 (June 1932): 523-47; also reprinted as vol. 7 of Facet Books Historical Series, ed. Richard C. Wolf. Philadelphia: Fortress, 1967.

Shelley, Bruce. "Sources of Pietistic Fundamentalism." *Fides et Historia* 5 (Fall 1972 and Spring 1973): 68-78.

D. Dissertations and Theses

Hand, George Othell. "Changing Emphases in American Evangelism from Colonial Times to the Present." Th.D. thesis, Southern Baptist Theological Seminary, Louisville, Ky., 1949.

McLoughlin, William Gerald, Jr. "Professional Evangelism: The Social Significance of Religious Revivals Since 1865." 2 vols. Ph.D. thesis, Harvard U., Apr. 1953.

Whalen, Robert Kieran. "Millenarianism and Millennialism in America: 1790-1880." Ph.D. thesis, State U. of New York at Stony Brook, Oct. 1971.

White, John Wesley. "The Influence of North American Evangelism in Great Britain between 1830 and 1914 on the Origin and Development of the Ecumenical Movement." Ph.D. thesis, Mansfield College, Oxford, 1963.

E. Privately Printed Papers

Dayton, Donald W. "Asa Mahan and the Development of American Holiness Theology." Read at the Wesleyan Theological Society on Nov. 2, 1973. Asbury Theological Seminary, Wilmore, Ky.

————. "From 'Christian Perfection' to the 'Baptism of the Holy Ghost'; A Study in the Origin of Pentecostalism." Read at the Society for Pentecostal Studies on Nov. 30, 1973, Lee College, Cleveland, Tenn.

INDEX OF NAMES

INDEX OF SUBJECTS